Carnegie Commission on Higher Education
Sponsored Research Studies

BLACK ELITE:
THE NEW MARKET FOR HIGHLY
EDUCATED BLACK AMERICANS
Richard B. Freeman

PH.D.'S AND THE
ACADEMIC LABOR MARKET
Allan M. Cartter

DEMAND AND SUPPLY
IN U.S. HIGHER EDUCATION
*Roy Radner and
Leonard S. Miller*

FACULTY BARGAINING:
CHANGE AND CONFLICT
*Joseph W. Garbarino and
Bill Aussieker*

COMPUTERS AND THE
LEARNING PROCESS IN
HIGHER EDUCATION
*John Fralick Rockart and
Michael S. Scott Morton*

WOMEN AND THE POWER TO CHANGE
Florence Howe (ed.)

THE USEFUL ARTS AND
THE LIBERAL TRADITION
Earl F. Cheit

TEACHERS AND STUDENTS:
ASPECTS OF AMERICAN
HIGHER EDUCATION
Martin Trow (ed.)

THE DIVIDED ACADEMY:
PROFESSORS AND
POLITICS
*Everett Carll Ladd, Jr.
and Seymour Martin Lipset*

EDUCATION AND POLITICS
AT HARVARD
*Seymour Martin Lipset
and David Riesman*

HIGHER EDUCATION AND EARNINGS:
COLLEGE AS AN INVESTMENT AND A
SCREENING DEVICE
Paul Taubman and Terence Wales

EDUCATION, INCOME, AND HUMAN
BEHAVIOR
F. Thomas Juster (ed.)

AMERICAN LEARNED SOCIETIES
IN TRANSITION:
THE IMPACT OF DISSENT
AND RECESSION
*Harland G. Bloland and
Sue M. Bloland*

ANTIBIAS REGULATION OF UNIVERSITIES:
FACULTY PROBLEMS AND THEIR SOLUTIONS
Richard A. Lester

CHANGES IN UNIVERSITY
ORGANIZATION, 1964–1971
Edward Gross and Paul V. Grambsch

THE INVISIBLE COLLEGES:
A PROFILE OF SMALL, PRIVATE COLLEGES
WITH LIMITED RESOURCES
Alexander W. Astin and Calvin B. T. Lee

AMERICAN HIGHER EDUCATION:
DIRECTIONS OLD AND NEW
Joseph Ben-David
*(Out of print, but available in paperback from The
University of Chicago Press.)*

A DEGREE AND WHAT ELSE?
CORRELATES AND CONSEQUENCES OF A
COLLEGE EDUCATION
*Stephen B. Withey, Jo Anne Coble, Gerald Gurin,
John P. Robinson, Burkhard Strumpel, Elizabeth
Keogh Taylor, and Arthur C. Wolfe*

THE MULTICAMPUS UNIVERSITY:
A STUDY OF ACADEMIC GOVERNANCE
Eugene C. Lee and Frank M. Bowen

INSTITUTIONS IN TRANSITION:
A PROFILE OF CHANGE IN HIGHER
EDUCATION
(INCORPORATING THE 1970 STATISTICAL
REPORT)
Harold L. Hodgkinson

EFFICIENCY IN LIBERAL EDUCATION:
A STUDY OF COMPARATIVE INSTRUCTIONAL
COSTS FOR DIFFERENT WAYS OF ORGANIZING
TEACHING-LEARNING IN A LIBERAL ARTS
COLLEGE
Howard R. Bowen and Gordon K. Douglass

CREDIT FOR COLLEGE:
PUBLIC POLICY FOR STUDENT LOANS
Robert W. Hartman

MODELS AND MAVERICKS:
A PROFILE OF PRIVATE LIBERAL ARTS
COLLEGES
Morris T. Keeton

BETWEEN TWO WORLDS:
A PROFILE OF NEGRO HIGHER EDUCATION
Frank Bowles and Frank A. DeCosta

BREAKING THE ACCESS BARRIERS:
A PROFILE OF TWO-YEAR COLLEGES
Leland L. Medsker and Dale Tillery

ANY PERSON, ANY STUDY:
AN ESSAY ON HIGHER EDUCATION IN THE
UNITED STATES
Eric Ashby

THE NEW DEPRESSION IN HIGHER
EDUCATION:
A STUDY OF FINANCIAL CONDITIONS AT 41
COLLEGES AND UNIVERSITIES
Earl F. Cheit

FINANCING MEDICAL EDUCATION:
AN ANALYSIS OF ALTERNATIVE POLICIES AND
MECHANISMS
Rashi Fein and Gerald I. Weber
(Out of print, but available from University Microfilms.)

HIGHER EDUCATION IN NINE COUNTRIES:
A COMPARATIVE STUDY OF COLLEGES AND
UNIVERSITIES ABROAD
*Barbara B. Burn, Philip G. Altbach, Clark Kerr,
and James A. Perkins*

BRIDGES TO UNDERSTANDING:
INTERNATIONAL PROGRAMS OF AMERICAN
COLLEGES AND UNIVERSITIES
Irwin T. Sanders and Jennifer C. Ward

GRADUATE AND PROFESSIONAL EDUCATION,
1980:
A SURVEY OF INSTITUTIONAL PLANS
Lewis B. Mayhew
(Out of print, but available from University Microfilms.)

THE AMERICAN COLLEGE AND AMERICAN
CULTURE:
SOCIALIZATION AS A FUNCTION OF HIGHER
EDUCATION
Oscar Handlin and Mary F. Handlin

RECENT ALUMNI AND HIGHER EDUCATION:
A SURVEY OF COLLEGE GRADUATES
Joe L. Spaeth and Andrew M. Greeley
(Out of print, but available from University Microfilms.)

CHANGE IN EDUCATIONAL POLICY:
SELF-STUDIES IN SELECTED COLLEGES AND
UNIVERSITIES
Dwight R. Ladd
(Out of print, but available from University Microfilms.)

STATE OFFICIALS AND HIGHER EDUCATION:
A SURVEY OF THE OPINIONS AND
EXPECTATIONS OF POLICY MAKERS IN NINE
STATES
Heinz Eulau and Harold Quinley
(Out of print, but available from University Microfilms.)

ACADEMIC DEGREE STRUCTURES,
INNOVATIVE APPROACHES:
PRINCIPLES OF REFORM IN DEGREE
STRUCTURES IN THE UNITED STATES
Stephen H. Spurr

COLLEGES OF THE FORGOTTEN AMERICANS:
A PROFILE OF STATE COLLEGES AND
REGIONAL UNIVERSITIES
E. Alden Dunham

FROM BACKWATER TO MAINSTREAM:
A PROFILE OF CATHOLIC HIGHER EDUCATION
Andrew M. Greeley

THE ECONOMICS OF THE MAJOR PRIVATE
UNIVERSITIES
William G. Bowen
(Out of print, but available from University Microfilms.)

THE FINANCE OF HIGHER EDUCATION
Howard R. Bowen
(Out of print, but available from University Microfilms.)

ALTERNATIVE METHODS OF FEDERAL
FUNDING FOR HIGHER EDUCATION
Ron Wolk
(Out of print, but available from University Microfilms.)

INVENTORY OF CURRENT RESEARCH ON
HIGHER EDUCATION 1968
Dale M. Heckman and Warren Bryan Martin
(Out of print, but available from University Microfilms.)

*The following technical reports are available from the Carnegie Commission on Higher Education, 2150 Shattuck Ave.,
Berkeley, California 94704.*

RESOURCE USE IN HIGHER EDUCATION:
TRENDS IN OUTPUT AND INPUTS, 1930–1967
June O'Neill

MAY 1970:
THE CAMPUS AFTERMATH OF CAMBODIA AND
KENT STATE
Richard E. Peterson and John A. Bilorusky

MENTAL ABILITY AND HIGHER EDUCATIONAL
ATTAINMENT IN THE 20TH CENTURY
Paul Taubman and Terence Wales

AMERICAN COLLEGE AND UNIVERSITY
ENROLLMENT TRENDS IN 1971
Richard E. Peterson

PAPERS ON EFFICIENCY IN THE MANAGEMENT
OF HIGHER EDUCATION
*Alexander M. Mood, Colin Bell, Lawrence Bogard,
Helen Brownlee, and Joseph McCloskey*

AN INVENTORY OF ACADEMIC INNOVATION
AND REFORM
Ann Heiss

ESTIMATING THE RETURNS TO EDUCATION:
A DISAGGREGATED APPROACH
Richard S. Eckaus

SOURCES OF FUNDS TO COLLEGES AND
UNIVERSITIES
June O'Neill

TRENDS AND PROJECTIONS OF PHYSICIANS IN
THE UNITED STATES 1967–2002
Mark S. Blumberg

THE NEW DEPRESSION IN HIGHER EDUCATION
—TWO YEARS LATER
Earl F. Cheit

PROFESSORS, UNIONS, AND AMERICAN
HIGHER EDUCATION
*Everett Carll Ladd, Jr. and
Seymour Martin Lipset*

A CLASSIFICATION OF INSTITUTIONS
OF HIGHER EDUCATION

POLITICAL IDEOLOGIES OF
GRADUATE STUDENTS:
CRYSTALLIZATION, CONSISTENCY, AND
CONTEXTUAL EFFECT
Margaret Fay and Jeff Weintraub

FLYING A LEARNING CENTER:
DESIGN AND COSTS OF AN OFF-CAMPUS SPACE
FOR LEARNING
Thomas J. Karwin

THE DEMISE OF DIVERSITY?:
A COMPARATIVE PROFILE OF EIGHT TYPES OF
INSTITUTIONS
C. Robert Pace

TUITION: A SUPPLEMENTAL STATEMENT TO
THE REPORT OF THE CARNEGIE COMMISSION
ON HIGHER EDUCATION ON "WHO PAYS?
WHO BENEFITS? WHO SHOULD PAY?"

THE GREAT AMERICAN DEGREE MACHINE
Douglas L. Adkins

AN OWL BEFORE DUSK
Michio Nagai

DEMAND AND SUPPLY IN UNITED
STATES HIGHER EDUCATION:
A TECHNICAL SUPPLEMENT
Leonard A. Miller and Roy Radner

The following reprints are available from the Carnegie Commission on Higher Education, 2150 Shattuck Ave., Berkeley, California 94704.

ACCELERATED PROGRAMS OF MEDICAL EDUCATION, *by Mark S. Blumberg, reprinted from* JOURNAL OF MEDICAL EDUCATION, *vol. 46, no. 8, August 1971.**

SCIENTIFIC MANPOWER FOR 1970–1985, *by Allan M. Cartter, reprinted from* SCIENCE, *vol. 172, no. 3979, pp. 132–140, April 9, 1971.**

A NEW METHOD OF MEASURING STATES' HIGHER EDUCATION BURDEN, *by Neil Timm, reprinted from* THE JOURNAL OF HIGHER EDUCATION, *vol. 42, no. 1, pp. 27–33, January 1971.**

REGENT WATCHING, *by Earl F. Cheit, reprinted from* AGB REPORTS, *vol. 13, no. 6, pp. 4–13, March 1971.**

COLLEGE GENERATIONS—FROM THE 1930s TO THE 1960s, *by Seymour M. Lipset and Everett C. Ladd, Jr., reprinted from* THE PUBLIC INTEREST, *no. 25, Summer 1971.**

WHAT'S BUGGING THE STUDENTS?, *by Kenneth Keniston, reprinted from* EDUCATIONAL RECORD, *American Council on Education, Washington, D.C., Spring 1970.**

THE POLITICS OF ACADEMIA, *by Seymour Martin Lipset, reprinted from David C. Nichols (ed.),* PERSPECTIVES ON CAMPUS TENSIONS: PAPERS PREPARED FOR THE SPECIAL COMMITTEE ON CAMPUS TENSIONS, *American Council on Education, Washington, D.C., September 1970.**

*The Commission's stock of this reprint has been exhausted.

INTERNATIONAL PROGRAMS OF U.S. COLLEGES AND UNIVERSITIES: PRIORITIES FOR THE SEVENTIES, *by James A. Perkins, reprinted by permission of the International Council for Educational Development, Occasional Paper no. 1, July 1971.**

FACULTY UNIONISM: FROM THEORY TO PRACTICE, *by Joseph W. Garbarino, reprinted from* INDUSTRIAL RELATIONS, *vol. 11, no. 1, pp. 1–17, February 1972.**

MORE FOR LESS: HIGHER EDUCATION'S NEW PRIORITY, *by Virginia B. Smith, reprinted from* UNIVERSAL HIGHER EDUCATION: COSTS AND BENEFITS, *American Council on Education, Washington, D.C., 1971.**

ACADEMIA AND POLITICS IN AMERICA, *by Seymour M. Lipset, reprinted from Thomas J. Nossiter (ed.),* IMAGINATION AND PRECISION IN THE SOCIAL SCIENCES, *pp. 211–289, Faber and Faber, London, 1972.**

POLITICS OF ACADEMIC NATURAL SCIENTISTS AND ENGINEERS, *by Everett C. Ladd, Jr., and Seymour M. Lipset, reprinted from* SCIENCE, *vol. 176, no. 4039, pp. 1091–1100, June 9, 1972.*

THE INTELLECTUAL AS CRITIC AND REBEL, WITH SPECIAL REFERENCE TO THE UNITED STATES AND THE SOVIET UNION, *by Seymour M. Lipset and Richard B. Dobson, reprinted from* DAEDALUS, *vol. 101, no. 3, pp. 137–198, Summer 1972.*

THE POLITICS OF AMERICAN SOCIOLOGISTS, *by Seymour M. Lipset and Everett C. Ladd, Jr., reprinted from* THE AMERICAN JOURNAL OF SOCIOLOGY, *vol. 78, no. 1, July 1972.*

THE DISTRIBUTION OF ACADEMIC TENURE IN AMERICAN HIGHER EDUCATION, *by Martin Trow, reprinted from* THE TENURE DEBATE, *Bardwell Smith (ed.), Jossey-Bass, San Francisco, 1972.*

THE NATURE AND ORIGINS OF THE CARNEGIE COMMISSION ON HIGHER EDUCATION, *by Alan Pifer, based on a speech delivered to the Pennsylvania Association of Colleges and Universities, Oct. 16, 1972, reprinted by permission of the Carnegie Foundation for the Advancement of Teaching.*

AMERICAN SOCIAL SCIENTISTS AND THE GROWTH OF CAMPUS POLITICAL ACTIVISM IN THE 1960s, *by Everett C. Ladd, Jr., and Seymour M. Lipset, reprinted from* SOCIAL SCIENCES INFORMATION, *vol. 10, no. 2, April 1971.**

THE POLITICS OF AMERICAN POLITICAL SCIENTISTS, *by Everett C. Ladd, Jr., and Seymour M. Lipset, reprinted from* PS, *vol. 4, no. 2, Spring 1971.**

THE DIVIDED PROFESSORIATE, *by Seymour M. Lipset and Everett C. Ladd, Jr., reprinted from* CHANGE, *vol. 3, no. 3, pp. 54–60, May 1971.**

JEWISH ACADEMICS IN THE UNITED STATES: THEIR ACHIEVEMENTS, CULTURE AND POLITICS, *by Seymour M. Lipset and Everett C. Ladd, Jr., reprinted from* AMERICAN JEWISH YEAR BOOK, *1971.**

*The Commission's stock of this reprint has been exhausted.

THE UNHOLY ALLIANCE AGAINST THE CAMPUS, *by Kenneth Keniston and Michael Lerner, reprinted from* NEW YORK TIMES MAGAZINE, *November 8, 1970.**

PRECARIOUS PROFESSORS: NEW PATTERNS OF REPRESENTATION, *by Joseph W. Garbarino, reprinted from* INDUSTRIAL RELATIONS, *vol. 10, no. 1, February 1971.**

. . . AND WHAT PROFESSORS THINK: ABOUT STUDENT PROTEST AND MANNERS, MORALS, POLITICS, AND CHAOS ON THE CAMPUS, *by Seymour Martin Lipset and Everett C. Ladd, Jr., reprinted from* PSYCHOLOGY TODAY, *November 1970.**

DEMAND AND SUPPLY IN U.S. HIGHER EDUCATION: A PROGRESS REPORT, *by Roy Radner and Leonard S. Miller, reprinted from* AMERICAN ECONOMIC REVIEW, *May 1970.**

RESOURCES FOR HIGHER EDUCATION: AN ECONOMIST'S VIEW, *by Theodore W. Schultz, reprinted from* JOURNAL OF POLITICAL ECONOMY, *vol. 76, no. 3, University of Chicago, May / June 1968.**

INDUSTRIAL RELATIONS AND UNIVERSITY RELATIONS, *by Clark Kerr, reprinted from* PROCEEDINGS OF THE 21ST ANNUAL WINTER MEETING OF THE INDUSTRIAL RELATIONS RESEARCH ASSOCIATION, *pp. 15–25.**

NEW CHALLENGES TO THE COLLEGE AND UNIVERSITY, *by Clark Kerr, reprinted from Kermit Gordon (ed.),* AGENDA FOR THE NATION, *The Brookings Institution, Washington, D.C., 1968.**

PRESIDENTIAL DISCONTENT, *by Clark Kerr, reprinted from David C. Nichols (ed.),* PERSPECTIVES ON CAMPUS TENSIONS: PAPERS PREPARED FOR THE SPECIAL COMMITTEE ON CAMPUS TENSIONS, *American Council on Education, Washington, D.C., September 1970.**

STUDENT PROTEST—AN INSTITUTIONAL AND NATIONAL PROFILE, *by Harold Hodgkinson, reprinted from* THE RECORD, *vol. 71, no. 4, May 1970.**

COMING OF MIDDLE AGE IN HIGHER EDUCATION, *by Earl F. Cheit, address delivered to American Association of State Colleges and Universities and National Association of State Universities and Land-Grant Colleges, Nov. 13, 1972.*

MEASURING FACULTY UNIONISM: QUANTITY AND QUALITY, *by Bill Aussieker and J. W. Garbarino, reprinted from* INDUSTRIAL RELATIONS, *vol. 12, no. 2, May 1973.*

PROBLEMS IN THE TRANSITION FROM ELITE TO MASS HIGHER EDUCATION, *by Martin Trow, paper prepared for a conference on mass higher education sponsored by the Organization for Economic Co-operation and Development, June 1973.**

*The Commission's stock of this reprint has been exhausted.

Black Elite

Black Elite

THE NEW MARKET FOR

HIGHLY EDUCATED BLACK AMERICANS

by *Richard B. Freeman*

Associate Professor of Economics
Harvard University

A Report Prepared for
The Carnegie Commission on Higher Education

MCGRAW–HILL BOOK COMPANY
New York   St. Louis   San Francisco
Auckland   Bogotá   Düsseldorf   Johannesburg
London   Madrid   Mexico   Montreal
New Delhi   Panama   Paris   São Paulo
Singapore   Sydney   Tokyo   Toronto

The Carnegie Commission on Higher Education
2150 Shattuck Avenue, Berkeley, California 94704,
has sponsored preparation of this report as part
of a continuing effort to obtain and present
significant information for public discussion.
The views expressed are those of the author.

BLACK ELITE
The New Market for Highly Educated Black Americans

This book was set in Palatino by University Graphics, Inc.
It was printed and bound by The Maple Press Company.
The designer was Elliot Epstein. The editors were Nancy Frank
and Janine Parson for McGraw-Hill Book Company and
Verne A. Stadtman for the Carnegie Commission
on Higher Education. Audre Hanneman edited the index.
Milton J. Heiberg supervised the production.

Library of Congress Cataloging in Publication Data

Freeman, Richard Barry, date
Black elite.

Bibliography: p.
  Includes index.
1. Afro-Americans—Employment. 2. Afro-American
college graduates. 3. Afro-Americans—Economic
conditions. I. Carnegie Commission on Higher Education.
II. Title.
E185.8.F74   331.6'3'96073   76-28702
ISBN 0-07-010116-7

123456789 MAMM 7

To W. E. B. Du Bois, Charles Johnson, and Horace Mann Bond

Contents

Foreword

Richard Freeman provides in this report the best current study of the emergence in American society of an expanding group of black professionals. This is an important development in the contemporary life of the nation, and one long overdue.

This historic change in the climate of opportunity results from the efforts of the blacks themselves and the new chances for them to obtain advanced education through colleges and universities; but above all, Freeman concludes, from the recent intervention of government on behalf of the American promise that all persons shall be given an opportunity to develop their talents.

In the midst of our national concentration on our failures, here is a documentation of one area of success. Richard Freeman has contributed his careful scholarship to an illumination of a most important aspect of American society.

Clark Kerr
Chairman
The Carnegie Commission
on Higher Education

January 1977

Introduction

How then shall the leaders of a struggling people be trained and the hands of the risen few strengthened? There can be but one answer: The best and most capable of their youth must be schooled in the colleges and universities of the land.

W. E. B. DUBOIS, 1903

Despite the widely assumed connection of discrimination with poverty, labor market differentials by race traditionally have been greatest at the top of the economic ladder. College-trained black men, in particular, have long suffered from low incomes and poor job opportunities. In 1959 the income of white male college graduates exceeded that of nonwhite graduates by 81 percent, while white grade school graduates had an advantage of just 46 percent (U.S. Bureau of the Census, 1963*a*, table 1). Young (24- to 34-year-old) nonwhite men earned $4,760 compared with $7,146 for young white degree recipients (ibid). With rare exception, black graduates were excluded from high-level jobs in major corporations and concentrated in low-paying professions. Nearly half of black male college seniors planned on teaching careers compared with one-seventh of white seniors. The potentiality for black economic progress through additional education and attainment of college and university training seemed small, indeed.[1]

---

[1]National statistics often refer to nonwhites rather than blacks. Wherever possible in this book I use data for blacks. However, in many cases, I am forced to examine statistics for nonwhites, especially when the data are from the 1950 and 1960 *Census of Population* reports. Because a reasonably large proportion of college-trained nonwhites are *not* black, this creates some biases in the analysis. When I examine changes over time using data on nonwhites for 1960 and for blacks in 1970, the bias will tend to understate black advance. When nonwhite data are used in the text to refer to the position of blacks, at a moment in time, on the other hand, they tend to overstate the relative standing of blacks. Still, I use nonwhite data to indicate the position of blacks when these are the only data available.

During the 1960s these discriminatory patterns underwent dramatic change. The demand for black college graduates increased enormously, with consequent improvements in job opportunities and salaries. For the first time, national corporations began to recruit black men and women for managerial and professional jobs, seeking employees at southern black colleges that had previously never seen corporate recruiters. Increasing numbers of black college men entered managerial and business-oriented professions, such as accounting and law, rather than the traditional teaching field. The income of black college graduates rose sharply relative to that of white graduates, ending the historic pattern of increasing racial income differentials with the level of education. The starting salaries of black college graduates reached parity with those of whites. The educational position of blacks also improved substantially as colleges and universities began recruiting black students and faculty. Black college enrollments skyrocketed, particularly in traditionally white national institutions. In short, there was a *dramatic collapse in traditional discriminatory patterns in the market for highly qualified black Americans.*

Black Elite is a detailed examination of this remarkable socioeconomic development. It documents the post-World War II gain of college-trained and related high-level black workers, investigates the response of black college students and qualified personnel to the new market setting, and explores the factors that transformed the market. The analysis and findings have important implications for understanding the operation of discrimination in the economy, the economic motivation of a discriminated people, and the role of government in reducing economic discrimination.

The book begins with an empirical analysis of the developments of the new market for highly qualified black workers. Chapter 1 shows how the income and occupational position of college-educated blacks improved relative to that of their white peers in the late 1960s and early 1970s. It finds that in the new market young black male college graduates and black female graduates attained rough economic parity with whites, after decades of substantial inequality. Chapter 2 concentrates on the transformation of the educational system that accompanied the new market, particularly the increased enrollment of blacks in colleges and universities. The way in which black Americans responded to the new opportunities is the subject of Chapters 3 and 4. Chapter 3 examines the impact of changed economic incentives on career and educational decisions and provides estimates of the elasticity of supply of blacks to higher education and to diverse occupations. Chapter 4 shows how traditional intergenerational patterns of social mobility were altered in the 1960s, as young black cohorts made significant gains relative to older cohorts.

The four succeeding chapters examine the extent of economic change in important high-level markets and seek to evaluate the impact of governmental and related antidiscriminatory activity on the increased demand for the black elite. Chapter 5 presents evidence that the rapid economic advance of black workers in the late sixties–early seventies was substantially affected by the diverse equal employment pressures that followed the 1964 Civil Rights Act. Chapter 6 relates the improved position of highly qualified blacks in public employment to black voting power, which increased greatly in the South after the Voting Rights Act of 1965. Chapter 7 turns to what has traditionally been the major occupation of black college graduates, elementary and secondary school teaching. It finds that despite desegregation of schools which could be expected to reduce demand for black teachers in the South, employment was maintained in the sixties in part because of increased black voting power. The next chapter investigates the market for college professors, where federal affirmative action and related pressures greatly increased demand for black academicians and created a nonnegligible premium in income for the most academically productive. While in each of these chapters the analysis is equivocal due to the problem of pinning down specific factors behind the "revolutionary" development of the new market, the evidence suggests a substantial role for federal antidiscriminatory policy, indicating that governmental activities can redistribute income and opportunities in the society.

The final chapter summarizes the main findings of the book and sketches out a new view of discrimination in the United States, designed to account for the rapid advances of the 1960s in contrast with previous decades of stability in black-white economic differentials.

In writing this book I have benefited from the assistance and comments of numerous persons. Franziska Amacher, Kathy

Burgoyne, Jerome Culp, Bruce Dunson, Eric Jones, Stephanie Sonnabend, among others, provided useful research assistance. Comments by R. Fogel, Z. Griliches and T. W. Schultz improved the study. Financial support by the Carnegie Commission and by grant No. G-00-0202 from the National Institution of Education enabled me to undertake the calculations and interviews necessary for the book.

Black Elite

1. The New Market for Highly Educated Black Americans

Long-standing economic differences between black and white Americans, which have traditionally been greatest among the highly educated and skilled, began declining in the 1960s. After decades of little economic advance relative to whites, blacks made significant progress in a wide variety of areas:

- In education, the average educational attainment of blacks moved closer to that of whites, with the proportion of high school and college graduates increasing significantly among the young.

- In the job market, ratios of black to white incomes rose substantially for most groups of workers. Black women enjoyed exceptionally great advances, which brought them economic parity with white women having comparable education or job skills. Young black men also obtained large gains in relative income while the income ratio for older men rose more moderately.

- Black and white occupational distributions tended to converge, as black women moved from domestic service to factory and clerical jobs and as black men increased their representation in craft, professional, and managerial jobs.

- In each region of the country, but notably in the South, income differences by race declined, although sizeable gaps remained, especially in the South.

In the college job market, the changes were even more dramatic, with the situation for blacks improving to the point where:

- Black college women reported higher income than their white counterparts in 1970.

- The income differential between black and white male graduates narrowed for all men and disappeared among young graduates.
- Major corporations recruited and hired black professionals and managers for the first time.
- Black male students entered traditionally closed fields such as law, management, accounting, and engineering, in large numbers.
- An increasing proportion of black young persons enrolled for undergraduate and graduate training.

These changes in the economic position of black Americans, which created a new market for the highly educated, are the subject matter of this chapter. While the chapter considers briefly the overall economic advance of blacks, it is principally concerned with college-trained and professional-managerial work forces, where economic differences were greatest and have declined most.

OCCUPATIONAL PROGRESS Black Americans have historically been concentrated in low-level occupations as a result of little and poor quality education, unfavorable family backgrounds, and job market discrimination. The highly educated were found in teaching and segregated professional services, but rarely in managerial or professional jobs in major corporations. From the period of slavery until the 1950s and 1960s, the occupational standing of blacks relative to that of whites improved little, if at all, save during World Wars I and II, and may even have deteriorated somewhat over the long run.[1] In the new market of the 1960s, the historic pattern of little or no occupational progress was finally broken. Blacks moved up the occupational hierarchy rapidly, with the highly educated breaking into previously "closed" managerial and professional occupations.

Overall Change The broad pattern of black advancement in the job structure is examined in Tables 1 through 3, which compare the occupational distribution of black (nonwhite) and total (white) workers from 1950 to 1974. Table 1 presents census of population data on the position of black and total men and women in 1950,

[1] For evidence of deterioration in the job structure of blacks through the depression see Freeman (1974). A detailed analysis of the economic history of blacks since the slavery period will be given in Freeman (forthcoming).

TABLE 1   *Distribution of men and women by major occupation and race, 1950–70*

	1950		1960		1970	
Occupation	Black	Total	Black	Total	Black	Total
Male						
Professional workers	2.1	7.3	3.1	10.3	5.9	14.3
Managerial workers	2.0	10.6	1.7	10.6	3.0	11.2
Clerical workers	3.1	6.5	5.5	7.0	8.1	7.7
Salespersons	1.1	6.4	1.3	9.6	2.1	6.9
Craftsmen	7.7	18.7	9.8	19.6	15.3	21.2
Operatives	21.1	20.1	24.4	19.9	29.9	19.5
Private household workers	1.0	0.2	0.7	0.1	0.4	0.1
Service workers	13.3	5.9	14.0	6.0	15.6	8.1
Laborers	23.3	8.1	20.3	5.3	15.8	6.6
Farmers	13.4	10.4	4.3	5.5	0.9	2.8
Farm laborers	10.4	4.9	6.9	2.7	3.5	1.7
Not reported	1.4	1.1	8.4	6.2	0.0	0.0
Female						
Professional workers	5.4	12.4	7.2	13.0	11.3	15.7
Managerial workers	1.4	4.3	1.0	3.7	1.5	3.7
Clerical workers	4.0	27.2	7.6	29.7	20.7	34.9
Salespersons	1.3	8.4	1.5	7.9	2.6	7.4
Craftsmen	0.6	1.5	0.7	1.2	1.4	1.8
Operatives	14.5	19.2	12.7	15.4	16.5	14.3
Private household workers	41.5	8.6	35.7	7.8	17.9	3.8
Service workers	18.9	12.2	21.4	13.5	25.5	16.6
Laborers	1.5	0.8	0.9	0.5	1.5	1.0
Farmers	1.7	0.8	0.6	0.6	0.2	0.2
Farm laborers	7.6	2.9	2.9	1.2	1.1	0.5
Not reported	1.6	1.8	8.2	5.7	0.0	0.0

SOURCES: 1950, U.S. Bureau of the Census (1956, pp. 29–36); 1960, U.S. Bureau of the Census (1963*b*, pp. 21–30); 1970, U.S. Bureau of the Census (1973*a*, pp. 739–745).

1960, and 1970. It reveals an enormous gap between black and total occupational attainment in 1950, which is greatly reduced among women but only moderately among men in the next two decades. At the outset, just 2 percent of black men are employed as professionals, 2 percent as managers, and 8 percent as craftsmen compared with 7, 11, and 19 percent of total men; among women the 1950 gap is even greater as 42 percent of black women, but just 9 percent of total women, are employed as domestics in the private household sector, and only 4 percent of black compared with 27 percent of total women held clerical jobs. Between 1950 and 1970, especially in the 1960s, there are substantial black gains in relative occupational positions, with black women improving their status especially rapidly. The proportion of black women employed in private households dropped sharply between 1960 and 1970 from 36 percent to 18 percent while the fraction in professional and clerical jobs rose equally dramatically from 7 and 8 to 11 and 21 percent. Among men, there is a similar but more modest gain in white collar jobs (9 percent are professionals or managers in 1970) and a striking movement into craft activities, whose share of black men doubled from 1950 to 1970, while the proportion of whites so employed was roughly stable.

To obtain an overall measure of the extent of black advance in the job structure in the fifties and sixties, I have calculated two summary statistics of the difference between the black and total distributions: the sum of the absolute percentage point differences between them, to be called the index of structural differences (ISD), and income-weighted indices valuing the distributions with black and total incomes by occupation.[2] The former statistic measures the difference in the composition of black and white job structures, regardless of whether the differences are likely to create large or small differences in income. The income indices, by contrast, show the overall dollar worth of the job distributions given black or total income weights. The ratio of income values with the same weights measures the difference in occupational status if blacks and whites received the same pay within occupations; the ratio with blacks given nonwhite weights and whites total weights (line 4 of Table 2) shows the overall difference in income due to differences in job structure and of income within occupational classes.

The summary statistics, which are given in Table 2, reveal substantially different rates of black occupational advance by decade and sex. In the fifties black men made, at best, a modest

---

[2] The index of structural differences is calculated as follows: Let α_i^B be the proportion of blacks employed in the ith occupation and α_i^W, the proportion of whites. Then the ISD is defined as $\Sigma \mid \alpha_i^B - \alpha_i^W \mid$. The income weighted index of the structure is $\Sigma \alpha_i W_i$ where W_i is the income weight of the ith occupation.

TABLE 2 *Differences between black and total job structures, 1950–1970*

Measure of structure	Male			Female		
	1950	*1960*	*1970*	*1950*	*1960*	*1970*
1. Absolute sum of percentage points	66.67	68.47	58.98	91.87	67.71	52.30
2. Income value of structure (total weights)						
Black	3,480	3,864	4,307	1,467	1,642	2,133
Total	4,531	4,857	5,007	2,406	2,469	2,594
Ratio of income values	0.77	0.80	0.86	0.61	0.67	0.82
3. Income value of structure (nonwhite weights)						
Black	2,417	2,774	3,066	1,344	1,526	1,991
Total	2,982	3,225	3,361	2,238	2,319	2,418
Ratio of income values	0.81	0.86	0.91	0.60	0.66	0.81
4. Ratio of income value of structures with nonwhite weights for blacks and total weights for whites	0.53	0.57	0.61	0.56	0.63	0.77

SOURCE: Income weights, U.S. Bureau of the Census (1963c, tables 25, 26).

relative advance in occupational standing: the ratio of the income value of their jobs to that of white men rose from 0.77 to just 0.80, while the index of structural differences was virtually unchanged; by contrast, in the 1960s both statistics indicate substantial advances, with relative income indices increasing from 0.80 to 0.86 and the ISD falling from 68 to 59. The low income of farmers, especially nonwhite farmers in 1959 ($2,202 for all farmers and $836 for nonwhites) makes the movement from agriculture to industry especially significant in improving the income-weighted occupational index of black men.

While black men did not make sizeable gains in the job structure until the 1960s, the position of black women improved significantly in the 1950s and at accelerated rates in the 1960s. Between 1960 and 1970 the ISD declined by about 40 percentage points, and the relative income-value of occupations rose from 0.61 to 0.82. In 1950 black women, working largely as domestics, differed more from white women in the job structure than did black from white men; in 1970 black women were more likely to be working in the same occupation as comparable whites than were black men. In 1950 the relative position of black women was much lower than that of men; in 1970 it was nearly the same.

The rapid upward movement of blacks in the job structure in the new market is examined further in Table 3, which compares the percentage of nonwhite and white workers in the major occupations in the late 1960s and early 1970s using Current

TABLE 3 *The changing percentage of nonwhite and white workers in occupations, 1966–1974*

Occupation	Negro and other races			White		
	1966	*1970*	*1974*	*1966*	*1970*	*1974*
Male						
Professional and technical workers	5.8	7.8	9.4	13.2	14.6	14.5
Managers and administrators except farm	3.4	4.7	5.4	14.5	15.3	14.8
Salespersons	1.7	1.8	2.0	6.1	6.1	6.4
Clerical workers	6.7	7.4	7.4	7.2	7.4	6.3
Craftsmen	12.6	13.8	15.8	20.7	20.8	21.4
Operatives	27.5	28.3	25.6	20.1	18.7	17.4
Nonfarm laborers	19.6	17.5	15.1	6.0	6.2	6.9
Private household workers	0.3	0.3	0.1	0.1	0.1	0.0
Other service workers	15.3	12.8	15.2	6.1	6.0	7.2
Farmers and farm managers	2.4	1.7	1.2	4.4	3.6	3.1
Farm laborers	4.9	3.9	2.8	1.9	1.7	1.8
Female						
Professional and technical workers	8.7	10.8	11.7	14.1	15.0	15.4
Managers and administrators except farm	1.5	1.9	2.4	4.9	4.8	5.3
Salespersons	1.9	2.5	2.7	8.0	7.7	7.4
Clerical workers	13.5	20.8	24.9	35.4	36.4	36.4
Craftsmen	0.7	0.8	1.4	1.0	1.2	1.6
Operatives	15.9	17.6	17.2	15.7	14.1	12.3
Nonfarm laborers	0.6	0.7	1.2	0.4	0.4	0.5
Private household workers	27.8	17.5	11.3	4.2	3.4	2.5
Other service workers	25.7	25.6	26.1	14.1	15.3	16.7
Farmers and farm managers	0.5	0.1	0.0	0.5	0.3	0.3
Farm laborers	3.3	1.5	1.0	2.0	1.5	1.2

SOURCES: 1966 and 1970, U.S. Bureau of Labor Statistics (1971, table 19); 1974, U.S. Bureau of Labor Statistics (January 1975, table 19).

Population Survey data.[3] The table shows a substantial black advance from 1966 to 1970, particularly into the professional and managerial ranks, and most importantly, continued, and possibly accelerated progress in the early seventies, despite the weakened job market. Between 1966 and 1970 the fraction of black men working as managers or professionals increased by 36 percent as compared with 8 percent for whites; from 1970 to 1973, the proportion of blacks employed as managers increased by 15 percent compared with a 3 percent drop for whites; the proportion of professionals went up by 21 percent (versus a 1 percent drop). Overall, the ISD between the male occupational distributions fell from 67 to 53 while the relative income index of occupational position rose from 0.84 to 0.88 (using 1959 income weights). Similarly, the proportion of black women in managerial and clerical jobs continued to rise from 1970 to 1974 while the proportion in private household work fell. In the entire 1966–1974 period black and white female job structures converged rapidly, with the ISD declining by 23 points and the ratio of income weighted indices increasing from 0.71 to 0.89.

Occupational Change: Cohorts and New Entrants

The process of occupational change in a population involves shifts in jobs by experienced cohorts and differences in the job distributions between retiring and entering workers. How important were these two forms of adjustment in the advance of blacks in the 1960s?

Table 4 presents data that suggest that the major adjustment occurred at the new entrant-retiring worker margin, which makes the career choice of young persons an especially important part of the story. Columns (1) and (2) record the proportionate distribution among major occupations of a single black cohort, persons aged 35–44 in 1960 and 45–54 in 1970; column (3) gives the difference in these distributions for each occupation, and column (4) the comparable change for total workers. The rest of the table focuses on new entrants and retiring workers, comparing the occupational distribution of persons entering the labor market in the 1960s (aged 25–34 in 1970) with those likely to retire in the decade (55–64 in 1960).

---

[3] Because survey methodologies differ, the Current Population Survey (CPS) and *Census of Population* figures diverge somewhat. I compare changes in CPS and in *Census of Population* data separately and try not to compare one with the other, which could give misleading pictures of the trends

TABLE 4
*Distribution in 1960
and 1970 of the
nonwhite work force
35–44 years old in
1960, and of retiring
workers and new
entrants, and
nonwhite and total
changes, 1960–1970*

Sex and occupation	Workers 35–44 years old in 1960			
	Distribution of nonwhites		Change, 1960–1970	
	1960 (1)	1970 (2)	Nonwhites (2) − (1) (3)	Total workers (4)
Females				
Professional and technical workers	0.08	0.09	0.01	0.00
Managers, officials, and proprietors, except farm	0.01	0.03	0.02	0.02
Clerical workers	0.09	0.10	0.01	0.00
Salespersons	0.02	0.02	0.00	−0.01
Craftsmen	0.01	0.01	0.00	0.00
Operatives	0.16	0.18	0.02	−0.04
Laborers except farm and mine	0.01	0.01	0.00	0.00
Farmers and farm managers	0.01	0.00	−0.01	0.00
Farm laborers and foremen	0.03	0.02	−0.01	0.01
Service workers except private household	0.24	0.29	0.05	0.02
Private household workers	0.34	0.26	−0.08	0.00
TOTAL	1.00	1.00	0.00	0.00
Males				
Professional and technical workers	0.05	0.06	0.01	0.01
Managers, officials, and proprietors, except farm	0.03	0.06	0.03	0.06
Clerical workers	0.06	0.07	0.01	0.00
Salespersons	0.01	0.01	0.00	−0.02
Craftsmen	0.13	0.16	0.03	0.00
Operatives	0.29	0.27	−0.02	−0.03
Laborers except farm and mine	0.21	0.18	−0.03	0.00
Farmers and farm managers	0.04	0.02	−0.02	−0.01
Farm laborers and foremen	0.05	0.03	−0.02	−0.01
Service workers except private household	0.12	0.14	0.02	0.00
Private household workers	0.01	0.00	0.01	0.00
TOTAL	1.00	1.00	0.00	0.00

NOTE: Figures are rounded and may not add to totals.
SOURCE: Freeman (1973).

Distribution of nonwhites		Net difference between entering and leaving cohorts, decade ending in 1970	
Retiring workers 55–64 years old in 1960 (5)	New entrants 25–34 years old in 1970 (6)	Nonwhites (6) − (5) (7)	Total workers (8)
0.06	0.15	0.09	0.05
0.02	0.01	−0.01	−0.03
0.03	0.25	0.22	0.14
0.01	0.02	0.01	−0.06
0.01	0.01	0.00	0.01
0.09	0.21	0.12	0.00
0.01	0.01	0.00	0.00
0.01	0.00	−0.01	−0.01
0.03	0.01	−0.02	0.00
0.20	0.23	0.03	−0.03
0.53	0.08	−0.45	−0.05
1.00	1.00	0.00	0.00
0.03	0.11	0.08	0.12
0.04	0.05	0.01	−0.01
0.03	0.08	0.05	0.00
0.01	0.03	0.02	−0.01
0.10	0.14	0.04	−0.02
0.20	0.35	0.15	0.03
0.22	0.14	−0.08	−0.01
0.08	0.00	−0.08	−0.07
0.08	0.02	−0.06	−0.01
0.19	0.09	−0.10	−0.02
0.01	0.00	−0.01	0.00
1.00	1.00	0.00	0.00

The major finding is that the greatest difference in the job structures is between entering and leaving cohorts—columns (7) and (8), which accounted for much of the gain in the black job structure. Measured by the ISD, the distributions of entering and leaving black cohorts differ by 68 points among men and 96 points among women. By contrast, the differences for all workers are more moderate, 30 points for both men and women. As a result, the income value of the occupational structure of black men in the 25- to 34-year-old group was 89 percent that of their white peers compared with just 76 percent in the 55- to 64-year-old group. Among women the entering cohort had a job structure worth 87 percent that of whites; the leaving cohort, just 63 percent. By contrast, while the occupational attainment of experienced blacks, particularly women, also improved in the sixties, the changes shown for these workers are much smaller. The ISD between the distributions of workers aged 35–44 in 1960 and 45–54 in 1970 is 20 and 21 points for nonwhite men and women, respectively, and 14 and 10 points for nonwhite women. Measured as income-weighted indices of job structure, the relative position of 35- to 44-year-old black men increased from 0.81 to 0.83 as they aged over the decade; the relative position of women improved by six percentage points, from 0.68 to 0.74 (Freeman, 1973).

In short, the major factor producing convergence in the black and white job structure was the greater similarity in the occupations of young workers than of retiring workers.[4]

MALE COLLEGE GRADUATES AND PROFESSIONALS

The black male college graduates of particular concern to this book made exceptionally large gains in the job structure in the period under study.

First, as Table 5 shows, there was a substantial increase in the fraction of black college men employed in the professional and managerial categories normally associated with college training

[4] The relative size of the various cohorts is also, of course, a critical factor in the overall impact of changes in experienced-worker job distributions and differences between entering and leaving workers. In the period under study, there were approximately 1 million black male and 0.8 million female entrants aged 25–34 and 0.8 million male and 0.28 million female workers whose age increased from 55 to 64 to greater than 65 compared with approximately 1.7 (male) and 1.4 (female) million workers in the intermediate age (35–54) bracket. Given these similarities in magnitude, the statement in the text holds, though obviously in weakened form.

TABLE 5 *Occupations of male college graduates, 1950–1970*

| | Percent of college graduates, male | | | | | |
| | 1950 | | 1960 | | 1970 | |
Occupation	Nonwhite	Total	Nonwhite	Total	Black	Total
Professional and technical workers	54.28	55.37	60.37	57.00	61.31	59.13
Managers	7.72	18.40	6.99	18.25	13.38	20.83
Clerical workers	9.89	6.09	9.36	5.32	7.78	4.59
Salespersons	3.06	8.42	2.53	8.39	3.34	8.52
Craftsmen	5.28	4.48	3.55	3.98	4.68	3.16
Operatives	5.19	2.19	3.39	1.35	3.62	1.21
Service workers	7.63	1.30	4.45	0.92	4.03	1.23
Farm laborers	0.53	0.32	0.23	0.15	0.14	0.14
Farm managers	2.08	2.10	0.62	1.17	0.19	0.80
Laborers	3.10	0.16	1.82	0.38	1.53	0.40
Not reporting	1.24	0.71	6.71	3.09	0.00	0.00

SOURCES: U.S. Bureau of the Census (1953*b*, table 1, pp 108–127; 1963*c*, table 8, pp. 136–168; 1973*c*, table 11, pp. 213–222).

and a decline in the proportion in less desirable jobs. In 1950 only 61 percent of nonwhite graduates were professionals or managers compared with 74 percent of all college men, a 13-point differential. By contrast, in 1970, 75 percent of nonwhite graduates worked as professionals and managers compared with 80 percent of all graduates, a 5-point differential. Much of the black gain in the 1960s occurred in management, where blacks have historically been heavily underrepresented.

Second, as Chart 1 depicts, the movement of black graduates into management, which has potentially great significance in view of the decision-making powers of managers, continued into the 1970s. The chart shows that the percentage of nonwhite college men working as managers quadrupled from 1965 to 1973, with much of the gain occurring in the early 1970s while the proportion of whites so employed rose only slightly. In 1965 just 5 percent of nonwhite college men held managerial positions; in 1969, 11 percent; in 1973, 20 percent. While the functions and responsibilities accorded newly hired black managers are obviously important in judging the nature of the change, it is clear that a major breakthrough into an important occupational area was made.

CHART 1 *Changes in the fraction of nonwhite and white college graduates employed as managers, 1959–1973*

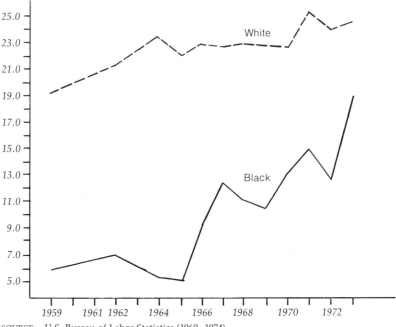

SOURCE: U.S. Bureau of Labor Statistics (1960–1974).

Third, while significant differences continue to exist in the specific professions of black and white college graduates, there was a substantial convergence in distributions at the level of very detailed jobs. Table 6 examines the relative distributions among detailed high-level occupations in 1950, 1960, and 1970. Columns (1) through (3) record "relative probabilities of employment," the ratio of the percentage of black to total male graduates employed in a field; columns (4) through (5) depict the ratio of these probabilities.[5] When the figures in columns (1) to (3) exceed 1, the black graduates have higher probabilities of being employed than whites. When the figures in column (4) or (5) rise above unity, the relative probability that black gradu-

---

[5] Because 1950 and 1960 Census data on occupation by education do not distinguish blacks from nonwhites, the number of black college men had to be estimated. I multiplied the percentage of nonwhites who were black in each occupation by the number of nonwhite college men to obtain the basic figures. These were summed and divided by the sum to get the probabilities. Data on the percentage of nonwhites who were black in the occupations were taken from U.S. Bureau of the Census (1956, table 3; 1963b, table 3).

TABLE 6 *Relative probability of employment of black men with four or more years of college in detailed occupations and changes in relative probabilities, 1950–1970*

	Relative probability of employment of men with four or more years of college			Changes in relative probabilities	
	1950 (1)	1960 (2)	1970 (3)	1950–1960 (4)	1960–1970 (5)
Professional	0.99	0.95	1.03	0.96	1.08
Accountants	0.16	0.24	0.52	1.50	2.17
Architects	0.39	0.17	0.49	0.44	3.47
Clergymen	2.00	1.31	1.21	0.66	0.92
College teachers	1.16	0.82	0.78	0.71	0.95
Dentists	1.11	0.97	0.88	0.87	0.91
Designers	0.22	0.51	0.73	2.30	1.43
Draftsmen	0.60	0.57	1.24	0.95	2.18
Editors and reporters	0.39	0.34	0.41	0.87	1.21
Engineers, technical	0.13	0.18	0.34	1.38	1.89
Civil	0.13	0.28	0.38	2.15	1.36
Electrical	0.23	0.20	0.45	0.87	2.25
Industrial	*	0.12	0.38	*	3.17
Mechanical	0.08	0.15	0.21	1.88	1.40
Funeral directors and embalmers	4.06	4.57	3.00	1.13	0.66
Lawyers and judges	0.40	0.40	0.41	1.00	1.03
Librarians	2.40	1.12	1.14	0.80	1.02
Musicians and composers	1.68	1.43	1.60	0.85	1.12
Natural scientists	0.26	0.64	0.87	2.46	1.36
Biologists	*	1.23	1.38	*	1.22
Chemists	*	0.76	1.13	*	1.49
Mathematicians	*	1.30	0.96	*	0.74
Personnel and labor relations workers	0.59	0.41	1.21	0.69	2.95
Pharmacists	0.86	0.83	0.77	0.97	0.93
Photographers	0.25	1.55	0.56	0.62	0.36
Physicians and surgeons	1.11	0.97	0.88	0.87	0.91
Public relations workers	*	0.30	0.70	*	2.33
Recreation workers	3.36	3.05	3.00	0.91	0.98
Social welfare workers	3.24	4.33	3.80	1.34	0.88
Social scientists	0.59	0.70	0.78	1.19	1.11

TABLE 6 *(continued)*

	Relative probability of employment of men with four or more years of college			Changes in relative probabilities	
	1950 (1)	1960 (2)	1970 (3)	1950–1960 (4)	1960–1970 (5)
Teachers, elementary	*	3.56	2.86	*	0.80
Secondary	*	2.00	1.83	*	0.92
Technicians, health	2.19	3.61	2.40	1.65	0.66
Electrical and electronic	*	1.78	1.25	*	0.70
Therapists	0.84	1.64	1.25	1.95	1.49
Managers (except farm)	0.39	0.32	0.65	0.82	2.03
Officials	0.72	0.61	1.34	0.85	2.20

*Not available.
NOTE: Data for 1950 and 1960 are estimates, as described in footnote 5.
SOURCE: U.S. Bureau of the Census (1956, tables 3, 10, 11; 1963*b*, tables 3, 9, 10; 1973*c*, tables 5, 6).

ates are in the occupation rose and conversely when they are less than unity.

The table reveals a striking change in the relative occupational distribution of black college men in postwar years. In occupations where exceptionally few black graduates were found in 1950 and 1960 relative probabilities increased substantially, especially in the sixties, while relative probabilities in traditional areas of employment—such as clergy, teaching, funeral directing and embalming—fell. The most impressive gains are in the business-oriented fields of accounting, engineering, management, and personnel and labor relations. In accounting, for example, the ratio of black to total proportions of college graduates jumps from 0.16 in 1950 to 0.52 in 1970. Overall, the result is a substantial decline in the difference between the distributions in the 1960–1970 period, with the index of structural differentiation between the underlying distributions dropping from 68 points in the former year to 45 points in the latter year.[6]

When the college population is divided into those with and without postbachelor's training, moreover, even smaller differences are found in 1970 for the latter group (see Table 7). In this

[6] In these calculations I have used the figures for engineers, natural and social scientists, and managers in total, rather than the more detailed distributions given in the table and include the percentages in other professions and all other fields as two additional groups.

TABLE 7 *Percentage distribution of black and total college-trained men, by years of college, 1970*

	Percentage distribution, 1970			
	College graduates, four years only		Post B.A. training, five or more years	
	Black (1)	Total (2)	Black (3)	Total (4)
Professional	54.49	46.66	68.61	72.60
Accountants	2.93	6.22	1.24	1.93
Architects	0.16	0.34	0.46	0.87
Athletes and kindred	0.25	0.13	0.06	0.07
Clergymen	1.91	0.80	3.87	3.94
College teachers	0.71	0.76	7.34	9.11
Dentists	0.13	0.19	2.29	2.41
Designers	0.35	0.43	0.18	0.32
Draftsmen	0.63	0.46	0.28	0.30
Editors and reporters	0.29	0.91	0.30	0.56
Engineers (technical)	3.90	12.36	3.34	8.72
Civil	0.65	1.90	0.53	1.18
Electrical	1.32	2.87	0.96	2.18
Industrial	0.51	1.66	0.50	0.97
Mechanical	0.39	1.82	0.28	1.22
Funeral directors and embalmers	0.27	0.08	0.20	0.06
Lawyers and judges	0.45	0.50	2.74	6.94
Librarians	0.20	0.08	0.29	0.36
Musicians and composers	0.32	0.15	0.23	0.19
Natural scientists	1.60	1.54	1.99	2.60
Biologists	0.31	0.14	0.37	0.36
Chemists	1.09	0.96	1.28	1.20
Mathematicians	0.25	0.23	0.24	0.28
Personnel and labor relations workers	1.60	1.65	1.70	1.06
Pharmacists	0.77	1.14	0.91	1.01
Photographers	0.11	0.13	0.00	0.05
Physicians & surgeons	1.27	1.90	8.86	11.77
Public relations workers	0.25	0.52	0.33	0.28
Recreation workers	0.63	0.19	0.31	0.13
Social welfare workers	3.31	0.85	3.22	0.88

TABLE 7 *(continued)*

	College graduates, four years only		Post B. A. training, five or more years	
	Percentage distribution, 1970			
	Black (1)	Total (2)	Black (3)	Total (4)
Social scientists	0.42	0.67	1.31	1.46
Economists	0.32	0.57	0.52	0.75
Pyschologists	0.02	0.02	0.63	0.51
Teachers, elementary	9.78	2.82	7.57	3.35
Secondary	12.71	5.29	12.96	8.83
Technicians, health	1.02	0.30	0.64	0.42
Electrical and electronic	0.17	0.16	0.13	0.08
Therapists	0.44	0.15	0.56	0.27
Other professional	7.56	5.94	5.30	4.63
Managers (except farm)	10.04	23.44	15.94	15.77
Officials	1.24	1.03	1.52	1.01
All other	35.47	29.90	15.45	11.63
Total	100.00	100.00	100.00	100.00

SOURCE: U.S. Bureau of the Census (1973c, tables 5, 6; 1963b, tables 9, 10).

case, the ISD shows that the occupational structure of black and total men with five years or more of college differs by 34 points while that for those with four years of training differs by 55 points. However, even with postgraduate training held fixed, there remained, in 1970, significantly fewer black graduates in very important professions such as accounting, law, engineering, social science, medicine, editing and reporting. Moreover, for bachelor's, but not postbachelor's, graduates there continued to be a greater likelihood of blacks' being employed as technicians, social and recreational workers, clergymen, funeral directors and embalmers, personnel and labor relations specialists, and less likelihood of being employed as managers. However, blacks with postbachelor's training were as likely to be managers as whites with the same education. In general, blacks were concentrated in professions where average levels of education and incomes were relatively low, where there were relatively many female workers, and where governmental employment was important.

Finally evidence on the black share of all male professionals and managers, given in Table 8, confirms the preceding picture of occupational progress.[7] In virtually every high-level occupation, black representation rises, with percentage gains in the 1960s varying from 71 percent in management and 140 percent in engineering to 200 and 300 percent in accounting, architecture, personnel and labor relations, and public administration. Even in the 1950s black representation in these fields increased

[7]These figures reflect differences in educational attainment as well as in the occupations of those with similar schooling and thus differ from those in Tables 6 and 7. The figures do not have to be adjusted for the black share of nonwhites as the data are reported specifically for blacks.

TABLE 8
Black proportion of professional and managerial male workers, and changes in proportions, 1950–1970

	Percentages		
	1950	*1960*	*1970*
Professional	2.49	2.50	3.49
Accountants	0.27	0.61	1.73
Architects	0.79	0.42	2.06
Clergymen	11.36	6.73	5.83
College teachers	2.55	2.48	2.48
Dentists	2.50	2.66	2.46
Designers	0.94	0.90	1.58
Draftsmen	0.52	1.03	2.58
Editors and reporters	0.89	0.73	1.74
Engineers, technical	0.31	0.48	1.12
Civil	0.32	0.78	0.30
Electrical	0.46	0.49	1.37
Industrial	0.00	0.35	0.99
Mechanical	0.19	0.34	1.01
Funeral directors and embalmers	9.15	8.56	8.04
Lawyers and judges	0.83	1.10	1.25
Librarians	5.23	4.28	5.76
Musicians and composers	7.55	6.17	7.76
Natural scientists	1.26	1.80	2.82
Biologists	*	3.34	4.10
Chemists	1.26	2.03	3.40
Mathematicians	*	3.82	3.13

TABLE 8
(continued)

	Percentages		
	1950	*1960*	*1970*
Personnel and labor relations workers	1.04	1.10	3.98
Pharmacists	1.46	1.82	2.14
Photographers	2.20	2.23	3.05
Physicians and surgeons	2.00	2.10	2.02
Public relations workers	*	0.70	2.84
Recreation workers	7.04	7.61	13.56
Social welfare workers	6.21	11.23	14.77
Social scientists	1.18	1.78	2.39
Teachers, elementary	6.40	9.88	8.31
Secondary		5.56	5.35
Technicians, health	2.44	7.99	10.46
Electrical and electronic		1.88	3.00
Therapists	4.79	6.58	16.30
Managers (except farm)	1.63	1.34	2.24
Officials	0.97	1.20	3.93

*Not available.
SOURCE: U.S. Bureau of Census (1956, table 2; 1963*b*, table 3; 1973*c*, table 2).

sizeably in percentage though not in absolute terms. These advances notwithstanding, however, the figures in Table 8 show that, except in lower-level professions, the black percentage of specialists was much below the percentage of the total male work force, indicating that attainment of a representative share of high-level jobs lies considerably in the future. For example, blacks constituted 15 percent of male social workers, 16 percent of therapists, 10 percent of health technicians, 8 percent of elementary school teachers, but just 1.7 percent of accountants, 2 percent of managers, and 1.3 percent of lawyers and judges. Between 1970 and 1974, however, data on the nonwhite fraction of all (male and female) professional workers shows further substantial advances. In 1970, 3.8 percent of accountants were nonwhite; in 1974, 5.6 percent; in 1970, 3.0 percent of engineers were nonwhite; in 1974, 4.6 percent (U.S. Bureau of the Census, 1973*c*, table 1; U.S. Bureau of Labor Statistics, 1975, table 1). The new market of the 1960s led to significant improvements in the occupational structure of college-trained and other highly qualified black men but did not eliminate black-white occupational differences.

FEMALE GRADUATES

In contrast to the situation among men, college-trained black women have traditionally had very similar job distributions to those of their white peers, as both black and white women have been concentrated in teaching, which accounted in 1970 for 60 percent of black female and 53 percent of all female college graduates. Comparisons of the distribution of female graduates by race in Table 9 show only slight and declining differences between them, not all unfavorable to blacks, who were under-represented not only as managers but also as clerical workers. While more detailed analysis of the teaching profession in Chapter 7 reveals significant changes in the opportunities for black college-trained women (and men) to obtain work outside of segregated southern schools, the important finding is that, in terms of occupational attainment, the disadvantages of being black are not added to those of being female in high-level labor

TABLE 9
Occupational distribution of female college graduates by race

	1950	1960	1970
Nonwhite/black			
Managerial	0.01	0.02	0.04
Professional	0.71	0.78	0.81
Teachers	0.57	0.59	0.60
Registered nurses	0.04	0.04	0.03
Social welfare workers	0.04	0.04	0.05
Clerical workers	0.11	0.09	0.09
Secretaries	0.04	0.03	0.02
Total			
Managers	0.04	0.04	0.05
Professional	0.70	0.75	0.77
Teachers	0.44	0.51	0.53
Registered nurses	0.06	0.04	0.04
Social welfare workers	0.03	0.03	0.03
Clerical workers	0.17	0.12	0.12
Secretaries	0.08	0.06	0.04

NOTE: 1950 and 1960 data are for nonwhites; 1970, for blacks.

SOURCE: U.S. Bureau of the Census (1956, tables 10, 11; 1963*b*, tables 9, 10; 1973*c*, tables 8, 9).

markets. The major market problems facing black women graduates result from sexual rather than racial differences in market opportunities.

Changes in Relative Incomes The ratio of black to white incomes also increased significantly in the new market, with black women in general and both black male and female high-level workers enjoying especially large gains. In 1973, in fact, the earnings of black female college graduates exceeded those of white graduates, while the traditional pattern of declining income ratios by level of skill among men was reversed. This section examines the broad pattern of change in relative incomes and then concentrates on college-trained and professional-managerial workers.

Overall Income Patterns Chart 2 provides a capsule view of the overall pattern of black-white wage and salary differentials from 1946 to 1974 for men and women separately. The chart shows a striking improvement in the relative position of black women, beginning in the mid-1950s, and a more modest advance for men. At the onset of the period, black women earned less than 40 percent as much as white women; at the end of the period, 98 percent. Black men, on the other hand, began with earnings 60 percent of white earnings and show no improvement until the late 1960s. Between 1965 and 1974, however, the male income ratio begins to rise, reaching a level of 0.71. Similar data on the earnings of year-round full-time workers, which provide a better fix on wage rates, show much the same pattern (U.S. Bureau of the Census, 1947–1975). In 1955 full-time black female earnings were just 57 percent of those of whites, compared with 94 percent in 1974. Among men the equivalent rise was from 0.64 (1955) to 0.74 (1974). As a result of the differential advance of black women and men, the ratio of male to female incomes fell substantially in the black but not in the white community, possibly contributing to the decline in the labor force participation of older black men and the "deterioration" of the black family structure.[8]

[8] The proportion of black homes headed by women rose sharply in the 1960s and early 1970s, while participation of older men fell sharply beginning in the mid-1950s (Freeman, 1973). The hypothesis that these are intertwined phenomena related to the change in male-female incomes is currently under study.

CHART 2 *Ratio of nonwhite to white median wage and salary income, 1946–1974*

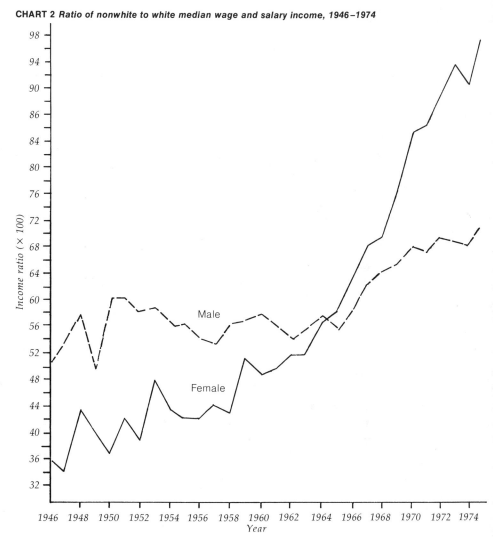

NOTE: 1974 data are preliminary.
SOURCE: U.S. Bureau of the Census *(Current Population Reports, Consumer Income,* various editions, 1947–1975).

COLLEGE GRADUATES

The moderate gains in income for all black men were far surpassed by those of the college-trained, who enjoyed the greatest increases in income of any group in the new market. Table 10 compares the median incomes and growth of incomes of college workers with those of high school and grade school graduates. The figures for 1949, 1959, and 1969(1) are from the various censuses of population; the 1969(2) and 1973 data are from

TABLE 10
Income by education, sex, and race, 1949–1973

Years of schooling and race	Median income				
	1949	*1959*	*1969(1)*	*1969(2)*	*1973*
Male					
Nonwhite/Negro					
Grade school graduate	$1,851	$2,911	$4,669	$4,293	$4,930
High school graduate	2,245	3,741	6,368	6,144	8,284
College graduate	2,633	4,447	9,025	8,567	11,294
Total					
Grade school graduate	2,533	3,892	5,503	5,453	6,371
High school graduate	3,285	5,441	8,554	8,434	10,832
College graduate	4,407	7,650	12,767	12,555	14,704
Female					
Nonwhite/Negro					
Grade school graduate	734	970	1,718	1,531	2,114
High school graduate	1,093	1,732	3,400	3,257	4,092
College graduate	2,103	3,743	6,937	6,747	7,987
Total					
Grade school graduate	909	1,120	1,709	1,645	2,220
High school graduate	1,584	2,184	3,369	3,240	3,970
College graduate	2,321	3,765	6,093	5,817	7,042

NOTE: 1949 and 1965 refer to nonwhite; 1969(1), 1969(2), and 1973 to Negroes. College graduates have four or more years of college.

SOURCE: 1949, U.S. Bureau of the Census (1953*a*); 1959, U.S. Bureau of the Census (1963*c*); 1969(1), U.S. Bureau of the Census (1973*b*); 1969(2), U.S. Department of Commerce (1970); 1973, U.S. Department of Commerce (1974).

current population reports. Columns (1) through (5) record the actual income; columns (6) through (9) give the ratio of percentage increases in each period to the percentage increase of the base group, nonwhite male high school graduates. Thus, the figure for nonwhite male college graduates in the last column shows a 22 percent greater increase in income for them than for total high school men. The exceptional improvement in the income of nonwhite college men is indicated by the fact that their incomes increased by 22 percent more than those of high school graduates over the entire period while, by contrast, the

Percentage change relative to the percentage change for nonwhite male high school graduates (× 100)

By period			Total period
1949– 1959	1959– 1969(1)	1969(2)– 1973	1949– 1973
85.9	85.2	85.2	61.7
100.0	100.0	100.0	100.0
103.3	147.1	91.4	122.3
80.5	58.6	48.3	56.5
98.5	78.6	81.6	85.5
110.4	95.7	48.9	87.0
48.2	110.0	109.5	69.9
87.7	137.1	73.9	101.8
117.0	121.4	52.9	104.8
34.8	75.7	100.6	46.1
56.8	77.1	64.7	56.1
93.4	88.6	60.6	75.5

incomes of other all male college graduates increased 13 percent more slowly.[9] As a result of the gains for black college men, they obtained about the same premium over high school graduates as did their white peers in 1973 (a 36 percent differential), reversing the long-standing pattern of declining black-white income ratios with education. In 1959, the ratios fell from 0.75 (grade school graduates) to 0.69 (high school graduates) to 0.58

[9]Despite problems of comparing *Census* and *CPS* data, the 24 years covered seem sufficiently long to permit trend analysis as in the text.

(college graduates). In 1973 they stood at 0.77, 0.76 and 0.77, respectively. Whereas in 1959 black college men earned 22 percent less than all high school graduates, in 1973 they earned 4 percent more, on average. One consequence of this change, to be pursued in Chapter 3, is that the rate of return to black male investments in college education, which had traditionally fallen short of the return to white male investments, rose above the white rate for young blacks at the onset of the 1970s.

Among women, there is a similar pattern of significantly greater gains for highly educated black than for other black or white women. Even in the 1950s, however, the table shows that black college women earned virtually as much as their white counterparts, and had larger premium over high school graduates than whites. In this case, the rapid gains of college graduates produced an advantage of 16 percent for blacks in 1973, while increases in high school incomes brought the income ratio of black to total high school graduates from 0.79 to virtual unity. While the income advantage of black college-trained women is certainly partly the result of greater hours worked, differences in the incomes of full-time workers in the 1970 census also suggest the possibility of a wage-rate advantage for blacks (U.S. Bureau of the Census, 1973d, tables 7 and 8). Specifically, the census data show that white women graduates working 50 to 52 weeks over the year earn 10 percent more than all white women with a college degree, while full-time black graduates earn 5 percent more than all black college women. If the same ratios held true in 1973, the black female college advantage would narrow by 5 percentage points, leaving a nonnegligible 10 percent black advantage, which may be the result of greater black commitment to the labor market over the life cycle as well as at a moment in time. In any case, it is evident that black female graduates, like male graduates, made enormous progress in the 1960s and early 1970s.

Income differentials by occupational position, summarized in Table 11, confirm the story of marked progress in high-level labor markets. Among male workers, the ratio of black-to-white incomes rises most rapidly for managers, from exceptionally low levels of 0.50 and 0.57 in 1949 and 1959 to 0.66 by 1969; it also increases substantially from 0.58 (1949) to 0.72 (1969) for professionals. In other occupations, the relative income of black men increased in the 1960s, though both total income and year-round full-time earnings remained substantially below 1.0 in virtually all cases. Despite the impressive gains, sizeable intraoccupational differences remained in 1969. If black men had the same job distribution as whites and were paid their 1969 income, the black-white income ratio would rise to 0.75, closing about one-third of the 36-percentage-point gap. Much of

TABLE 11 *Median nonwhite income as percentage of median white income, by sex and occupation, various years, 1949–1969*

Occupation	All income recipients			Year-round full-time workers
	*1949**	*1959†*	*1969‡*	*1969‡*
Male				
Professional and technical workers	57.5	68.5	72.3	72.6
Managers, officials, and proprietors	50.0	57.1	66.0	67.2
Clerical workers	83.6	84.0	84.7	86.1
Sales workers	54.8	55.6	64.2	67.6
Craftsmen	62.6	65.7	72.4	74.6
Operatives	72.1	70.1	81.6	80.7
Service workers except private household	77.6	75.5	85.5	79.5
Private household workers	91.1	104.9	102.9	88.6
Laborers except farm and mine	81.0	83.4	90.5	82.6
Farm laborers and foremen	71.6	71.4	72.5	68.9
Female				
Professional and technical workers	84.9	96.7	102.3	103.9
Managers, officials, and proprietors	44.6	56.2	95.3	96.7
Clerical workers	95.2	99.2	98.1	100.4
Sales workers	74.5	97.7	112.7	101.5
Craftsmen	78.7	82.4	87.9	87.6
Operatives	76.9	79.1	92.6	89.5
Service workers except private household	86.8	95.4	117.5	99.1
Private household workers	100.5	99.3	116.8	101.2
Laborers except farm and mine	88.5	84.1	98.0	94.4
Farm laborers and foremen	88.0	91.8	71.6	79.4

*Nonwhite medians as percentage of medians for total labor force. Medians for whites are not separately available.

†Negro medians as percentage of medians for total labor force.

‡Data are for Negroes rather than nonwhites.

SOURCE: Freeman (1973).

the remaining differential could, however, result from different occupational positions within the broad census categories.

Relative income data for women in Table 11 show black incomes equaling or surpassing white incomes even among year-round full-time workers. In some occupations, notably the professions, black women earn more overall than whites but the same when both work year-round full-time. Increases in income from 1949 to 1969 eliminated racial differences in wage rates in the female labor market so that if black women had the same occupational skills as whites, they would have the same total income.

Male Income Differentials in High-Level Occupations

The pattern of black-white male income differentials in the professional occupations of concern to this book is examined in Tables 12 and 13. Columns (1) through (3) of Table 12 record the ratios of nonwhite (black) to total incomes in 1949, 1959, and 1969, respectively, while columns (4) and (5) give the changes in the ratios from 1949 to 1969 and from 1959 to 1969. Mean income ratios and changes in ratios are presented in columns (6) through (8). What stands out in the table are the sizeable increases in the relative income of high-level black workers in virtually all occupations, which closed much of the initial income gap. Between 1949 and 1969 the nonwhite (black) to total median income ratio rose by 10 or more points in 23 of 26 occupational groupings; between 1959 and 1969 it rose by that many points in 16 cases while the mean income ratios increased by at least 10 points in 7 of 17 cases. In 1949, the median ratio exceeded 0.80 in just 3 occupations and 0.90 in no case; in 1969, by contrast, the ratio stood above 0.80 in 20 cases and above 0.90 in 8. As might be expected, the greatest increases occurred in those occupations where blacks had initially relatively low incomes (medical professions, management, architecture, and editing and reporting), though sizeable increases are also found in teaching. Even with these changes, however, black-white income ratios remained below 1.00 in all but one detailed profession.

Table 13 pursues the analysis of income differentials by examining the positions of black (nonwhite) male college graduates in high-level occupations in 1959 and 1969. Columns (1) and (2) record the mean income of 25- to 64-year-old nonwhite and all college graduates in each occupation while columns (3) through (5) give the ratio of incomes in 1969 and 1959 and the change in ratios. The general pattern is similar to that in the preceding table, with nonwhite-total college male income ratios increasing except in engineering but remaining below unity. Nonwhite college-trained managers made, in particular, especially large gains as did those in the health professions.

Additional data on incomes in the early 1970s show that the pattern of advance in the professional and managerial occupations continued into the seventies. The income of black managers, in particular, increased especially rapidly in the 1969–1973 period, far surpassing the increase for white managers. In 1969, black managers obtained just 59 percent as much as white managers, according to the *Current Population Reports* survey; in 1973, black managers obtained 78 percent as much—a remarkable 18-point gain in the span of four years (U.S. Bureau of the Census, 1970, table 50; 1974, table 65). The relative income of black professionals, by contrast, rose more modestly from 0.69 to 0.74 in the same period.

In sum, there were sizeable increases in the ratio of nonwhite to total male income in high-level jobs in the new market. The increases did not, however, eliminate all of the initial black-white differences, which remained large in many occupations.

Economic Parity for Starting College Men

While economic differences persisted among all highly qualified men, the evidence in this section shows that these differences disappeared among young college graduates, whose position is especially sensitive to changes in the job market. Census statistics on income, special survey data from southern black colleges obtained as part of the *Black Elite* study, and interviews with college placement directors at those institutions reveal a collapse in labor market discrimination against starting black male graduates in the late 1960s, which, if continued, marks the end of discrimination in high-level labor markets.

The census data on the improved position of young black college graduates is contained in Table 14, which records the ratios and changes in the ratios of incomes of black to total male college graduates in the 1959–1969 period. Lines 1 through 3 show ratios of median incomes for persons with four or five or more years of college; lines 4 and 5 deal with mean incomes. Because the Census reported the mean incomes of nonwhites with four or more years of college, by occupation, in 1960 rather than those with four or five and more years, the comparisons in line 5 are crude: they relate the same income ratios in 1959 (for

TABLE 12 *Black-white* *income ratios* *among men,* *1949–1969*		*Ratio of median incomes*		*Changes* *in ratios*
				Column (3) *− column (1)*
	1949 *(1)*	*1959* *(2)*	*1969* *(3)*	*(4)*
Professional, technical, & *kindred*	0.57	0.68	0.74	0.17
Accountants	0.72	0.85	0.83	0.11
Architects	0.68	0.71	0.97	0.29
Artists and art teachers	0.57	0.76	0.81	0.24
Clergymen	0.58	0.64	0.86	0.28
College professors	0.76	0.76	0.79	0.03
Dentists	0.61	0.65	0.88	0.27
Draftsmen and designers	0.82	0.91	0.85	0.03
Editors and reporters	0.64	0.59	0.77	0.15
Engineers	0.70	0.86	0.80	0.11
Funeral directors	0.63	0.50	0.69	0.06
Lawyers and judges	0.65	0.57	0.69	0.04
Musicians and music *teachers*	0.68	0.66	1.00	0.32
Natural scientists	0.53	0.79	0.81	0.28
Chemists	0.77	0.82	0.86	0.09
Personnel and labor *relations*	0.66	0.69	0.79	0.13
Pharmacists	0.68	0.78	0.89	0.21
Photographers	0.72	0.65	0.88	0.16
Physicians and surgeons	0.59	0.41	0.87	0.28
Social welfare, recreation, *and group workers*	0.84	0.89	0.96	0.12
Social scientists	0.73	0.83	0.92	0.19
Sports instructors	0.66	0.70	0.76	0.10
Teachers	0.72	0.79	0.89	0.17
Elementary	*	0.82	0.91	*
Secondary	*	0.77	0.90	*
Technicians, health	0.71	0.85	0.97	0.26
Electrical and electronic	0.84†	0.81	0.96	0.12
Managers	0.50	0.57	0.68	0.18

*Not available.
†1950 estimated using testing technicians' data.
SOURCE: U.S. Bureau of the Census (1956, tables 19, 21; 1963*b* tables 25, 26; 1973*b* tables 25, 26; 1973*c*, tables 1, 17).

Column (3) − column (2) (5)	Ratios of mean incomes		Changes in mean ratios
	1959 (6)	1969 (7)	(8)
0.06	0.63	0.77	0.14
−.02	0.76	0.73	−.03
0.26	*	*	*
0.05	*	*	*
0.22	0.67	0.86	0.19
0.03	0.81	0.83	0.02
0.23	0.70	0.99	0.29
−.16	0.83	0.87	0.04
0.18	*	*	*
−.06	0.83	0.86	0.03
0.19	*	*	*
0.12	*	0.78	*
0.34	0.67	0.73	0.06
0.02	0.74	0.78	0.04
0.04	0.80	0.81	0.01
0.10	*	*	*
0.11	*	*	*
0.23	*	*	*
0.46	0.48	0.70	0.22
0.07	*	0.92	*
0.09	*	0.81	*
0.06	*		*
0.10	0.78	0.90	0.12
0.09	0.83	0.88	0.05
0.13	0.77	0.88	0.11
0.12	0.80	0.87	0.07
0.15	0.94	0.95	0.01
0.11	0.51	0.68	0.17

TABLE 13 *Income of male college graduates, by occupation and race, 1960–1970*

Occupation	Nonwhite (1)	Total (2)	Ratio (3)	Mean income ratio 1960 (4)	Change in ratio (5)
		Mean income, 1970			
Professional	$11,469	$14,853	0.77	0.61	0.16
Accountants	10,264	13,966	0.73	0.67	0.06
Clergymen	7,004	7,214	0.97	0.85	0.12
College professors	12,752	10,835	0.84	0.81	0.03
Dentists	24,870	25,243	0.99	0.66	0.33
Draftsmen	8,582	10,128	0.85	*	*
Designers	12,772	13,534	0.94	*	*
Editors and reporters	11,142	13,803	0.81	*	*
Engineers	12,752	15,299	0.83	0.84	−0.01
Civil	12,339	15,199	0.81	0.84	−0.03
Electrical	13,043	15,623	0.85	0.86	−0.01
Mechanical	13,961	16,438	0.85	0.89	−0.04
Lawyers and judges	18,208	22,958	0.79	0.63†	0.16
Natural scientists	10,722	13,812	0.78	0.74	0.04
Chemists	10,690	13,348	0.80	0.79	0.01
Physicians and surgeons	21,559	30,800	0.70	0.48	0.22
Social and recreation workers	962	9,837	0.98	*	*
Social scientists	10,835	12,860	0.81	*	*
Teachers, elementary	8,155	9,217	0.88	0.82	0.06
Secondary	8,623	9,826	0.88	0.77	0.11
Technicians, health	9,202	10,684	0.84	*	*
Electrical and electronic	10,431	11,720	0.89	*	*
Managers	12,798	17,956	0.71	0.49	0.22

*Not available.
†Used median income.
NOTE: 1970 figures are averages of means for those with four and five or more years of college.
SOURCES: 1970, U.S. Bureau of the Census (1973*d*, table 1); 1960, U.S. Bureau of the Census (1964, table 9; 1963*b*, table 32).

those with four or more years of college) to the ratios for those with four and five or more years, separately.

This problem notwithstanding, the table tells a clear story of extraordinary gains in the relative income of young black workers in the decade, which brought the youngest cohorts to rough equality with whites. Among workers with four years of college, the median income ratios jumped by 34 points in the 22- to 24-year-old group (line 1) while mean income ratios rose by 20 points among 18- to 24-year-olds (line 3), with the result that black incomes equaled or exceeded those of whites by small amounts in each of the youngest groups considered. Among persons with five or more years of college, a comparable pattern is found, with the median income ratio for 25- to 29-year-olds

TABLE 14
Ratio of income of young black to all male college graduates, 1959–1969

Age and group	1959	1969	Δ
1. *Median income, 22 to 24*			
4 years of college	0.70	1.04	0.34
2. *Median income, 25 to 29*			
4 years of college	0.70	0.87	0.17
5 or more years of college	0.61	0.90	0.21
3. *Median income, 30 to 34*			
4 years of college	0.64	0.75	0.11
5 or more years of college	0.71	0.78	0.07
4. *Mean income, 18 to 24*			
4 years of college	0.80*	1.00	0.20
Professionals	0.86	1.02	0.16
5. *Mean income, 25 to 34*			
4 years of college	0.67*	0.77	0.10
Professionals	0.72	0.82	0.10
Managers	0.64	0.73	0.09
Engineers	0.90	0.92	0.02
Teachers	0.81	0.94	0.13
5 years of college	0.67*	0.86	0.19
Professionals	0.72	0.88	0.16
Managers	0.64	0.84	0.10
Engineers	0.90	1.02	0.13
Teachers	0.81	0.94	0.13
Doctors	0.48	0.91	0.43

*Data in lines 4 and 5 are for men with 4 or more years of college in 1959, providing only crude comparisons to the 1969 figures.

NOTE: 1959 data are for nonwhites relative to all men.

SOURCE: Lines 1–3, U.S. Bureau of the Census (1963c, table 6; 1973b, table 7); line 4, U.S. Bureau of the Census (1963e, table 5; 1973d, table 5); line 5, U.S. Bureau of the Census (1963e, tables 1, 2; 1973d, tables 1, 2).

rising from 0.69 to 0.90 (line 2). The more experienced workers, aged 30–34 and 25–34, also obtained sizeable economic gains, on the order of 11 to 22 percentage points on average, but in general did not reach parity, except in a few occupations such as engineering, where postbachelor blacks aged 25–34 earned $13,133 in 1969 compared with $12,843 for whites. From these data it appears that while all young black graduates obtained substantial income advances, only the most recent graduates, roughly those who entered the market in the period following the 1964 Civil Rights Act, obtained income parity with their white peers.

Actual starting salaries for the college classes of 1968–69 and 1969–70 contained in Table 15 confirm this finding. In the new

TABLE 15 *Starting salaries of black college graduates, by field and school, 1968–1970*			
Field and school	*Salary of black graduates*	*Compar-able national salary*	*Relative salary*
Howard (1968–69)			
Civil engineering, B.S.	$ 800	$ 797	1.00
Electrical engineering	805	826	0.98
Mechanical engineering	810	820	0.99
Accounting	758	761	1.00
Other business fields	666	687	0.97
Mathematics, chemistry, and physics	706	784	0.90
Other liberal arts	644	667	0.97
North Carolina A&T (1969–70)			
Engineering	800	873	0.92
Texas Southern (1969–70)			
Industrial engineering, B.S.	833	849	0.98
Business, B.B.A. (males)	816	836	0.98
Liberal arts	615	682	0.98
Pharmacology, B.S.	876	*	*
Texas Southern Graduate			
Law, J.D.	1,050	988	1.06
M.B.A.	1,097	1,026	1.07

*Not available.

SOURCES: Black salaries, college placement counselors at various schools; national salaries, College Placement Council (1969–70).

market male graduates from southern black colleges received the same starting salaries as other college workers in their area of employment, with some groups (from law and business schools) doing a bit better than average and others (from physical sciences and liberal arts areas) doing a bit worse. Even in such out-of-the-way places as Alabama A&M (Normal, Alabama) placement offices report "salary offers . . . comparing favorably with national averages in the College Placement Council Survey," which contrasts sharply with the status of earlier black graduates. Black men in the class of 1958, for example, earned just 72 percent as much as comparable whites two years after graduation (Sharp, 1970 p. 65).

THE COLLEGE-
INCOME
PREMIUM
The rapid increase in the income of young black college graduates substantially increased the earnings differential between college and high school men at the outset of their careers, and thus the economic incentive for college going. Table 16 examines this important development for the period 1959–1969 using *Census of Population* data and for the year 1973 using tabulations from the *Current Population Survey (CPS)* of March 1974.[10] It records the mean income of 25- to 29-year-old black and white college and high school graduates and the absolute dollar differential between these incomes (which according to human capital analysis is the relevant measure of the incentive for college)[11] in 1959, 1969, and 1973. The table displays a striking increase in the college premium for blacks from 1959 to 1969 and through 1973, when the depressed job market for college graduates substantially reduced the advantage of college education for white men (Freeman, 1975). In 1959, when 25- to 29-year-old black college men earned just 71 percent as much as white college men, they had a noticeably smaller premium over their high school peers than did white graduates. By 1969, black graduates earned 83 percent as much as whites and, because black high school graduates suffered a greater income disadvantage relative to whites, the college premium was $210 greater for blacks than whites. The 1973 figures, which are

[10]The *Current Population Reports* survey of incomes is a monthly survey of about 49,000 households. It is described in detail in U.S. Bureau of the Census (1947–1975). I tabulated the figures in the text from the March 1974 survey tapes.

[11]In this analysis individuals are motivated by differences in discounted values of lifetime income streams, which clearly depend on differences in mean incomes.

TABLE 16
Mean incomes
and differences in
mean incomes of
25- to 29-year-old
black and white
college and high
school men,
1959–1973

	Incomes (in 1973 dollars) and ratios of income		
Group and year	Black men	White men	Black-white ratio
1959*			
1. College	$ 6,419	$ 9,158	0.71
2. High school	5,121	7,574	0.69
3. Difference (1 − 2)	1,298	1,584	0.82
1969			
4. College	9,120	11,022	0.83
5. High school	7,157	9,269	0.77
6. Difference (4 − 5)	1,963	1,753	1.12
1973			
7. College	11,168	10,242	1.09
8. High school	7,700	9,702	0.79
9. Difference (7 − 8)	3,468	540	6.42

*Incomes in 1959 are based on medians. I have adjusted them to means by multiplying by 1959 ratios of mean to median incomes from U.S. Bureau of the Census (1963a, table 1).
SOURCES: U.S. Bureau of the Census (1963c, table 6; 1973b, table 7) and Current Population Survey computer tapes from March 1974 Survey, for 1973 incomes.

based on a smaller sample and thus subject to greater possible errors of measurement, reveal an even more striking development: an increase in the premium for blacks coupled with a decrease for whites. In the *CPS* data, black college men aged 25–29 earned 9 percent more than their white peers and had an income premium over six times that for whites. Among older graduates, however, the differential advantage of white college men persisted throughout the period. While the 1973 data may possibly exaggerate the extent of the change in the market,[12] the overall finding of a sizeable increase in the economic incentive for black men to go on to college, absolutely and relative to whites, cannot be denied. The effect of the changed income position of young graduates on the rate of return to investments in college and enrollments is analysed in detail in Chapter 3.

New Recruitment Policies

Underlying the attainment of parity in starting salaries and higher relative incomes of young black graduates are significant changes in the recruitment practices of national corporations,

[12] The *CPS* data show occasional, puzzling ups and downs, which presumably reflect sampling error and thus must be treated cautiously.

who began hiring blacks for managerial and professional jobs in the sixties. Historically, relatively few corporations had sought workers at the southern black colleges and those that did generally limited their search to Howard or Tuskegee. This discriminatory pattern came to a rapid end in the new market, when, as Table 17 shows, the number of companies recruiting at the southern black colleges skyrocketed; in 1960 barely four company recruiters appeared per campus; in 1965, about 30; in 1970, nearly 300, a remarkable change in recruitment and

TABLE 17
Recruitment visits of representatives of corporations to predominantly black colleges and universities

College	Number of representatives of corporations interviewing job candidates		
	1960	*1965*	*1970*
Atlanta University	0	160	510
Howard	*	100	619
Clark	0	40	350
Alabama A&M	0	0	100
Alabama State	0	7	30
Hampton	20	247	573
Jackson State	*	*	280
Johnson C. Smith	0	25	175
Morehouse	*	*	300
Miles	0	12	54
Norfolk State	5	100	250
North Carolina A&T	6	80	517
Prairie View	*	*	350
Southern	0	25	600
Southern, New Orleans	0	5	75
Texas Southern	0	69	175
Tuskegee	50	85	404
Virginia State	0	25	325
Winston-Salem	*	*	25
Virginia University	5	25	150
Xavier	0	44	185
Average per school	4	50	297

*Not available

SOURCE: Survey and interviews conducted for *Black Elite* study in 1970.

hiring policies that was the direct cause of equality in starting salaries.

Interviews with the placement directors of some of the major southern black colleges and universities in 1970 confirm the impact of the new recruitment practices on economic opportunities. According to the placement directors, the opportunities facing the graduates of 1970 were substantially better than those for graduates at the outset of the decade. Thirteen of twenty-one directors noted a "great improvement" and five, a moderate improvement in the opportunities facing their graduates. Nineteen reported that students from their school obtained starting salaries equal to national averages while two reported salaries above average. The fields with the greatest perceived improvement in job opportunities and salaries were business administration and engineering, traditionally "closed" occupations which were opened by new corporate recruitment and hiring policies. The 1970 student body expected and were likely, in the placement directors' eyes, to do as well in the job market as other college graduates.

Future Economic Status Will the newly established parity in starting salaries be maintained in the future as the classes of the late 1960s and early 1970s grow older or will the relative status of young black male graduates deteriorate over the life cycle?

There is only limited evidence available on this critical question. Census income data examined in Chapter 5 show that in the 1949–1959 and 1959–1969 decades the relative income of nonwhite male cohorts was roughly constant as the cohort aged and time passed. In the fifties, when black-white economic differences were relatively stable, there was no change in the ratio of cohort income, despite the cross-sectional pattern of declining relative incomes by age. In the sixties, some older black cohorts experienced small increases in relative incomes, though again the overall impression is of generally stable cohort income differentials (Freeman, 1973). While this evidence suggests that the gains of starting graduates will be maintained over the life cycle, the serious danger of future discrimination in promotion decisions cannot be denied. Two-thirds of the placement directors in the *Black Elite* survey expressed concern that at least some black graduates being offered good jobs in

1970 could face dead-end careers 10 years hence. "Exclusion from intermediate- and upper-level executive positions" was uniformly viewed as the chief problem with which black graduates would have to contend in the future. Even granting these possibilities, however, the achievement of equal starting salaries in the late 1960s was a major advance over the experience of previous generations and past decades.

REWARDS TO GRADUATE TRAINING At the top of the educational hierarchy black workers with graduate training obtained increases in income far above those of comparable whites, with the result that the economic incentive for black investments in postbachelor's study came to exceed that for white investments.

Table 18 records the differential rate of increase in incomes between black and white workers with five or more years of college in the 1960s. Despite the fact that the black increases are biased downward due to the use of nonwhite rather than black incomes in 1959 when nonwhites received higher pay than blacks, blacks had significantly greater increases in income than

TABLE 18 Percentage changes in incomes of black and total workers with five or more years of college, 1959–1969

Age group	Black	White
Male		
25–29	127.2	74.0
30–34	103.8	76.8
35–44	113.0	98.7
45–54	115.5	112.8
55–64	109.3	122.5
Female		
25–29	83.9	66.1
30–34	85.5	65.6
35–44	82.3	67.6
45–54	87.5	65.6
55–64	n.a.	63.2

NOTE: 1959 data are from nonwhites due to the absence of income data for blacks; 1959 income for all persons used for whites; 1969 income for persons with five years of college obtained as weighted average of incomes of persons with five years of college and persons with six or more years of college.

SOURCE: U.S. Bureau of the Census (1973*b*, tables 7, 8; 1963*c*, tables 6, 7).

whites, especially among young men, with the gains among the young wiping out an initial income disadvantage. Among women, the rates of change in the incomes of blacks with more than five years also exceeded those of whites even though in 1959 highly educated black women were already doing roughly as well in the labor market as highly educated white women. By 1969, black women in all age brackets with graduate training were earning more than white peers, in some cases by as much as 16 percent (U.S. Bureau of the Census, 1973*d*, tables 7, 8). Even with the rapid increases in the sixties, however, among men, only young black graduates did as well as or better than their white peers.

Differences in income ratios do not, however, necessarily imply differences in the economic incentive to attend graduate school. As noted earlier, what matters are differences in the income stream of those with and without training. If blacks with graduate training have a greater income advantage over bachelor's graduates than whites, even if they earn less, the incentive to invest will be larger. Table 19 compares the income streams of black and white workers with and without graduate

TABLE 19 *Earnings of black and white workers with four and five or more years of college, 1969*

Age group	Black			White		
	(1) *5 or more years*	*(2)* *4 years*	*(3)* *(1) − (2)*	*(1)* *5 or more years*	*(2)* *4 years*	*(3)* *(1) − (2)*
Men						
Total, 25–64	$11,755	$8,652	$3,103	$16,145	$14,225	$1,920
18–24	6,142	4,767	1,375	5,060	4,777	283
25–34	9,401	8,188	1,213	11,097	10,808	289
35–54	12,984	9,148	3,836	18,687	16,086	2,601
55–64	11,954	8,307	3,647	19,464	16,120	3,344
Women						
Total, 25–64	$ 8,412	$6,545	$1,867	$ 8,144	$ 6,453	$1,691
18–24	4,462	4,250	212	4,432	4,182	290
25–34	2,220	6,219	1,001	6,883	5,940	943
35–54	8,800	6,820	1,980	8,486	6,527	1,959
55–64	8,954	6,667	2,287	9,366	7,594	1,772

SOURCE: U.S. Bureau of the Census (1973*d*, tables 1, 2, 5, 7, 8, 11).

training in 1969. It reveals a much greater return to black than to white graduate training. Overall, black men having over five years of college obtain $3,103 more per year than those with just four years (a 36 percent advantage) compared with a much smaller $1,920 (13 percent) gain for whites with some graduate training. Age group by age group, the differences between postgraduate and bachelor's income streams are greater for blacks, though the most marked differences are among the young. As a result, given similar cost of attendance, the economic rewards for black men to go on to graduate training exceeded those for white men in 1969 by sizeable amounts. In contrast, the income differences for women reveal only a modest black advantage, which suggests a rough similarity in the return to black and white female investment in graduate education.

The finding that blacks with graduate degrees do relatively well in the job market is confirmed by National Science Foundation data on the salaries of black doctorates in scientific areas (NSF, 1975, table B-10). Overall, in 1973 black Ph.D.'s reported a median income of $21,200 compared with $21,000 for whites. In 5 of 6 specific fields for which data were available, blacks earned more, with the greatest differential occurring among social scientists ($2,500). While these data are not corrected for differences in age, sex, and related factors, it is apparent that by 1973 there was at the least no black income disadvantage among all (not just young) Ph.D.'s.

Additional evidence from the American Council of Education survey of faculty, which is the basic source of data on faculty incomes, examined in detail in Chapter 8, also reveals a premium to black faculty, though a relatively modest one.[13] Apparently with the supply of black Ph.D.'s and potential faculty relatively inelastic in the new market due to the period of training, increases in demand due to such factors as federal affirmative action programs raised salaries, creating a premium, for the more able.

CONCLUSION This chapter has documented the emergence of a new market for highly qualified black workers in the 1960s. Its statistics reveal rapid advances in relative occupational position and

---

[13] These data are obtained from the American Council on Education data tapes, as described in detail in Chapter 8.

income, particularly for young college graduates and all black female workers and a substantial divergence between the market of the sixties and that of previous decades—which potentially makes the period a watershed in economic discrimination against black Americans. These developments and those in the education market, to be described next, constitute the empirical phenomenon on which the rest of the book focuses.

2. Transformation of the Educational System

In addition to advancing in the job market black Americans also made substantial gains in education in the period under study. Their years of schooling completed rose rapidly, closing a century-old gap. Large numbers of young persons enrolled in colleges, many in northern institutions and others in previously segregated southern white schools. For the first time, the majority of black students obtained college training outside the predominantly black colleges of the South.

LONG-TERM INCREASE IN EDUCATIONAL ATTAINMENT Since the period of slavery, when blacks were forbidden to read or write, their educational attainment has fallen far short of that of whites, placing them at a severe disadvantage in the job market. Discrimination in the allocation of educational resources by white-controlled southern states maintained an enormous gap in black and white attainment, which did not begin to diminish rapidly until after World War II. In the postwar period, as Chart 3 shows, there was a sizeable increase in the median years attained by nonwhites relative to whites. In 1952 nonwhite men had 7.2 years of education compared with 10.8 for white men; nonwhite women had 8.1 years compared with 12.1 for white women, yielding the two-thirds attainment ratio in the chart. The increase in years completed among blacks was so great in the ensuing decades that by 1973, the male attainment ratio rose to 0.95 (11.9 years versus 12.5 years) and the female ratio reached 0.98 (12.2 years versus 12.5 years).

Because the number of years of schooling has a peculiar distribution due to legally mandated attendance, "median years" tends to overstate the closeness of educational attainment.[1] To

---

[1] With many persons graduating from high school, median years will concentrate around 12, although many more whites than blacks will have more than 13 years.

CHART 3 *Ratio of nonwhite to white median years of education of civilian labor force, 1952–1973*

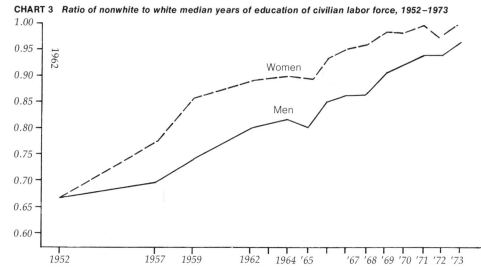

SOURCE: U.S. Department of Labor (1974, table B-9).

obtain a better picture, I compare actual distributions of years completed in Table 20. The table shows that blacks made significant relative gains in years completed from 1950 to 1970 but that a larger gap remained in 1970 than the median years indicates. The proportion of black men and women with high school degrees or better rose from 11.3 to 28.5 percent and from 13.7 to 32.0 percent, respectively, but still lagged behind the proportion for all persons (51.9 percent for men and 52.9 percent for women). Similarly, while the fraction of black college-trained workers roughly doubled, many fewer blacks had one to three or four or more years of college in 1970. Using the index of structural differentiation rather than median years to measure the difference between the distributions, the figures show a convergence from 70 to 55 points (men) and 58 to 45 points (women) but indicate a sizeable difference to be made up.

The potential impact of the increase in black attainment on income differences is considered in Table 21, which transforms the distributions into income-weighted indices, using 1959 total and nonwhite incomes by education as weights. When each distribution is given the same weights, the increased relative black attainment is seen to have a large impact on potential incomes: with total weights, for example, black male incomes would have risen by 35.3 percent from 1950 to 1970 as a result of additional schooling compared with a 21.0 percent gain for total men; with nonwhite income weights the black gain is 23.1 percent versus 12.2 percent for whites. When each distribution is weighted by its own income, however, the fact that in 1959 blacks obtained only modest gains in income with additional schooling produces a very different pattern; in this case the rate of change in income is about the same for the two groups (23.1 versus 21.0 percent). Despite the increased relative educational attainment of blacks, the low return to schooling meant that additional schooling was not a viable means of reducing income inequality, as was widely noted (Weiss, 1970; Freeman, 1972). By contrast, because black women obtained about as much additional income from increased education as white women, regardless of the weights used, their relative

TABLE 20
Relative educational attainment of black and total persons 25 and over, 1950–1970

Years of school completed	Black 1950	Black 1970	Total 1950	Total 1970
Males				
4 or more years of college	1.9	3.9	7.1	13.5
1–3 years of college	2.6	5.8	6.8	10.6
4 years of high school	6.8	19.8	17.6	27.8
1–3 years of high school	11.5	23.0	16.4	18.6
8 years of elementary school	10.7	10.2	20.8	12.9
5–7 years of elementary school	26.5	19.3	16.4	10.5
1–3 years of elementary school	28.7	14.0	9.3	4.4
0 years of elementary school	7.4	4.0	2.6	1.6
Not reported	3.9	0.0	3.0	0.0
Females				
4 or more years of college	2.3	4.5	5.0	8.1
1–3 years of college	3.0	5.6	7.5	10.7
4 years of high school	8.4	21.9	22.0	34.1
1–3 years of high school	14.4	26.6	17.5	20.0
8 years of elementary school	12.1	10.8	19.8	12.6
5–7 years of elementary school	29.2	18.4	15.5	9.5
1–3 years of elementary school	22.7	9.4	7.4	3.4
0 years of elementary school	5.3	2.7	2.4	1.6
Not reported	2.6	0.0	2.4	0.0

SOURCES: U.S. Bureau of the Census (1953*a*, table 5, pp. 42, 44; 1973*b*, table 1, pp. 3, 6).

TABLE 21 *The impact of increased black educational attainment on incomes, 1950–1970*

Income weights and group	Income value of education position				Percent increase in income due to changes in educational distributions	
	Males		Females			
	1950	1970	1950	1970	Males	Females
Black						
Nonwhite 1959	$2,382	$2,913	$1,031	$1,318	23.1	27.8
Total 1959	3,217	4,354	1,205	1,584	35.3	31.5
Total						
Nonwhite 1959	3,075	3,449	1,342	1,596	12.2	18.9
Total 1959	4,141	5,009	1,579	1,876	21.0	18.8

SOURCES: Income weights, U.S. Bureau of the Census (1963c, tables 6, 7); distributions, Table 19 of this volume.

income rises. Convergence in years completed meant convergence in income for women but not for men, which also required increases in the income of highly educated blacks, as in fact occurred in the new market.

Causes of the Trend   Two major factors underlie the relative increase in black educational attainment in the post–World War II period: the movement of the black population to the North and the increase in spending for the education of blacks on the part of southern states after a half-century of extraordinary discrimination.

Migration north improved black attainment because levels of enrollment and years completed were higher in the North than in the South for all students and also because blacks appear to have gotten a fairer share of the northern than of southern school resources.[2] In 1960, black men aged 25 and over born in the North had 10.4 median years of education compared with 7.1 for southern-born blacks and 9.5 years for southern-born whites. Blacks from the South trailed their white peers by 2.4 years and were half as likely to graduate from high school (15 versus 30 percent) while northern-born blacks trailed whites by 0.9 years and were only moderately less likely to graduate high

[2] Differences between the resources given black and white children in the South are described in Freeman (1974a & forthcoming) and in Welch (1973). While good data on black schooling in the North are not readily available, it is obvious that whatever differentials existed in the North did not approach those in the South.

school (36 versus 45 percent) (U.S. Bureau of the Census, 1963c, table 3). While not all these differentials are due to "pure geographic" forces, such as differences in public educational resources, blacks obviously benefited, in terms of educational attainment, by moving to the North.

Relative increases in spending on black education in the South began in the 1940s, prior to the 1954 Supreme Court decision that made de jure segregation illegal, in part to prove that "separate but equal" was socially viable. After decades of extremely large discrimination—expenditure differentials on the order of 5:1 (Mississippi) and 6:1 (Alabama) in favor of whites—an enormous reallocation was required to redress past inequalities, which ranged from failure to provide public high schools for blacks in most of the South through the 1930s to unequal numbers of books, teachers per pupil, and so forth. By the 1960s, current expenditures on education in primarily black and white schools was roughly equalized throughout the South (Freeman, 1974b).

DEVELOPMENTS IN HIGHER EDUCATION

In the higher educational system, which is of special concern to this study, there was an equally dramatic transformation in the position of black Americans. In the early fifties, relatively few black youngsters enrolled in college; enrollments were concentrated in the financially and academically weak southern black colleges; southern white colleges and universities were usually legally segregated, and only a small number of blacks attended northern institutions. Two decades later the proportion of blacks in college, while below that of whites, was sizeable and rising rapidly; the bulk of blacks studied in predominantly white colleges; black colleges received large influxes of federal and foundation moneys; and colleges and universities were desegregated in the South, and in some cases were eagerly recruiting black students.

Spurt in College Enrollments

Table 22 examines the most important aspect of these changes, the extraordinary increase in black college enrollments in the 1960s. It records the absolute number of black and white college students and the proportion of those aged 18–19 in college. What stands out in the table is the sharp increase in black enrollments, which more than quadrupled over the period, while white enrollments, particularly among men, increased

		Number and percentage of population		
		*1960**	*1965*	*1970*	*1974*
Male					
Black					
1.	*Number enrolled, 3–34*	90	126	253	422
2.	*Percent 18- to 19-year-olds enrolled*	12.9	16.3	17.6	21.5
White					
3.	*Number enrolled, 3–34*	2,214	3,326	4,065	4,367
4.	*Percent 18- to 19-year-olds enrolled*	39.0	42.9	43.4	35.0
Female					
Black					
5.	*Number enrolled, 3–34*	84	148	269	392
6.	*Percent 18- to 19-year olds enrolled*	12.7	16.7	25.4	24.7
White					
7.	*Number enrolled, 3–34*	1,128	1,191	2,693	3,413
8.	*Percent 18- to 19-year-olds enrolled*	25.7	31.9	35.7	33.9

TABLE 22
Enrollment in college, 1960–1973

*1960 black figures estimated by multiplying data on nonwhites by black share of non-white college enrollees and population in 1964 from Series P-20, No. 148, which is the first report giving Negro data separately.

NOTE: Odd lines deal with all college enrollments. Even lines with 18- to 19-year-olds only.

SOURCE: U.S. Bureau of the Census (Current Population Reports, *School Enrollment in the U.S.,* series P-20, numbers 110, 148, 162, 222, 278, table 5).

only modestly. In 1960 just 12.9 percent of 18- to 19-year-old black men and 12.7 percent of 18- to 19-year-old black women were enrolled compared with 30.0 and 35.7 percent of their white peers. By 1974, the percentage of young blacks in college had risen to 21.5 and 24.7 for men and women, respectively, closing the bulk of the gap in enrollment between the races. Perhaps most importantly, even in the early seventies when the college job market entered a sizeable recession, causing white male enrollments to fall as a proportion of the college-age population (Freeman, 1976), black male youngsters continued to flock to higher education. From 1970 to 1974, the proportion of 18- to 19-year-old black men in college rose by 22 percent while the comparable white proportion fell by 21 percent. Whereas in 1965 at the outset of the new market white 18- to

Percentage change in numbers		
1960–1965	*1965–1974*	*1960–1974*
40.0	244.9	368.9
26.4	31.9	66.7
50.2	26.8	97.2
8.6	−18.4	−10.3
76.2	164.9	366.7
31.5	47.9	94.5
76.5	186.6	202.6
24.1	6.3	31.9

19-year-olds were over 150 percent more likely to go to college than blacks, in 1974 they were 60 percent more likely. Blacks made up 5 percent of college students in 1960 and 9.5 percent in 1974.

Much of the increase in enrollments occurred in predominantly white institutions (Table 23), causing a sharp break with the past. In the 1930s, 85 percent of black college students attended predominantly Negro schools, usually in the South; in the 1950s, 80 percent of those enrolled in college were in the southern Negro schools; by 1970, however, 75 percent of the black student body, 378,000 of 520,000, were educated in predominantly white colleges, including many in the once legally segregated schools of the South. Ninety-two percent of the increase in black enrollments from 1964 to 1970 occurred in integrated national institutions and just 8 percent in the largely

TABLE 23
Enrollment of
black students in
predominantly
white colleges in
the 1960s

	1964	1966	1968	1970
Estimated total black enrollments (in thousands)	234	282	434	522
Number in nonblack schools	114	148	278	378
Percent in nonblack schools	48.7	52.5	64.1	72.4

SOURCE: U.S. Bureau of the Census (1971*b*, table 69, p. 83).

black southern schools. In part because of greater opportunities for engineering, science, and business training and in part because of higher quality education, relatively many black male students, especially those with high socioeconomic and financial backgrounds and high academic skills, were enrolled in primarily white schools.

In the North the new pattern of training was sparked by a shift in the recruitment and admission policies of private and public institutions, many of which sought in the late sixties to discover and attract able black youngsters. The new policies took various forms: several prestigious eastern colleges set up the Cooperative Program for Educational Opportunities to recruit black students "qualified for one of the colleges but who would not apply without encouragement." The principal midwestern colleges began "working actively to enroll minority students" (Willingham, 1970). Many colleges used existing black students to "pass the word" about new opportunities and get qualified students to apply. In prestigious Ivy League schools such as Yale, Brown, and similar institutions like MIT, the proportion of freshmen who were black jumped from less than 1 to 6 and 10 percent between 1960 and 1970, indicating a desire for roughly proportionate representation of blacks in the college classes.[3] In the major public institutions of the Midwest, the proportion of blacks also rose, though less impressively (Willingham, 1970). While some methods for accomplishing these changes, introduction of informal quotas and preferential admission, are not desirable in the long run they were presumably needed to transform the educational system after decades of discrimination or neglect of the black population.

[3]Data on minority admission to these schools were obtained by personal interviews. At Brown in the freshman class of 1974–75, 11 percent were black; at MIT, 6 percent; at Yale, 7 percent.

Desegregation of Southern Colleges and Universities

The increased enrollment of blacks in predominantly white southern colleges in the 1960s culminated a long legal effort to open these institutions.[4] Long before the *Brown vs the Board of Education* decision (1954) the Supreme Court demanded equal professional and graduate facilities for blacks under the "separate but equal" doctrine. In the Murray case (1935) a black law student was admitted to the University of Maryland law school as the state failed to provide alternative modes of legal training to blacks. In the Gaines case (1938) out-of-state scholarships were ruled unequal treatment under law, and Missouri was ordered to admit blacks into the state law school in the absence of "separate but equal" schools. In the Sweatt case (1950) the creation of a new Negro law school lacking "the reputation of faculty, experience of administration, position and influence of alumni, standing in the community, traditions, and prestige" of the University of Texas Law School was ruled unequal treatment for blacks. Strict application of the "separate but equal" doctrine forced states to choose between the expense of establishing new *equal quality* graduate or professional schools or desegregating existing white institutions. In each case, the cost of new schools exceeded the desire for segregation and black students were admitted for graduate or professional study. Prior to 1954 at least 17 colleges and universities in the South and 9 in border states were desegregated as a result of these developments (Johnson, 1954, p. 320). Following the Court's ruling, colleges and universities in the border states and in much of the South desegregated rapidly, and blacks were soon enrolled, in small numbers, in most southern institutions. Although there was die-hard segregationist opposition in Alabama, South Carolina, and Mississippi, none of which desegregated until 1964–65 under the threat of federal government suits and cutoff of funds under the 1964 Civil Rights Act, desegregation was relatively rapid, as Table 24 makes clear. By 1970, 20 percent of blacks attending public colleges in the southern and border states were enrolled in traditionally white public institutions, University of Texas rather than Texas Southern, for example (U.S. Department of Commerce, 1971, table 20). Concurrently the fraction of whites attending the public Negro institutions also rose, to about 8 percent of the student body at

[4]For a detailed account of public desegregation and opposition, see McCord (1969).

	Year and nature of desegregation			
State and number of institutions	*1948– 1953*	*1954– 1955*	*1956– 1957*	*1958– 1959*
Alabama (8)			C	
Arkansas (8)	C	7V		
Delaware (1)		V		
Florida (24)				C
Georgia (18)				
Kentucky (8)	2C, V	2V	3V	
Louisiana (10)	C	3C		C
Maryland (16)	C, V	6V	4V	2V
Mississippi (19)				
Missouri (18)	2C, V	9V	V	3V
North Carolina (13)	C, V		2V	V
Oklahoma (22)	C	18V	3V	V
South Carolina (6)				
Tennessee (6)	C		4V	V
Texas (49)	6V, C	C, 6V	3C, 5V	V
Virginia (5)	4V, C			
West Virginia (10)		10V		

TABLE 24
Numbers of public colleges and universities desegregating in southern and border states 1948–1965

NOTE: *V* stands for Voluntary desegregation, *C* for Court-ordered desegregation.

SOURCE: Southern Educational Reporting Service (Nov. 1961, updated Feb. 1962 & Nov. 1964).

the undergraduate level and 21 percent at the graduate level (Office of Advancement of Public Negro Colleges, 1969). Desegregation was evidently easier to carry out at the college and university than at the elementary and secondary school level.

Southern Black Colleges

Despite the movement of black youngsters into primarily white institutions, southern black colleges were not neglected in the new market. Their financial support was increased as the federal government and foundations, after years of shortchanging the schools, began to provide the additional dollars needed to upgrade the institutions. In 1966 predominantly black colleges had a current fund income of $1,773 per pupil compared with $2,144 for other colleges—a relative income of 83 percent com-

1960–1961	1962–1963	1964–1965
	C	2C, 4V
4V	5V	14V
C, V	5V	11V
	C	C, 3V
2V		
	C	18C
	2V	
3V	4V	V
	2C	4V
C, 3V	9V, 2C	8V

pared with a 1940 differential of 49 percent.[5] More importantly, perhaps, the 1966 difference in income per pupil was due entirely to the absence of sizeable research and development activities at campuses and the concurrent lack of federal research and development support: black schools received just $6.25 million in research support compared with $2.5 billion dollars in overall research support (Bowles & DeCosta, 1971, p. 157). Exclusive of research and development, spending per pupil in the southern black schools equaled that of other colleges in the late 1960s—$1,201 compared with $1,214. Indeed, despite the lopsided distribution of research and development,

[5] Figures for 1940 are from Badger (1951). Those for 1966 are obtained from Bowles and Decosta (1971), with numbers of pupils and current fund revenues fror Table 19. I made the calculations from the basic statistics.

private black institutions outspent public predominantly white schools by over 20 percent per student (calculated from data in Bowles & DeCosta, p. 157).

Among major programs initiated in the late 1960s to aid the southern black colleges were the Ford Foundation support of $10 million to raise several of the institutions to the level of national universities, U.S. federal aid, and, in some states like North Carolina, special funding to make up for the cumulated deficit in resources that resulted from past discrimination.

The predominantly black colleges were, however, also negatively affected in several ways by the changes of the 1960s. They lost their most able students to predominantly white national colleges and universities, limiting their role to educator of those from the poorest families and those with the most severe academic shortcomings. They also ran into difficulties in holding the most able faculty or in attracting first-rate black scholars due to the increased employment opportunities available at primarily white colleges and universities. While some schools may in fact achieve the rank of first-rate national institutions, most southern black colleges are likely to remain at the bottom of the educational ladder, providing compensatory schooling for the disadvantaged.

GRADUATE TRAINING

A substantial effort to increase the graduate and professional school opportunities of black students was also initiated in the late 1960s. Many major universities made black (and other) minority representation in graduate schools an institutional goal, assigning the task of minority recruitment to particular administrators, initiating special fellowship programs for minority students, waiving application fees, and actively seeking qualified applicants in various ways (for instance, by writing to all those scoring well on the Graduate Record Examination). Preferential treatment in admissions became sufficiently widespread that *Graduate and Professional School Opportunities for Minorities,* published by Education Testing Service (1971), recommended that minority students "identify your minority group" on applications when the law prohibits schools from requesting ethnic and religious information. To increase minority representation in business schools, several universities banded together in consortia which provide financial aid and engage in recruiting activities (Council for Opportunity in Graduate Management Education, Accelerated Business Leadership Education, Consortium for Graduate Study in Management). Law and medical schools have also undertaken joint action to increase the number of minority students in their fields. Perhaps the most striking indication of the changed environment is the statement by the School of Medicine of the University of Mississippi that "for equal abilities, we would give preference to a minority student" in awarding fellowships, surely a far cry from past policies (Educational Testing Service, 1971, p. 189).

As Tables 25 and 26 show, this "transformation" appears to have had a substantial impact on the number of blacks taking graduate work, particularly black men. Between 1967 and 1973, black male graduate enrollment roughly doubled while white male enrollments for five or more years of college grew only modestly (Table 25). Relative to the number of 22- to 29-year olds, the graduate age population, or to the number of graduates less than 34 years of age, black male graduate enrollments rose, while those for whites fell. Among women, the pattern is,

TABLE 25
Graduate enrollments, 1967–1973

	Male		Female	
	1967	*1973*	*1967*	*1973*
Black				
Number enrolled five or more years in college (in thousands)	18	37	14	24
As percentage of population, 22- to 29-year-olds	1.9	2.9	1.7	1.5
As percentage of college graduates less than 34 years old	27.7	37.2	14.1	26.5
White				
Number enrolled five or more years in college (in thousands)	662	827	228	465
As percentage of population, 22- to 29-year-olds	8.1	7.5	2.5	4.0
As percentage of college graduates less than 34 years old	28.2	23.2	14.6	16.0

SOURCE: U. S. Bureau of the Census, *Current Population Reports: Population Characteristics* ("School Enrollment in the U.S.," various editions, for enrollment data; "Educational Attainment," for graduate data).

TABLE 26 Black graduate enrollments as percent of all enrollments by discipline, 1973	*Percentage black, 1973*
Doctorate institutions, all fields	4.4
Physical sciences	1.4
Engineering	1.2
Life and health sciences	2.8
Social sciences	4.1
Arts and humanities	2.8
Education	7.2
Professions	5.1
Law school, first-year	5.1
Medical school, first year	7.1
Business school, total	1.0–2.2

SOURCES: American Council on Education (1974) and interviews with the National Medical Association, the Institute for Education Development, the Council on Legal Educational Opportunities, and the Council on Graduate and Management Education.

however, different as both black and white women increased their graduate enrollments in the new market. The figures in Table 25 are, it must be stressed, based on a small sample, which makes the magnitude though not the direction of change subject to considerable sampling error.

Additional evidence from diverse scattered sources, summarized in Table 26, confirms the picture of increased black graduate enrollments in the new market. According to the table, blacks constituted a nonnegligible share of graduate students in doctorate, law, and medical school programs in 1973, which contrasts sharply with their relatively slight representation in the stock of workers in these areas. At the doctorate level, for example, blacks constituted 4.4 percent of students in Ph.D.-granting institutions compared, for example, with a bare 2.9 percent of all Ph.D.'s (National Academy of Sciences, 1973). In each Ph.D. specialty, the fraction enrolled greatly exceeds the fraction of Ph.D.'s, though black graduate students remain exceedingly rare in some fields, notably physical sciences and engineering, and underrepresented relative to the black share of the population in all. The professional school enrollment figures tell a similar story, though the black share in business schools is still slight. At one major university, Harvard, blacks constituted 9.8 percent of the entering law class of 1973, up from just 3.0 percent of the class of 1965; and 12.7 percent of the entering medical students; but just 3.5 percent of business school and 3.1 percent of arts and science students. Many of the most able black undergraduates preferred legal and medical studies, which promise high pecuniary rewards, to academic studies, with those in the latter areas tending to concentrate in more vocational fields.

THE POPULATION OF COLLEGE GRADUATES While black graduate and undergraduate enrollments increased rapidly in the new market, blacks continue to be significantly underrepresented in the college graduate work force. In 1972, 7.1 percent of black men and 4.8 percent of black women attained four or more years of college compared with 15.4 and 9.1 percent of all men and women, so that blacks constituted 3.2 and 5.2 percent of male and female graduates, respectively (U.S. Bureau of the Census, 1972c). Among young (25- to 29-year-old) workers, the black shares were markedly higher: 4.4 percent of male graduates and 6.4 percent of female graduates, though still below the shares of the population. Since in 1950, just 2.3 percent of the male and 4.1 percent of the female college population was black (U.S. Bureau of the Census, 1953, table 5); the 1972 figures show a marked gain in the fifties and sixties, though one that will not yield roughly proportionate black representation in the foreseeable future.

With respect to the graduate-trained black population, *Current Population Survey* data tell a similar story. In 1964, 2.7 percent of men with five or more years of college were black; in 1972, 3.0 percent. Among the young (25- to 34-year-olds in these data), the number of black men with five or more years of college increased from 14,000 to 32,000 during 1964–1972. In the former year 1.9 percent of 25- to 34-year-old men with five or more years of college were black; in the latter, 2.6 percent—a 37 percent increase, but one still showing large underrepresentation of blacks in that group (U.S. Bureau of the Census, 1972c). The picture for women is quite different: in 1972 5.8 percent of women with five or more years of college and 7.3 percent of those aged 25–34 were black. As for the group at the top of the education pyramid, Ph.D.'s, the growth of black enrollments has yet to augment significantly the supply. In 1973 blacks constituted just 1.4 percent of all Ph.D.'s and 2.9 percent of new doctoral graduates[6] (National Academy of Sciences, 1974).

The underrepresentation of blacks, particularly of black men, in the college and graduate-trained labor force thus remains a substantial bottleneck for the goal of increasing the relative number of blacks in many high-level occupations. Because of the long supply adjustment needed to raise the educational attainment of an entire population, significantly fewer blacks than whites are likely to be found in most graduate-level fields for several decades. While the educational opportunities and academic attainment of blacks increased greatly in the new market period, attainment of parity with whites will not be achieved for some time to come.

CONCLUSION The principal theme of this chapter, that blacks made significant progress in education, has been shown in various ways: increased black educational attainment, particularly among the young; growth of the black college and graduate student population; the shift of black students to primarily white northern colleges and universities; new recruitment and admission policies in higher education favorable to blacks; desegregation of southern white colleges; increased funding of southern predominantly black colleges.

[6]Because data on all doctorates by ethnic origin are hard to come by, the 1973 percent of all Ph.D.'s is a rough estimate. I multiplied the percent of all Ph.D. scientists and engineers who were black from National Academy of Sciences (1974, table 11) by the ratio of the percent of 1973 Ph.D.'s who were black to the percent of science and engineering Ph.D.'s who were black and United States citizens (ibid., Appendix, table 2). This assumes that blacks are represented in the total Ph.D. population proportionately to their representation in 1973 Ph.D.'s between sciences and other fields.

3. Supply Responses to New Opportunities

The road to the top is through higher education—not black studies. . . . let the clever young black go to a university to study engineering, medicine, chemistry, economics, law, agriculture.

SIR ARTHUR LEWIS, 1969

How have black students and qualified personnel responded to the improved educational and job opportunities of the late 1960s and early 1970s? To what extent are educational and career plans the result of economically rational supply behavior in the new market setting? Have young college-trained blacks followed the strategy of Sir Lewis or have they chosen less vocational black study curricula?

This chapter uses statistical and survey tools of analysis to investigate these and related questions about the impact of the new labor market on the black elite. It provides fairly conclusive answers to the questions of concern, which can be summarized in two basic propositions:

- *Proposition 1:* The career and educational decisions of black male students and qualified personnel were substantially altered in the new market, as large numbers chose "traditionally closed" business and technical occupations.

- *Proposition 2:* The changes in decisions resulted largely from economically rational supply responses to new income and employment opportunities, which produced an elastic supply of black workers to professional and managerial jobs.

CHANGED CAREER DECISIONS Evidence on the fields of study and careers selected by students and on the occupations of young high-level black workers provides compelling support for the first proposition.

First, as Table 27 shows, there was an extraordinary change

57

TABLE 27   Occupations and fields of study of male black college graduates or students, 1961–1975

Panel A: Prospective occupations

Distribution of new graduates

	1975		1964		1961	
Occupation	Black	Nonblack	Black	Nonblack	Black	Nonblack
Businessman	20.0%	16.0%	12.0%	28.0%	7.3%	23.7%
Teacher, including college	11.0	8.1	31.0	14.0	46.3	15.9
Doctor, dentist	6.3	6.4	3.7	4.0	2.5	4.1
Engineer	8.3	9.7	8.0	14.0	7.2	13.9
Lawyer	8.9	6.7	4.0	9.0	3.2	5.8
Scientist	2.2	3.4	14.0	10.0	7.4	8.4

Panel B: Prospective* and actual† fields of study

Percentage distribution

	1975		1967‡		1962‡	
Field of study	Black	Nonblack	Blacks at PNCs§	Nonblack	Blacks at PNCs§	Nonblack
Business	24.1%	18.0%	12.5%	17.5%	6.4%	20.0%
Education	8.2	4.5	30.1	8.8	39.1	11.1
Engineering	9.9	13.4	4.2	10.8	3.9	14.4
Mathematics	2.1	2.6	8.0	4.0	7.7	4.5
Physical sciences	1.6	3.1	5.6	4.4	4.7	6.0
Social science (including history)	17.5	10.4	24.1	18.4	18.3	17.1
Biology	3.5	4.5	6.3	5.9	10.4	5.3

*"Prospective" refers to 1975.

†"Actual" refers to 1967 and 1962.

‡In some Negro colleges many black students majored in industrial arts. They are not included in the reported catgories.

§PNCs refer to Predominantly Negro Colleges.

NOTE: I have subtracted female from total figures given in Fichter (1964) to obtain estimates of male career plans in 1971.

SOURCES: 1961, Fichter (1964, p. 51; 1965, p. 73); 1964, U.S. Department of Health, Education, and Welfare (1965, p. 12A); 1962, U.S. Department of Labor, (1965, p. 266); 1967, calculated from data in U.S. Office of Education (1969); 1975, based on plans of freshman class of 1971 in American Council on Education (1972, p. 26).

in the career plans and fields of study of black male college students in the new market. Both the actual and prospective occupations of black students given in Panel A and the actual and prospective fields of study in Panel B reveal a tremendous shift into business-oriented fields. In the class of 1961, for example, 7.3 percent of black students chose business careers compared with proportionately three times as many white students (23.7 percent). A decade or so later, 20 percent of black freshmen in the class of 1975 (who entered in 1971) planned on business careers, 25 percent *more* than their white peers. A similar pattern is found in the field-of-study data in Panel B, where the fraction of blacks intending to major in business in the class of 1975 was five times as great as the proportion of graduates in 1962, while the nonblack fraction remained roughly the same. In engineering, there was a marked increase in the number of black majors, from 3.9 to 9.9 percent, and a narrowing in the gap between the black and nonblack proportions intending permanent careers in the field; a differential of nearly 2.0 to 1.0 in 1962 (13.9 versus 7.2 percent) drops to 1.16 to 1 by 1978 (9.7 versus 8.3 percent). Another traditionally closed area in which blacks pursued careers is law. In 1961 just 3.2 percent of black students sought legal careers; in the class of 1975, 5.8 percent. As in business, the black proportion rises from much below to somewhat above the white proportion in the new market. Counterpoise to the swing into business, engineering, and law is a precipitous decline in the number of blacks intending to teach. Between 1961 and 1972 the fraction of students seeking teaching careers fell from 46 to 18 percent (Panel A) while the expected number of education majors plummeted from 39 percent of the class of 1962 to 11 percent of the class of 1975. The once overwhelming importance of teaching to black male graduates came to an end.

Second, data for classes entering in the mid-seventies show continuation of the sudden concentration of blacks in vocationally oriented, previously closed occupations. In the class of 1978, who entered college in 1974 (for whom data on blacks are restricted to those at predominantly black colleges), 25 percent of black men intended to major in business, 10 percent in engineering compared with 20 and 12 percent of all male freshmen; 24 percent of the black students planned on business careers, 7 percent on careers as engineers, and so forth[1] (American Council on Education, 1974*b*). Data on actual rather than planned behavior confirm this picture. Between 1969 and 1974 the num-

---

[1]While there are differences between career and field-of-study plans by black male students in primarily black and other colleges, American Council on Education data (1972, p. 26) suggest that they are not sufficiently different to make the numbers in the text misleading.

ber of black freshmen in engineering increased 180 percent
(Planning Comission . . . , 1974, pp. 87, 97; Scientific Manpower Commission, 1975, p. 16) so that by fall 1974, 4.3 percent
of the freshmen engineering class were black, a figure that
implies a smaller movement into an engineering career than
that shown in the data on career plans but still one of substantial change relative to the past.

Third, in part as a result of changes in student career plans,
there was a significant shift in the occupational distribution of
young, 25- to 34-year-old, black male college graduates in the
1960s toward management and engineering and away from
teaching and traditionally segregated professional services.
Tables 28 and 29 summarize census of population evidence
regarding this shift, with the former comparing the distributions for the young in 1960 and 1970 in major professions for
which 1960 data are available and the latter giving the distribution of graduates among detailed professions in 1970. According to the estimates in Table 28, the proportion of young black
graduates in engineering and managerial occupations went up
twofold or more in the sixties and began to approach the
proportions among all 25- to 34-year-old male graduates while
the fraction of blacks teaching or employed in "other" occupations fell to levels closer to those of whites. As a result of these
changes, there was a considerable convergence in the occupational distributions of the two groups. The more detailed data

TABLE 28 *Changes in the occupational distribution of black and all college graduate men aged 25–34,
1960–1970*

| | Percentage distribution | | | | | |
| | Black men | | | Total men | | |
	1960*	1970	1970/1960	1960*	1970	1970/1960
Professionals	64.9	69.7	1.07	59.7	64.4	1.08
Engineers	5.3	10.3	1.94	12.9	11.0	0.85
Natural scientists	1.8	3.6	2.00	3.3	2.3	0.70
Physicians and surgeons	3.5	4.8	1.37	3.2	2.6	0.81
Teachers, elementary	7.0	6.6	0.94	3.5	3.8	1.09
Secondary	10.5	10.2	0.97	6.3	9.1	1.44
Managers	3.5	9.2	2.63	13.5	14.8	1.10

*1960 data relate to nonwhite men.

SOURCE: U.S. Bureau of the Census (1962, table 1; 1973*d*, table 1).

TABLE 29
Occupational
distribution of 25-
to 34-year-old
black and total
male college
graduates, 1970

	Percentage distribution	
	Black graduates 25–34	*Total graduates 25–34*
Professional, technical, kindred	66.1	64.4
Accountants	2.5	4.7
Architects	0.4	0.6
Clergymen and religious workers	1.4	1.8
College teachers	4.1	5.6
Dentists	0.3	0.9
Designers	0.4	0.5
Draftsmen	0.7	0.5
Editors and reporters	0.4	0.9
Engineers	4.8	11.0
Civil	0.8	1.5
Electrical	1.4	2.9
Mechanical	0.4	1.6
Lawyers and judges	1.1	3.2
Natural scientists	2.4	2.3
Chemists	1.8	1.1
Pharmacists	0.8	1.0
Physicians and surgeons	1.5	2.7
Social welfare and recreation	3.8	1.3
Social scientists	0.8	1.3
Teachers, elementary	10.5	3.8
Secondary	15.1	9.1
Technicians, health	0.9	0.5
Electrical and electronic	0.3	0.1
Managerial	10.1	14.8
Officials	1.3	1.1
All other	23.8	20.8

SOURCE: U.S. Bureau of the Census (1973c, tables 5, 6, 8, 9).

in Table 29 tell a similar story, as the proportion of young blacks in the occupations is much closer to the proportion of young whites than is true for all black and white workers. For example, the difference in the proportion of blacks and whites working as engineers in the table is 6.2 points, which compares with a difference of 8.8 points, for all workers; similarly the difference drops in secondary school teaching from 5.5 to 4.0 points, and most importantly, in management from 12.0 to just 4.7 points.[2] Measured in relative probabilities, the data reveal a similar though less striking development. While the changes in occupational attainment are not as dramatic as the changes in student decisions because 25- to 34-year-olds in 1970 chose their fields prior to the new market improvements, they still show considerable occupational adjustment.

Finally, estimates of the proportion of young, black professionals and managers in detailed fields presented in Table 30 show that, regardless of the level of education, young highly qualified blacks tended to move rapidly into traditionally closed business careers in the postwar period. In accounting, black representation increased sixfold between 1950 (0.35 percent of all 25- to 34-year old accountants) and 1970 (2.11 percent); in drafting, by nearly four times (0.78 to 3.0 percent); in chemistry, threefold (1.43 to 4.81 percent). Similar gains are shown in engineering (0.34 to 1.45 percent), management (1.55 to 2.92 percent), and most strikingly, in personnel and labor relations (0.82 to 5.35 percent), where black specialists may have opportunity to help shape hiring and firing policies in the future.

Between 1950 and 1960 there are also substantial increases in the share of young black social welfare and recreation workers; and in the 1960–1970 decade, in the share of black editors and reporters. At the other end of the spectrum, the share of young black professionals fell in the areas of medicine, theology, and college teaching and jumped erratically among lawyers and judges. Presumably the movement into traditionally closed business-oriented occupations was at the expense of professional services.

[2] For men with two or more years of college in 1970, the fraction of blacks (total men) in the occupations described in the text are:

Accounting 0.9 (3.8)
Engineering 2.0 (10.8)
Secondary school teaching 11.1 (5.6)
Management 5.7 (17.7)

The figures for 1970 are calculated from U.S. Bureau of the Census (1973c, tables 5, 6); those for 1960 are obtained from U.S. Bureau of the Census (1963b, tables 9, 10) and are adjusted, by occupation, from the percentages of nonwhites who are black in Table 3. See footnote 5 in Chapter 1.

TABLE 30 *Relative number of 25- to 34-year-old men who were black in detailed professions and changes in the relative number, 1950–1970*

	Ratio of black to total 25- to 34-year-olds			Changes in ratio	
	1950* (1)	1960* (2)	1970 (3)	1970/1950 (4)	1970/1960 (5)
Professional	2.23	2.91	3.71	1.48	0.80
Accountants	0.35	0.81	2.11	1.76	1.30
Architects	1.39	0.82	2.28	0.89	1.46
Clergymen	4.11	2.61	2.68	−1.43	0.07
College teachers	2.85	2.67	2.26	−0.59	−0.41
Dentists	2.37	2.57	1.21	−1.16	−1.36
Designers	1.49	0.56	2.13	0.64	1.57
Draftsmen	0.78	1.28	3.00	2.22	1.72
Editors and reporters	0.46	0.72	2.06	1.60	1.34
Engineers	0.34	0.65	1.45	1.11	0.80
Civil	0.45	1.22	1.80	1.35	0.58
Electrical	0.32	0.64	1.58	1.26	0.94
Mechanical	0.14	0.45	1.19	1.05	0.74
Lawyers and judges	0.33	2.57	1.14	0.81	−1.43
Natural scientists	1.43	2.35	3.51	2.08	1.16
Chemists	1.43	2.59	4.81	3.38	2.22
Personnel and labor relations	0.82	1.38	5.35	4.53	3.97
Pharmacists	2.52	3.34	2.72	0.20	−0.62
Physicians and surgeons	2.11	3.39	1.80	−0.31	−1.59
Public relations	†	1.19	3.97	†	2.78
Recreation workers	7.37	11.22	13.75	6.38	2.53
Social welfare workers	7.30	14.41	14.05	6.75	−0.36
Social scientists	1.02	1.66	2.35	1.33	0.69
Teachers, elementary	†	9.20	8.75	†	−0.45
Secondary	†	5.79	5.25	†	−0.54
Technicians, health	3.69	1.16	4.14	0.45	2.98
Electrical and electronic	†	†	3.06	†	†
Managerial	1.55	1.31	2.92	1.37	1.61

*Obtained by multiplying nonwhite proportion of 25- to 34-year-olds by black fraction of all nonwhites in the profession.
†Not available.

SOURCE: U.S. Bureau of the Census (1956, tables 6, 7; 1963*b*, tables 6, 7; 1973*c*, table 40, 41).

In sum, as asserted in proposition 1, great changed occurred in the occupational decisions of young black students and in the job distribution of qualified young black workers in the new market. Since in an important sense, *the decisions of the young represent the economic present and are in equilibrium with respect to existing wages,* the new career patterns of the young provide an exceptional measure of the changes in discrimination and in the state of the market.

ECONOMIC INCENTIVES AND SUPPLY DECISIONS

To what extent are the observed changes in the educational and occupational decisions of qualified blacks the result of economically rational supply decisions? How responsive are black male graduates to economic incentives? What determines the share of black men in a professional field?[3]

This section examines these questions in the context of the economic theory of career choice, which directs attention to the role of expected incomes on human capital investments and career decisions. According to this theory a decision maker can be viewed schematically as (1) estimating his potential lifetime income in each occupation on the basis of market wages and personal ability; (2) evaluating the goods which can be bought with the income and with initial wealth; (3) evaluating the nonmonetary characteristics of work in the occupations; (4) selecting the career with the highest total utility. Since individuals differ in tastes and ability, the *reservation wage* at which they enter one occupation also differs, producing an aggregate supply schedule which is the cumulative of the distribution of reservation wages. Since changing the wage in a single occupation only affects those working in it, *ceteris paribus,* changes necessarily have a "substitution" effect in supply, increasing or decreasing the number selecting the occupation.[4]

Discrimination in educational or employment opportunities which alters the structure of wages can be expected to induce blacks to make different educational and career decisions than

---

[3] This discussion deals solely with black men because the vast majority of black (and white) female graduates choose teaching, which provides little variation in occupational choice.

[4] This argument postulates a 0 to 1 discontinuous career decision in which the individual devotes full-time to a single occupation. See Freeman (1971, Ch. 1) for a discussion of this model. With 0 to 1 choices, only substitution effects are operative.

whites. When the costs of human capital formation are high, due say to educational discrimination, or when the absolute dollar returns to investments in skills are lowered by job market discrimination, which cuts the wages of skilled and less skilled black workers at least proportionately, the rate of return and black investments in human capital will be reduced.[5] Only if discrimination operates as a "lump sum" tax, lowering black wages by the same amount in all occupations and time periods will it be neutral with respect to human capital investment decisions. Even here, however, the "shrinkage" of black opportunities is likely to lead to a distinctive pattern of career decision making, since lower black incomes will have an "income effect" in career decisions, causing individuals to accept less pleasant work and more onerous jobs. Background differences in initial wealth will also induce "income effects," pushing blacks with low nonwage wealth into relatively less pleasant jobs. More importantly, perhaps, discrimination that reduces opportunities and income in some occupations more than in others is likely to have substantial substitution effects in career decision making, inducing blacks with the same human capital as whites to enter those occupations least affected by discrimination. The higher the ratio of black-to-white wages in a profession, the higher should be the relative number of qualified blacks as a result of supply behavior.

Economic analysis, while recognizing tastes, abilities, and related factors, suggests that differences in income and market opportunities account for the differential career decisions of blacks and whites and, ipso facto, that changed opportunities underlie observed changes in decisions.

The Rate of Return As the first step in linking the increase in black male college enrollments to economic incentives, I have estimated the rate of return to investments in four years of college in the new market. If the growth of enrollments is the result of rational supply behavior, the return would be expected to rise from the low levels of the 1950s (Weiss, 1970). Because the improvement in the relative income of blacks was concentrated among the

[5]If discrimination operates like a proportionate or progressive tax and the income differential between persons with and without training is reduced, and if costs of training are fixed or reduced by a smaller amount, the incentive to invest must decline.

young (see Chapter 1), however, with a consequent "twist" in the cross-sectional profiles usually used to estimate rate of returns, the standard estimates are suspect. By definition, rates of return and discounted present values are *foward-looking* concepts, which require forecasts of future incomes—a risky and uncertain undertaking of the type which economists have not excelled in in the past. In periods of stability, when cross-sectional profiles are stable and likely to parallel actual cohort changes, there is no problem in using cross-sectional data. In a period of substantial change, however, when the position of the young is drastically altered, alternative assumptions about future income possibilities will be critical in estimation. If young blacks maintain their improved position in the future, for example, their incomes will far exceed those of older black graduates (suitably adjusted for "normal" growth of real incomes), yielding rates of return much above those from cross-sectional profiles. If, on the other hand, the position of young blacks deteriorates in the future to approach that among older generations of black college men, the return will have been only moderately raised by the achievement of roughly equal starting salaries in the 1960s and early 1970s.[6]

To provide some notion of the range of possibilities dependent upon alternative postulates about the future, I report in Table 31 discounted present values and internal rates of return for 1973 under five alternative assumptions about future income streams and compare the estimated rate of return as of 1973 with the one obtained for 1959 by Hanoch (1967). Columns (1) through (3) give the discounted present values of the income of black men with four years of high school and four years of college and the direct cost of college in 1973, using a 10 percent interest rate. Column 4 gives the net present value of the black male college investment—the difference between discounted income from college less direct costs and that from high school. Column (5) gives the approximate internal rates of return for the black male investments and column (6) the comparable return to white male investments.

The five assumptions about future income streams are, line

---

[6] Deterioration in the relative income of young black graduates would be likely if the increased income of new entrants were due to reduced investments in on-the-job training rather than improved demand for blacks. The reduced training hypothesis is inconsistent with the bulk of the evidence in this book.

TABLE 31 *Alternative estimates of discounted present values and internal rates of return, 1973*

| | Discounted incomes of black men in thousands of 1973 dollars, with 10 percent interest rate | | | | | |
| | Discounted present values, 1973 private after tax | | | Net present values† | Approximate private rates of return* (to ½ percent) | |
Assumed income path	High school	College	Direct cost‡ of college	1973	Black men, 1973	White men, 1973
1. Actual cross-sectional profile with 1.5% growth	$72.6	$ 78.6	$3.2	$ 2.8	11%	10%
2. White male cross section, with 1.5% growth, applied to blacks	73.3	102.6	3.2	26.1	15+	10
3. 1959 cross section, with 1.5% growth, nonwhite for blacks, total for whites	89.8	74.6	3.2	12.0	14	8
4. 1959–1969 cohort gains, nonwhite for blacks, total for whites	87.6	72.7	3.2	11.7	14	8
5. 1963–1973 white cohort gains applied to blacks	98.0	76.2	3.2	18.6	15	7.5

*Private returns and private discounted values obtained by using *after*-tax incomes, obtained by adjusting incomes by tax liability reported in U.S. Bureau of the Census (*Statistical Abstract 1973*, p. 393, table 631) with interpolations between income changes. I used the married couple, independent incomes tax liabilities.

†Net present values obtained by subtracting discounted value of high school and direct costs from discounted value of college income values.

‡Direct cost obtained as sum of tuition and fees and estimated cost of books and transportation. Assumed the same for whites and blacks. Data from U.S. Bureau of the Census (1975*b*, p. 4, table F, figures for full-time male students in four-year colleges and universities).

NOTES: Line 1—Income profiles using actual cross sections with blacks given black (nonwhite) cross-sectional profile and whites given the white (total) male cross section. Line 2—Whites, same as line 1; blacks obtained by applying white cross section to blacks. Line 3—Applied 1959 actual cross sections to *all* years, with nonwhite data used for blacks and total male data for whites. Line 4—Applied 1959–1969 cohort gains to initial income at ages 25–29, with nonwhite (black) and total (white) incomes used for 1959 and 1969. Line 5—Whites, same as line 4; blacks obtained by applying white gains to blacks.

SOURCE: U.S. Bureau of the Census, computer tapes for March 1974, *Consumer Population Reports Survey*.

by line: (1) that they follow actual cross-sectional profiles in each year with a 1.5 percent growth due to increases in real earnings per worker. This is the most "pessimistic" assumption, as it assumes that young blacks rapidly lose the gains of the new market over their life cycle; (2) that future incomes follow *white* cross-sectional profiles, again with the 1.5 percent growth in overall productivity; (3) that the profiles in each year increase according to the 1959 black (or white) cross-sectional relation, with 1.5% growth—since 1959 preceded the development of the new market, this amounts to taking the presixties cross section as the appropriate indicator of "normal" life cycle income paths; (4) that black and white incomes increase at 1959–1969 actual cohort gains, an "optimistic" assumption for blacks due to the development of the new market; and (5) that both blacks and whites obtain the same "white" 1963–1973 cohort income gains. I choose this period because it covers both the booming college market of the 1960s and the market bust of the early 1970s (Freeman, 1975). In each case the income profiles were generated by applying the relevant changes to the incomes of 25- to 29-year-olds in five-year (ten-year) intervals.[7] That is, I estimate the income of 30- to 34-year-olds by multiplying the income of 25- to 29-year-olds by the life-cycle growth over five years and then take that figure, multiply it by the life-cycle growth from 30–34 to 35–39 to obtain the next figure, and so forth. In intermediate years, I interpolated by simple linear procedures. For comparability, in lines 3 through 5, I apply the same income profile to the different cohorts so that differences in incomes are due solely to differences in starting position.

To take account of the years in school, I tabulated from the CPS tapes the income of men, by individual age for 1973, in school and out of school. For ages 18 to 21, college men are given the income of college students while high school men are given the income of high school graduates out-of-school. For the age 22 (when college men presumably work part year) they are both given the income of out-of-school men. Private benefits are obtained by applying tax rates to incomes, and private costs from a recent census publication (U.S. Bureau of Census, 1975*b*), adjusted for earlier years as described in table notes. To focus on the effect of the postschool labor market changes on the return, for the ages 18–23 I employ the same 1973 cross-sectional profiles in each calculation. This can be modified in the cohort calculations to obtain a better fix on either historic returns or potential future returns. Finally, the cross-sectional estimates are adjusted for potential increases in real income in

---

[7] Because the *Census* and *CPS* data relate to previous years' incomes, the ages should be reduced by one to obtain the actual age to which earnings relate. For comparability with other statistics in this book, I report the data by age during the survey week rather than during the period of earnings.

the future by a growth factor of 1.5 percent per year. Larger or smaller factors will alter the estimated present values and returns but are unlikely to affect the substantive results. Since cohort incomes are based on actual income gains, no such adjustment is made in lines 4 and 5.

The computations show that as a result of the improved market for young black college men, the internal rate of return to black male investments in college, however calculated, came to exceed those for white male investments by 1973. Even in line 1, where young black graduates are assumed to obtain relatively slight increases in income in the future, as their position deteriorates to approach that of the older cohorts, the return to black college investments rises to *exceed* that for whites by 1 percent. In line 2, where blacks are assumed to obtain the life-cycle gains in the white male profile of the same year, the return to blacks rises even more sharply, by 5+ percentage points. Because the income of young white college men was depressed in 1973 (Freeman, 1975), however, the 1973 white profile is unusually steep and unrealistic. It assumes very rapid life-cycle income increases after ages 25–29 and 30–34, which appear implausible. The potentially most realistic assumptions are in lines 3 through 5, where blacks are expected to obtain life-cycle income gains at the rates shown by the 1959 cross-sectional profiles and by 1959–1969 and 1963–1973 cohort income gains. Here the return for blacks rises to the extent that they have significantly greater incentive than whites to enroll in college in 1973. While the depressed college job market in the early 1970s greatly reduced the potential rewards to white male investments in college, a strong return for black graduates was maintained.

That the high return to black investments arose in the new market is seen by comparing the estimates in Table 31 with those of Hanoch (1967) from 1959 *Census* cross-sectional profiles. His calculations suggest a return to nonwhites of 6 percent in 1959 compared with 10.1 percent for whites. While Hanoch's method of calculation differs from that of Table 31 due to differences in data and adjustments, the basic result that black rates of return rose *relative* to whites is unlikely to be affected by these differences.

The reason for the sharp rise in the return to black male college investments in 1973 is found in the changed income of black male graduates aged 25–29, the key "pivot" group in the estimates. In 1973 these black men had slightly *higher* earnings, according to the *CPS* data, than white male college graduates ($11,168 versus $10,242) while black male high school graduates trailed their white peers by about $2,000 ($7,700 versus $9,702). Since the calculations (save in line 1) extrapolate these patterns into the future they yield much higher rates of return for blacks than for whites. As long as black college graduates do about as well as their white peers, while black high school graduates do noticeably worse, the return to black college-going will be particularly high.

I want to stress, however, that the calculations in the table are only rough order of magnitude "guestimates" based on alternative possible future developments. While the cross-sectional profile calculations in line 1 are probably too pessimistic, requiring young blacks to experience unprecedented declines in income relative to white graduates over the life cycle, those in the other lines may be too optimistic, assuming *no* such deterioration.[8] What is important is not the precise estimates or which turns out to be closest to future reality but rather the fact that *all* show a marked improvement in the incentive for young black men to enroll in college in the period under study, consistent with observed behavior.

The Market and Increased Enrollments

A more formal test of the link between the improved job market for black graduates and college enrollments is given in Table 32, which records the results of regressing the percentage of 18- to 24-year-old nonwhite men in college and the ratio of the nonwhite to white percentages in college on one indicator of the changing opportunity for nonwhite college men, the fraction (relative fraction) obtaining jobs as managers. Both regressions include a lagged dependent variable to allow for lags in adjustment to changing opportunities. The table shows that the incentive variables account for much of the increase in enroll-

[8]Two forces are likely to operate in the future to produce rates different from those in the projections. On the one hand, as noted in Chapter 9, the increased supply of black graduates may reduce incomes in the late seventies and early eighties, cutting the high rates shown in the table. On the other, the career paths of black graduates are highly unlikely to follow the cross-sectional profiles, which depend on the position of older graduates trained in primarily black colleges and excluded from jobs in national corporations, causing the low rates. Thus the figures in Table 31 probably bracket the future.

TABLE 32 *Economic incentives and black college enrollment, 1959–1972*

Equation and group	Constant	Percentage of college graduates as managers*	Lagged enrollment	R^2	SEE
1. Percentage of 18- to 24-year-old nonwhites enrolled	1.97	0.64 (0.10)		0.82	0.12
2. Percentage of 18- to 24-year-old nonwhites enrolled	1.37	0.44 (0.17)	0.40 (0.26)	0.85	0.12
3. Ratio of percentage of 18- to 24-year-old nonwhites enrolled to whites enrolled	−.27	0.51 (0.11)		0.70	0.12
4. Ratio of percentage of 18- to 24-year-old nonwhites enrolled to whites enrolled	−.08	0.39 (0.13)	0.40 (0.26)	0.77	0.11

*Percentage of nonwhite graduates as managers in lines 1 and 2. Ratio of percentages of nonwhite to total graduates as managers in lines 3 and 4.

NOTE: Numbers in parentheses are standard errors; years 1960, 1961, and 1963 were deleted due to lack of data.

SOURCES: U.S. Bureau of the Census (*Current Population Reports,* series P-20, various editions, 1960–1973) and U.S. Department of Labor Statistics (*Educational Attainment of Workers,* various editions, 1960–1973).

ments. Statistically, over 80 percent of the variation in the fraction of 18- to 24-year-old black men in college and 70 percent of the variation in the relative fraction are attributable to the simple incentive measures. The elasticity of enrollments to the percentage in managerial jobs is on the order of 0.4 in the short run and 0.7 in the long run in the context of the partial adjustment model.[9] Despite the crude measures used, the evidence supports the relevance of proposition 2 to the growth of black male college enrollments.

The problem of estimating future lifetime incomes in a period of sharp change in starting salaries, which led to the various estimates in Table 31, is pursued further in Table 33, which compares actual income expectations of black students obtained by a special survey for this study[10] and two possible future streams, based on *Census of Population* data. The census actual estimates for blacks assume that the economic position of new black graduates deteriorates to that of older graduates in the future; the "total" estimates assume that the black income

[9] The long run elasticity is obtained by dividing the coefficient by one minus the parameter on the lagged term.

[10] The *Black Elite* male survey covered 2,500 male students in selected black colleges. There was a response rate of 25 percent. Despite the low rate, the questionnaires provide useful supplementary information to the data in this book. Eric Jones cross-checked the findings by interviews with placement directors at the schools and discussions with students.

	Salaries		
	Foregone income	*Initial*	*With 15 years' experience*
Black undergraduates, 1970 *expected*	$5,811	$10,154	$20,733
Census "actual," 1969 *black B.A.*	5,686*	9,517†	15,051‡
Census "actual," 1969 total *B.A.*	5,690*	10,482†	25,681‡

*Estimated from income of full-time (total) 18- to 24-year-old men with one to three years of college, using 1969 census data, raised by 7.2 percent, for increases in the income of such men from 1969 to 1970.

‡Census income of black (total) men aged 35–44 in 1969 forecasts 18 years into the future change in college incomes from 1969 to 1972 (the approximate year of graduation for the sample). Black figures used for blacks; total male figures for totals.

‡Census income of black (total) men aged 35–44 in 1969 forecasts 18 years into the future from 1969 at a rate of growth of 2.75 percent per annum—the rate of growth of real total male college incomes from 1959 to 1969.

SOURCE: U.S. Bureau of the Census (1970; 1973*d*, table 5; 1973*b*, table 7; 1963*c*, table 11; 1973*j*) and *Black Elite* survey.

profile follows that of all male workers. To take account of potential changes in real income, the estimates for persons with 15 years experience extrapolate the 1969 census data at a rate of increase of 2.75 percent per annum, the observed gain in real college incomes throughout the sixties.

Columns (1) and (2) of the table show that student expectations and actual incomes foregone or starting salaries are in close concordance. Black undergraduates expected to earn $5,811 if they left school in 1969 compared with "actual" earnings of about $5,700. They expected starting salaries of about $10,000 compared with the estimate of $9,500 for blacks and $10,500 for all men in 1972, the approximate years they would graduate. By contrast, the figures in column (3) show a large divergence, with black students expecting earnings much above those they would receive by extrapolating the position of older blacks in 1969 yet below those based on the incomes of all comparable male graduates. This suggests that the students are roughly averaging the two possibilities or possibly forming expectations in a more complex way that yields such a result.

Finally, in response to direct questions about the improvement in opportunities in the new market and the economic benefits of college, black college students reveal considerable knowledge and concern about the job market, as would be expected according to proposition 2. In the *Black Elite* survey, the vast majority (93 percent) were aware of moderate or great "improvements in job opportunities" or (89 percent) of moderate or great "improvement in income opportunities." Two-thirds of black college students expected to earn the average college graduate salary in their field, and only 16 percent expected to have lower earnings because of discrimination, with others citing personal ability or willingness to take low pay for minority community goals as likely causes of deviations in salaries from average. As Table 34 shows, moreover, black college students place a great stress on economic factors in going to college, with 85 percent of male and 86 percent of female students giving "to get a better job" and 56 and 40 percent "to make more money" as very important reasons for going to college—percentages above those for nonblack students presumably because of the lower family income of black youngsters. In sum, the survey data provide additional support for the "responsive supply" interpretation of the 1960s and the growth in enrollments of the early 1970s.

OCCUPATIONAL CHOICES

Can the movement of black men up the occupational ladder also be attributed to economically responsive supply decisions? To answer this question I have estimated supply equations relating 1960s changes in the number of black men in approximately 50 detailed occupations, largely, though not entirely, in the professional and managerial areas, to measures of economic incentives, using data from the 1960 and 1970 censuses. The occupations covered range from specialized professions, such as architecture, to the broad laborer category, and include the bulk of the male work force. In the decade under study, the data show considerable variation in the rate of change of black

TABLE 34
Reasons noted as very important for going to college

	Males		Females	
	Black	Total	Black	Total
Get a better job	84.8%	76.5%	86.0%	68.8%
Make more money	68.8	56.3	63.8	39.8
Prepare for graduate or professional school	53.9	38.1	57.9	27.1

SOURCE: American Council on Education (1972, pp. 27, 35).

employment, ranging from expansions exceeding 100 percent in such fields as accounting and engineering to declines in farming. To pin down changes in the career decisions of men with specified levels of schooling, as opposed to changes associated with increased attainment, men with grade school training only, and high school and college graduates, are examined separately. The basic regression calculations appear in Tables 35 and 36 which focus, respectively, on logarithmic changes in the number of black men in each occupation from 1960 to 1970 and on the logarithms of the 1970 proportion of blacks in the occupations. The log form is chosen to yield elasticities. The

TABLE 35
Coefficients for the supply of black male workers to occupations, 1960–1970

Variable	Constant	Income
1. Total nonwhites and their 1969 incomes*	−6.34 (1.03)	0.92 (0.10)
2. Total nonwhites and their 1959 incomes	−7.52 (1.41)	0.99 (0.13)
3. Total nonwhites and their 1969 estimated incomes‡	−8.02 (1.43)	1.04 (0.13)
4. Total blacks and their 1969 incomes	−6.37 (0.76)	0.91 (0.08)
5. Total blacks and their 1969 estimated incomes	−8.20 (0.90)	1.11 (0.09)
6. Grade school nonwhites and their 1969 incomes	−9.38 (1.46)	1.02 (0.15)
7. High school nonwhites and their 1969 incomes	−10.89 (1.75)	1.32 (0.18)
8. College nonwhites and their 1969 incomes	−10.52 (1.65)	1.21 (0.18)
9. Nonwhites, ages 25–34 and their 1969 incomes	−9.84 (1.56)	1.36 (0.15)

*Calculated from census data on total and white incomes.
†Ordinary least squares.
‡Estimated by instrumental variable technique described in text.
§Instrumental variable.
NOTE: The dependent variable is the change in the log of the number of black workers. The numbers in parentheses are standard errors. The number of observations varies with the availability of data for the specified group. In equations 1, 2, and 3, there are 46 occupations; in 4 and 5, 34; in equations 6 and 8, 50. Equation 7 contains 49 observations, with farmers and farm managers omitted because the income of nonwhite high school graduates in farming, as calculated from the census data on total and white incomes, was implausibly high—nearly twice the income reported for Negro farmers.
SOURCE: Freeman (1973).

key independent variable, designed to measure economic incentives, is the income of black workers or the income of blacks relative to all workers in each occupation. In addition, the lagged (1960) number or proportion of blacks is entered in the calculations to take account of differences in the size of occupations—the fact that in general large occupations will have smaller percentage changes in numbers than small occupations. In regressions with 1960–1970 changes in numbers as the dependent variable, the lagged number is expected to obtain a negative coefficient; in regressions with the 1970 proportion as the dependent variable, it should obtain a positive coeffi-

Number of black workers, 1960	R^2	Standard error of estimate	Estimating technique
−0.10 (0.03)	0.77	0.29	OLS†
−0.10 (0.04)	0.70	0.32	OLS
−0.09 (0.04)	0.70	0.32	IV§
−0.12 (0.03)	0.75	0.25	OLS
−0.11 (0.03)	0.71	0.26	IV
0.01 (0.04)	0.50	0.32	OLS
−0.04 (0.02)	0.66	0.19	OLS
(0.01 (0.04)	0.50	0.33	OLS
−0.16 (0.04)	0.78	0.37	OLS

TABLE 36
Coefficients for
relative supply of
black men to
occupations, 1970

Variable	Constant	Black income	White income
1. *Total nonwhites and their 1969 incomes*	3.91 (1.37)	1.82 (0.28)	−2.24 (0.41)
2. *Total nonwhites and their estimated 1969 incomes*	4.60 (1.43)	2.03 (0.30)	−2.54 (0.43)
3. *Total blacks and their 1969 incomes*	1.78 (0.67)	1.27 (0.14)	−1.54 (0.20)
4. *Nonwhite grade school graduates and their 1969 incomes*	3.15 (0.75)	1.56 (0.12)	−1.98 (0.12)
5. *Nonwhite high school graduates and their 1969 incomes*	2.88 (2.00)	0.40 (0.33)	−0.72 (1.65)
6. *Nonwhite college graduates and their 1969 incomes*	1.67 (2.10)	0.78 (0.49)	−1.01 (0.50)
7. *Nonwhites ages 25–34, and their 1969 incomes*	6.09 (2.35)	1.55 (0.29)	−2.30 (0.50)

*Ordinary least squares.

†Instrumental variable.

NOTE: The dependent variable is the log of the number of nonwhite (or black) workers. The numbers in parentheses are standard errors.

SOURCE: Freeman (1973).

cient less than one. By subtraction, these two forms are of course identical.[11] Observations are weighted by the number of blacks in the occupation in 1960 so that large changes in small fields (architecture, for instance) do not dominate the regressions.

The equations are expected to identify supply (rather than demand) behavior because the demand for black labor shifted substantially in the 1960s, due in part (it will be argued in succeeding chapters) to antidiscriminatory activity. The shift in demand presumably occurred unevenly across occupations, being most pronounced in occupations in which blacks had previously been sparse (construction trades and college teaching, for example), and least marked in traditional areas of black employment (such as farming and services). In general, sizeable shifts in demand trace out the relevant supply schedule in a body of data, unless the latter also shifted considerably. To

[11] Formally, I am simply rewriting the equation $X = aX(-1)$ as $X - X(-1) = (a -1) X(-1)$. The different forms yield the same coefficients, but different R^2 as the variable being explained is "different."

Total number of workers, 1970	Relative number of nonwhites, 1960	R^2	Standard error of estimate	Estimating technique
0.98 (0.03)	0.70 (0.07)	0.97	0.20	OLS*
0.99 (0.04)	0.67 (0.07)	0.97	0.20	IV†
0.99 (0.02)	0.59 (0.05)	0.99	0.15	OLS
1.02 (0.02)	0.59 (0.05)	0.99	0.12	OLS
0.96 (0.02)	0.67 (0.05)	0.99	0.16	OLS
0.92 (0.04)	0.40 (0.08)	0.93	0.34	OLS
0.99 (0.05)	0.39 (0.07)	0.94	0.29	OLS

minimize that possibility or its effect on the estimates, several techniques were used. First, analysis was focused on specific groups, persons of the same age or with the same amount of schooling, who would be expected to have a more stable and better-defined supply schedule than the broad population. Because young persons, in particular, have just entered the labor force, they can be regarded as responding to a given wage structure that they have not yet significantly influenced. Second, since in many occupations lengthy training periods cause changes in supply to lag behind economic incentives, 1969 income is replaced in some calculations by 1959 income. Use of the 1959 wage structure avoids problems of two-way causation; it may have affected the flow of manpower to occupations in the 1960s, but could not have been affected by that subsequent flow. Finally, the computations were also made with the statistical technique of instrumental variables.[12] Even with these

---

[12] The instruments include, in addition to the exogenous variables in the equation, the percentage of workers in an occupation employed by the government, the percentage employed by private industry, and 1959 incomes.

refinements, the calculations are offered as crude first-order approximations to the behavior under study. For one thing, total income, rather than the more appropriate rate of return of investment in the occupation, is used as a measure of incentives; second, the cross-sectional calculations implicitly assume that workers considering an occupation compare wages with the average for all occupations, rather than with some close alternatives.

Regression Results The regression results strongly support the hypothesis that the occupational structure of the black work force was significantly affected by economic incentives in the period under study. In all of the diverse computations, the income incentive variable obtains a large and reasonably well-defined positive coefficient.

The basic regression evidence is contained in Table 35. Lines 1 through 3 record the results of regressions of the proportionate change in the number of nonwhite men between 1960 and 1970 on the number in 1960 and on several income variables: income for either 1969 or 1959, or in line 3, an estimate of 1969 income obtained from the instrumental variable regression. In all cases, the estimated elasticity of supply to income is approximately unity; and the lagged employment variable is generally accorded a small negative coefficient. While the bulk of the variation in employment changes among occupations is accounted for by the regressions, the standard error of estimate, on the order of 0.30, indicates that considerable unexplained change remains. The regressions in lines 4 and 5 replace the nonwhite male variable with Negro men and nonwhite income with Negro income, with little substantive change in the results. Lines 6 through 9 decompose the nonwhite male population into more narrowly defined groups, by education and age, to obtain a better fix on responses. Here, changes in the number of nonwhite male grade school, and college graduates, and of 25- to 34-year-olds in various occupations are regressed on the income of workers with those characteristics. The resultant coefficients are similar to those in previous lines, yielding large and significant income coefficients with somewhat higher elasticities for the more educated and younger workers. The elasticity for those aged 25–34 is 50 percent larger than that for all men, while by contrast, grade school graduates have the smallest estimated elasticity. These calculations are thus consistent with the argument that the greater gains of younger black men reflect, in part, the greater flexibility of their career decisions in response to economic change.

Relative Supply

Table 36 presents an analogous set of computations for the relative number of black workers within given occupations. The dependent variable is the number of blacks, with the total size of the occupation introduced on the right-hand side of the equation. Since the coefficient on the total size emerges from the calculations rather than being predetermined as unity, the specification of the relative supply function can be "tested"; a coefficient of unity implies a reasonable specification. Since the lagged share of nonwhites in the occupation is also an explanatory variable, the regressions could also be written in log change form, simply by subtracting that variable from both sides. The R^2 would, of course, decline, but the standard error of estimate and coefficients would remain the same.

The regression results in Table 36 confirm the hypothesized effect of black and white incomes on relative supply, yielding positive coefficients for the former and negative coefficients for the latter. That is, an increase in black income in an occupation raises the proportion of blacks; an increase in white income depresses it. In addition, the coefficient on total size is about unity, as required in the model. Moreover in all the regressions the 1960 proportion of nonwhite (or black) workers is accorded a marked effect on the 1970 proportion, with a coefficient below unity whose size promises some notion of the speed with which past occupational distributions are altered. The estimated coefficients on the order of 0.6 to 0.7 indicate that after four decades only traces of the initial distribution survive so that, in the absence of discrimination, about 40 years would be required for past discriminatory differences in the occupational structure essentially to disappear.[13]

While the overall results support the hypothesized supply behavior, some of the calculations, such as equation 5 for high school graduates, yield small and poorly determined income coefficients. This suggests the value of further study of the

[13] This is calculated by treating occupational employment as a Markov process with an effect of the past of 0.6 to 0.7. In forty years the impact of the current number employed is $(0.6)^4$ or $(0.7)^4$ or 0.13 to 0.24. As the bulk of the current work force will have retired in 40 years, the result is reasonable.

supply of black and white workers within education and age categories. Analysis of the factors that determine expected income prospects in a period of substantial change for blacks is, in particular, needed to provide better estimates of the relevant supply elasticities. These provisos and problems notwithstanding, the regressions support the proposition that responses to economic incentives underlie new patterns of black career decisions in the 1960s.

SURVEY EVIDENCE Finally, to close the case for proposition 2, I examine the explicit role of economic factors in the career decisions of young black men with evidence from the *Black Elite* and other surveys and from interviews with placement directors and guidance officials at 16 predominantly black schools. This evidence shows that black students had the career information, income expectations, and economic motivation required for rational supply behavior in a period of change.

With respect to information, the isolation of southern black colleges, which lacked adequate guidance and placement services and had virtually no ties to national corporate recruiters and the low socioeconomic background of most black students, which limited information from families and friends, created a potentially serious information gap at the outset of the new market. The need to provide channels of information was recognized in the mid-sixties, leading the Ford Foundation, national corporations, and the black colleges to organize the College Placement Services, Inc., to develop and upgrade career counseling programs, and a College Assistance Fund to provide money for colleges lacking funds for placement programs. Innovative programs were introduced, with, for example a number of colleges bringing recent graduates working in business back to campus to tell students of their work experiences. Another program established an annual career day to focus attention on job opportunities. At Alabama State a bulletin was distributed to each dormitory and department listing employers and job openings. In 1969–70 an IBM–Southern Regional Education Board project was initiated to expose freshmen to career information and orient them toward choosing an occupation. Under the aegis of the Federal Career Outlook program, federal government agencies have made well-publicized recruiting trips. A College Placement Service film entitled "Do They Really Want

Me?" is shown to freshmen at some of the colleges and to high school seniors in surrounding communities.

While the net effect of the organized placement and information programs cannot be easily disentangled from that of informal labor market channels, the *Black Elite* survey suggests that they played a significant role in eliminating the potential "information gap." First, in the 1970 survey students at the black colleges reported heavy reliance on placement offices and college faculty in obtaining career information: 35 percent cited the college placement offices and 47 percent the faculty as major sources of career information compared with just 22 percent who cited their family. This contrasts with results for all students from a 1967 survey which showed 7 percent relying on placement and a third on family sources (Freeman, 1971). Second, measured by the number of students who foresee a change in career plans with better information—one possible indicator of inadequate information—the black college students did not differ from other students. The 1970 survey revealed that 28 percent of the blacks saw a change as "quite likely," 50 percent as "possible," and 22 percent as "not likely" compared with 29, 34, and 18 percent of all students in the 1967 survey (Freeman, 1971). Third, while students' views of the adequacy of information may be suspect, it is of some significance that the students at the black colleges were at least as satisfied with their information as other students. In 1970, 71 percent of the blacks regarded career information as "reasonably adequate" compared with 62 percent of all students in 1967.

A more direct test of the adequacy of any career information is given in Table 37, which compares students' views of the economic opportunities and changes in opportunities in six important professions with census evidence on the market for blacks in these occupations. The students were asked to rank MS engineers, doctors, lawyers, MBS businessmen, college professors and high school teachers in terms of earnings after 15 years of work experience, initial salaries, improvements in job opportunities, and the extent to which discrimination limits opportunities. Their rankings are compared with the income of black men in the census, the earnings of 25- to 34-year-old college graduates, the rate of increase in black male college employment, and the ratio of the proportion of black to total college graduates in an occupation, respectively. If students

TABLE 37
Student
perceptions of
the market for
black workers in
six important
careers

		Earnings after 15 years*			Initial earnings†	
Career	Student ranking	Census median black income	Actual ranking	Student ranking	Census mean income for nonwhite college graduates ages 24–34	Actual ranking
M.S. engineer	3	$12,668	3	1	$11,127	2
Doctor	1	23,158	1	2	10,437	3
Lawyer	2	13,977	2	3	11,796	1
M.B.A. businessman	4	10,909	4	4	9,986	4
College professor	5	9,910	5	5	7,911	5
High school teacher	6	8,201	6	6	7,630	6

*Spearman rank correlation between student and actual rank, 1.00.
†Spearman rank correlation between student and actual rank, .83.
‡Spearman rank correlation between student and actual rank, .66.
§Spearman rank correlation between student and actual rank, .73.
SOURCES: Student data, *Black Elite* survey. Comparison data, U.S. Bureau of the Census (1973*c*, tables 6, 11; 1973*d*, table 1; 1963*b*, table 10).

have reasonable career information and realistic perceptions, their ranking of the careers will parallel the actual ranking.

In fact, each of the measures of the labor market is closely linked with the actual ranking, indicating that the black students were quite aware of "market realities." Student ratings of earnings after 15 years are perfectly correlated with actual earnings; initial salaries show a slight divergence between the student and census ranks (the Spearman coefficient is 0.83); the more amorphous "improvement in opportunities" and "discrimination limits opportunities" also show a strong concordance between perceived and actual market characteristics. In short, the evidence shows black students to be well-informed about the economic situation in these well-known professions at the outset of the 1970s.

The next issue to consider is the explicit role of income and economic factors in the career decisions of black students. Are economic incentives explicitly as important in decision making as the regression calculations suggest? Survey evidence from the *Black Elite* questionnaire and other sources suggest that they are. Consider first Table 38, which records the percentage

	Improvement in job opportunities‡			Opportunities limited by discrimination§	
Student ranking	Census change in black college male employment	Actual ranking	Student ranking	Relative probability of employment of black college men	Actual ranking
1	178%	2	2	0.34	1
5	− 2	6	4	0.88	5
3	40	5	3	0.41	2
2	238	1	1	0.65	3
4	131	3	5	0.78	4
6	58	4	6	1.38	6

of black and white students who regard various characteristics of a career as important in decision making and gives black students' evaluation of how their chosen career compares with its closest alternative in the career. The table indicates that black students are highly economically motivated in occupational as well as educational decisions. Nearly two-thirds of black students regard income as "important" and virtually all as "important or somewhat important" in career decisions; 82 percent are concerned with income and employment stability; and 38 percent with entering costs. These figures, particularly those for income, far exceed comparable proportions for white students. Consistent with the hypothesized marginal effect of income, moreover, the majority of students regarded income in their chosen career as being higher than in its closest alternative.

National survey data from the Educational Testing Service (1971) corroborate the apparently greater weight attached to income by black than white students. In the ETS survey black students were roughly twice as concerned with income, security, and occupational status or prestige in career decision

TABLE 38 *Factors affecting black students' career decisions*

Characteristic	Percentage students viewing characteristic as:		Percentage students rating chosen or alternative career as "superior"	
	"Important"	"Important or somewhat important"	Chosen	Alternative
Level of income	63 (16)	96 (65)	54	22
Stability of income or employment	82 (21)	98 (68)	47	23
Cost of entry	38 (17)	80 (61)	32	29
Interest in work	95 (82)	99 (94)	60	8
Need of black community	67	96	94	5
Contains black workers	17	50	20	23
Discrimination	61	85	29	15

NOTE: Numbers in parentheses are nonblack.

SOURCES: *Black Elite* survey and Freeman (1971).

making than white students. By the economic analysis sketched out on pages 64–65, this concern is to be expected, given the low family income of blacks.

As for the other factors in Table 38, there is relatively little difference in the proportion of blacks and whites citing interest in work as important and relatively few blacks concerned with whether or not an occupation has many black workers presently. On the other hand, a large number are concerned with the "need" of the black community and possible career discrimination. Whether the former reflects actual decision making or the rhetoric of the time, however, is difficult to tell. In the comparisons of a career with its closest alternative in columns 5 and 6, the fraction of students who regard their career as superior in terms of need is too high to reflect a reasonable rating. Not all careers can be higher in need, suggesting that students are evaluating need in terms of their choice rather than choosing on that basis—along cognitive dissonance theory lines. Interestingly, less than 5 percent of the students actually anticipated receiving lower salaries as a result of the sacrifice of income for the need of the community; and only one in five placement directors who were asked to evaluate the factors entering into student decisions thought need was important.

The potential effect of discrimination on career choices in the new market should also be viewed cautiously. For one thing, in Table 38 relatively more students regard discrimination as being higher in their chosen career than in its closest alternative, indicating that, concern notwithstanding, discrimination is no longer a major factor in actual choices. For another, in response to the question of how they would react to potential changes in various factors likely to affect career decisions, two-thirds of the black college students did not believe that elimination of discrimination in jobs would influence them at all. The proportion who regarded changes in career plans as likely given elimination of market discrimination (19 percent) was no greater than that citing such relatively innocuous changes as "better grade school education" (17 percent), "better high school education" (21 percent), "opportunities for part-time or summer work to try jobs" (21 percent), and so forth. All of this implies that discrimination is not as major a factor in the career decisions of blacks as it has been in decades past.

SUMMARY The econometric and survey evidence in this chapter presents an arresting picture of the supply behavior of black college students and professionals, validating the propositions with which we began. As asserted, the career decisions of the black elite changed greatly in the new labor market, apparently in response to economic incentives. As far as can be told from our data, the convergence in the occupational distributions of black and white college men are attributable to changes in employment and income opportunities.

4. New Patterns of Social Mobility

Discrimination aside, most black Americans are disadvantaged by coming from families of low socioeconomic status which are unable to provide many of the background resources that facilitate success in economic life.[1] Black children are, in particular, more likely than white children to be brought up in broken homes; to have parents with little education, poor jobs, and low family income; and to reside in urban slums. In 1972, 39 percent of black children were living with only one parent compared with 11 percent of whites (U.S. Bureau of the Census, 1973g, p. 73); nearly one-third of black children compared with just 8 percent of white children were born to unwed mothers (calculated from U.S. Bureau of the Census, 1971a, tables 58 and 61). Over half of blacks resided in central cities in 1970 compared with less than one-third of whites (U.S. Bureau of the Census, 1971b, table 7). Despite the low social origins of most black Americans, however, only a moderate fraction of black-white economic differences is usually attributed to the burden of poor background. Moreover, evidence on the relation between background and achievement in years past suggested that "the Negro family is less able than the white to pass on to the next generation its socio-economic status" (Duncan, 1971, p. 85).

How has the new market affected traditional intergenerational mobility patterns? Have blacks from better family backgrounds made greater progress in the 1960s? What are the family background characteristics of the black young men going to college and attaining "elite" jobs in the late 1960s?

---

[1] The low socioeconomic status of black families is itself a result of *past* discrimination. In this chapter I distinguish between the effects of *current* market discrimination and low socioeconomic origins.

87

This chapter analyzes these questions by comparing the background and socioeconomic achievement among young black and white male cohorts (aged 17–27 in 1969) who entered the market in the 1960s, with the achievements of older black and white men (aged 48–62), whose position was essentially determined decades earlier, using data from the National Longitudinal Survey (NLS).[2] The chapter focuses on two key variables: attendance in college and attainment of professional-managerial job status, though some attention is also given to more continuous measures of socioeconomic success, such as wages. A detailed analysis of changes in socioeconomic mobility in the "new market" which deals with the overall educational attainment, income, and occupational position of young blacks is given in Freeman (1976*b*). The results of that study and of Hauser and Featherman (1975) are consistent with those for the more limited "elite" achievement variables reported in this chapter.

The major empirical finding is that the process of socioeconomic attainment underwent substantial change for black Americans in the new market. Family background factors became the major cause of differences in college going and overall educational attainment and, together with schooling, of the labor market achievement of young blacks in the late 1960s, in contrast with their previous relative unimportance. As a result, "class" differences among black Americans appear to have been enhanced in the period and black disadvantages in background resources to have become the main deterrent to attainment of socioeconomic parity with whites.

SAMPLES AND VARIABLES   At the outset, it will be fruitful to examine in some detail the data set under investigation and their strengths and drawbacks. The NLS survey contains questions on the labor market position, family background, and diverse other variables for 5,000 men in each of the two cohorts. It has the advantage of oversampling blacks in a 3 to 1 ratio, providing a relatively large number of both older and younger black respondents whose market success and background can be compared. Each of the samples, however, has some data problems: the older male survey lacks parental education information for a large part of

[2] For a detailed discussion of the survey, see U.S. Department of Labor (1970).

the population; the younger male survey relates to a young age cohort (17 to 27 in 1969), some of whom entered the job market before the 1964 Civil Rights Act altered opportunities and some after and some of whom had not yet taken full-time jobs in 1969.

Several measures of key variables and several samples are used to deal with these problems. Table 39 describes the major characteristics of the young and older male samples. Because of the value of doing the analyses with the largest possible number of persons, three subsamples were employed: one with all persons reporting information on education and on parental occupation; a second with persons who also report information on parental education; and a third sample limited to those reporting labor market information as well.

These groupings have different effects on the size of the samples as described in the table notes. Because of the youth of the 17- to 27-year-old group, nonnegligible numbers were enrolled in 1969, and thus could not report final years completed. Their attainment was estimated by the number of years they "expect to complete." To make sure that the calculations are not substantially affected by this proxy variable, additional regressions limited to the out-of-school population or based on assigning the enrolled their current year as an estimate of final attainment were also made, with results similar to those reported herein.

The number in school also substantially reduces the size of the working population in the final sample, which could lead to biases in estimates of the differing effect of background on black and white achievement if the in-school groups differed between them. This possibility is checked by analyzing the relation between background and expected occupation at age 30, for which information exists for nearly all respondents, as well as between background and actual occupation and income. Griliches' results (1976) with NLS data suggests that expected occupation has properties similar to actual occupation in equations. The restriction to the sample reporting parental education reduces the number of black respondents by 15 percent and the number of whites by 5 percent.

Turning to the older male group, data for 1966 rather than 1969 were employed so as not to lose respondents to retirement, death, or not reporting. Here, the losses of respondents due to

TABLE 39
Characteristics of
young and older
male samples

	Young men		Older men	
	Blacks	Whites	Blacks	Whites
General characteristics				
Age	20.7	21.3	51.3	51.3
Years in school	11.5	13.2	6.8	10.5
Percent in college	17	33	4	13
Percent professional or managerial	8	22	5	29
Logarithm of:				
Income	7.94	8.46	8.13	8.83
Wages	5.40	5.68	5.22	5.86
Occupation*	8.63	8.84	8.62	8.92
Background characteristics				
Percent from:				
Broken home	40	12	39	19
South	74	30	91	37
Rural areas	33	27	69	33
Parental occupation†	7.66	8.46	7.19	8.25
Parental years of education	7.9	10.5	5.1	7.7

*Own occupation measured by the log of male income in three-digit occupations in 1959 with *total* male income used for *both* whites and nonwhites (U.S. Bureau of the Census, 1963b, tables 25, 26).

†Parental occupation measured by the log of male incomes in three-digit occupations in 1959 with total male income used for whites and nonwhite for blacks (U.S. Bureau of the Census, 1963b, tables 25, 26).

NOTE: The sample size for the various characteristics differed. Among the young men, all background characteristics except parental education and labor market data came from samples of size 1,221 (blacks) and 3,403 (whites). Parental education is from samples of size 1,024 (blacks) and 3,292 (whites). The labor market data are from samples of size 634 (blacks) and 1,607 (whites). Among older men data on parental years of education are from a sample of size 653 (blacks) and 2,099 (whites); other data are from sample sizes of 979 (blacks) and 2,131 (whites). Income is the sum of income from the ratio of income of hours worked over the year, from one's own business or farm. Wages are income per hours worked over the year. For older men experience is the number of years since the respondent started his first job after ending high school. For younger men, experience is obtained by adding the number of weeks worked per year from 1966 to 1969 to years since first job in 1966.

SOURCE: Calculated from National Longitudinal Survey tapes for older and younger men.

the lack of data on parental education are greater, with the samples reduced by 52 percent (black) and 34 percent (whites). Again, however, results were duplicated for the larger as well as smaller groups, with essentially similar findings.

The table shows blacks trailing whites in education, labor market achievement, and background resources in both age groups, though young blacks are closer to their white counterparts than older blacks. Among 17- to 27-year-olds, blacks lagged whites in years of schooling by 1.7 years compared with a 3.7 year gap among 48- to 62-year-old men. The ratio of black to white probabilities of college going rises twofold (from 4/13 to 17/33), though the absolute difference increases. The difference between young blacks and whites in the logarithm of income and wages is much smaller than that between older black and white men (.52 versus .70 in income, .28 versus .64 in wages). The 24 percentage difference in attainment of professional and managerial jobs drops to 14 percentage points between the two cohorts.

With respect to family background, blacks trail whites in all dimensions. The parents of older blacks had 2.7 years less schooling than those of older whites; the parents of young blacks had 2.6 years less. Measured in terms of an income index of parental occupation, blacks trailed whites by large amounts in both samples (1.06 for older men and .80 for younger men, where the income variable is in log units).[3] The large differential in parental occupational attainment results, in part, it should be noted, from the fact that *black parental status is measured by nonwhite median incomes while white parental status is measured by total median incomes* in the various occupations. I have chosen this measure, as opposed to using the same weight for both groups, because of the potential importance of family income in socioeconomic success and the lack of data on income as well as parental occupational standing. Parental occupation weights are taken from the 1960 census, as most of the young men were in their parents' homes in the fifties and early sixties. Experiments with income from the 1940 and 1960 censuses yielded similar results. For comparability the older male parents were also given 1960 income weights. The final family background variable—presence or absence of father at age 14— also shows a substantial black disadvantage with 40 percent of the black youngsters living in father-absent homes at age 14 compared with just 12 percent of white youngsters.

The major dependent variables in the analysis are entrance into college and attainment of professional-managerial jobs. Because these variables are dichotomous, linear regression is

[3] This index attaches to black or white parent the median income in the three-digit occupation in which they work. It is reported in logarithmic units because the ensuing equations focus on the elasticity of son's achievement with respect to it.

not appropriate, though the linear probability model may provide useful information about the effect of exploratory variables.
A more appropriate model for a 0-1 dichotomous variable is the
logistic probability model. Let P be the probability of attaining
college or professional-managerial job status and X_i be an
explanatory variable with coefficient β_i. The estimated equation
is:

$$P = 1/(1 + \exp{-\Sigma\beta_i X_i}) \qquad (1)$$

for explanatory X_i, where $dP/dX_i = \beta_i(P)(1-P)$. The advantage
of the model over, say, the linear probability model, is that it
correctly bounds the effect of variables ($0 < P < 1$, for all values
of X_i) and takes account of the binomial nature of the residuals.[4] Rather than estimating Eq. (1) with an expensive maximum likelihood search procedure, I have followed the sugges-
tion of Nerlove and Press and of Haggstrom of transforming
estimated linear probability coefficients into logistic coefficients
by using an inverse Taylor approximation. The approximation
appears quite adequate for the purposes at hand, as maximum
likelihood estimates of related equations yield similar results
(Freeman, 1976*b*).

In addition to these variables, I also examine the impact of
background on total years of schooling and the logarithm of
annual wage and salary income, wage rates, and an index of
occupational standing, the median income in 1969 of the individual's three-digit occupation. Because pay and occupational

---

[4] The simplest way to derive the relation between β_i and dP/dX_i is to note that
since $P = 1/(1 + \exp{-\Sigma\beta_i X_i})$,

$$P(1 + \exp{-\Sigma\beta_i X_i}) = 1$$

so that

$$dP/dX_i \, [1 + \exp{-\Sigma\beta_i X_i} - P\beta_i \exp{-\Sigma\beta_i X_i}] = 0$$

upon differentiation by X_i. Then

$$dP/dX_i = [P\beta_i \exp{-\Sigma\beta_i X_i}]/(1 + \exp{-\Sigma\beta_i X_i})$$

But since $1-P = \exp{-\Sigma\beta_i X_i}/(1 + \exp{-\Sigma\beta_i X_i})$,

$$dP/dX_i = P\beta_i(1-P)$$

standing are separate variables, I use the same total income figures to reflect black and white occupational achievement.

When educational attainment is the dependent variable, explanatory variables include region and size of community residence at age 14, designed to reflect the geographic origins of persons and particularly the southern rural background of blacks;[5] age; and parental education or occupation. In the income and occupational attainment computations, years of work experience is entered as an explanatory variable, with the experience of the young estimated from the longitudinal information on the NLS tapes on actual weeks worked per year and the total years of experience for older men estimated by retrospective information on the years they began their first job.

The Cross-Sectional Inference Problem
While the NLS sample is well-suited for comparisons of the family background of black and white young men going on to college or high-level occupations in the late 1960s, it has one serious drawback for analyzing social mobility patterns over time. Since the data relate to two age groups in a cross-section rather than the same age group at two different times, normal life-cycle changes in the relation between background and attainment could be mistaken for the changes over time of concern. Since few persons enroll in college after age 25, there is unlikely to be a serious bias in using the data on the older men to indicate their propensity to enroll in college decades earlier in comparison to that in the young male sample. Changes in occupational standing and income over the life cycle, however, do create a potential inference problem. As I am primarily concerned with changes in the differential impact of background on black as compared with white attainment, however, interpretation of results in terms of time series changes would be marred only if the races have different life-cycle patterns in a particular time period. To deal with this difficulty, evidence from other studies regarding actual cross-sectional life-cycle patterns *prior* to the development of the new market is examined, and the findings of Hauser and Featherman in comparing

[5] The region of residence at age 14 was not reported in the young male sample and has to be inferred from regions of high school or current residence for those not reporting high school region. The question for older men relates to age 15. To minimize complication I refer to age 14 throughout.

the 1962 and 1973 Occupational Change in a Generation (OCG) data files are reviewed. The results in these studies tend to support our interpretation of the NLS data as reflecting changes in intergenerational mobility patterns in the new market.

COLLEGE ENROLLMENT

The first issue to consider is the impact of parental background on the probability of going to college. To what extent did family background affect black as opposed to white college going in the new market? Has background become a more important determinant of black college attainment in the period of rapid growth of black enrollments?

Table 40 contains calculations designed to answer these questions. It records the β_i coefficients on parental occupation and education estimated for the logistic curve using the inverse Taylor approximation from the least squares linear probability estimates.[6] Lines 1 and 2 record estimates of the β_i coefficients for the logistic form on the key parental years of schooling and occupational attainment variables of concern. Lines 3 and 4 give the least squares computations. The estimated parameters show a substantial change in the importance of parental occupation on the probability of college going for blacks and whites between the two cohorts. Among 48- to 62-year-old black men, parental occupational income has a negative insignificant effect on college going; while among 17- to 27-year-old blacks, parental occupational income has a sizeable significant effect on the probability of college going (lines 1 and 2). By contrast, the parental occupation coefficients decline between the older and younger white male samples. As for the coefficients on parental education, they are the same for blacks in the two samples but slightly smaller for younger than for older white men. Overall, whereas parental status has a markedly greater impact on the attainment of older white than black men, the situation among the young men is unclear: a greater effect of parental years of schooling on whites contrasted to a greater effect of parental occupational income on blacks. If the total effect of background on enrollment of young men in college is measured by the sum

---

[6]The approximation involves a simple transformation of the regression coefficients from the linear probability model. Let n = number of observations; SSR = sum of squared residuals from the linear model; and b_i = the linear regression coefficient of X_i. Then the estimated coefficient of X_i in the logistic form is just $\beta_i = [n/SSR]b_i$.

TABLE 40
Estimates of the effect of parental background on college going, logistic curve, and linear probability regression coefficients, 17- to 27-year-old men, by race

		Parental status			
		Years of schooling	Occupational income*	Sample size	F
Estimated logistic					
1.	17- to 27-year-olds				
	Black	.14 (.03)	.47 (.21)	1221	8.7
	White	.19 (.01)	.21 (.10)	3292	44.2
2.	48- to 62-year-olds				
	Black	.14 (.06)	−.22 (.51)	653	2.5
	White	.21 (.02)	.49 (.16)	2099	24.9
Least squares linear probability					
3.	17- to 27-year-olds				
	Black	.019 (.004)	.062 (.027)	1221	8.7
	White	.038 (.002)	.040 (.01)	3292	44.2
4.	48- to 62-year-olds				
	Black	.004 (.002)	−.007 (.016)	653	2.5
	White	.021 (.003)	.048 (.15)	2099	24.9

*Parent's occupational position measured by the log of 1959 median income of parents of three-digit occupations, with the total income figures used for whites and nonwhite incomes for blacks.

NOTES: All equations include variables for age, broken home, and eight region and size of residence dummies. Samples restricted to those reporting parental education. Numbers in parentheses are standard errors. Coefficients estimated by the inverse Taylor transformation of ordinary least squares estimates, as described in Haggstrom (1974). The coefficients relate to the logit equation, $P = 1[\exp(-\Sigma\beta_i X_i)]$ where X_i refers to the explanatory variable and β its coefficient; $dP/dX_i = \beta_i P(1 = P)$. All equations include additional variables reflecting age, broken-home status, and region and size of community of residence at age 14. Results for similar equations, with a slightly different sample, given in Freeman (1976b, table 3) yield virtually the same results using a maximum likelihood search procedure.

of the beta weights on the parental education and occupation coefficients, the logistic curve estimates yield roughly similar background effects for the races; since, however, relatively more whites than blacks go on to college, the impact of a standard deviation increase in parental education and occupation on the probability of attendance remains greater for whites. Even so, it is clear that the traditional inability of black families to pass on their socioeconomic status to their children was greatly changed with respect to college enrollments. Despite all the attention given to enrollment of the ghetto poor into college, it was the children of better educated and wealthier parents who went in increasing numbers in the 1960s.

Total Years of Schooling

To make sure that the increased importance of background in educational attainment is not limited to the college decision, I have also regressed the total number of years of education that an individual has completed or expected to complete on parental family background, dummies for region and size of residence at age 14, and age. The parental status coefficients given in Table 41 support the findings shown for college enrollment with regard to changes in the effect of background on years of education by race. In the older male sample, the coefficients on both parental education and occupation are larger for whites, whereas in the younger male sample, the parental occupation coefficient becomes larger for blacks. Hence there is a clear tendency toward convergence in the effect of background between the races. To determine whether parental background, measured by occupation and education, had a greater effect on whites than blacks in the young male sample, it is necessary to "average" the regression coefficients. One reasonable method is to multiply, as before, the coefficients by their standard

TABLE 41
Effect of parental years of schooling and occupational attainment on sons' years attained, older and younger male sample, by race

		Regression coefficient on parental:			
		Years of schooling	*Occupational income**	*Size of sample*	*R^2*
1.	*17- to 27-year olds*				
	Black	.20	.84	1,221	.18
		(.03)	(.21)		
	White	.31	.49	3,292	.202
		(.01)	(.11)		
2.	*48- to 62-year-olds*				
	Black	.21	.70	653	.272
		(.04)	(.30)		
	White	.30	1.42	2,099	.319
		(.02)	(.181)		

*Parent's occupational position measured by the log of 1959 median male income of three-digit occupations, with the total income figures used for blacks from U.S. Bureau of the Census (1963*b*, tables 25, 26).

NOTE: All regressions include variables for age, broken home, and dummies for region and size of residence at age 14. Regressions for older men are for 1966.

SOURCE: Calculated from NLS data tapes.

deviations in the sample, divide by the standard deviation of years attained and sum the resultant weights to obtain the effect of a standard deviation increase in each on years attained. With this metric, a change in parental occupation and education is found to raise black and white years completed by nearly the same amount among the young (0.46 for whites compared with 0.40 for blacks.)

One additional change in the relation between background and total years, not shown in the table but considered in detail in Freeman (1976*e*), deserves some attention: this is the change in regional coefficients between the younger and older male samples. For older black men, being brought up in the South and in rural areas had a tremendous negative effect on educational attainment. By contrast, in the young male sample coming from the South actually enhanced the total years attained by blacks slightly (Freeman, 1976*b*, table 2) while the negative effect of rural residence diminished to approximately equal that for whites. Presumably because of the decline in discriminatory allocation of school resources in the rural South, the burden of southern rural background was greatly reduced for blacks to about the same as for whites (Welch 1973; Freeman 1974).

Home Educational Resources
Family background presumably influences educational attainment through explicit household resources and activities, such as investment of parental time with children or presence of reading material, which are only roughly related to parental occupation and education. Addition of explanatory variables relating to specific home factors should increase the explanatory power of the background-education relation and help delineate the routes by which parental status determines years attained. In the NLS young men sample, questions regarding the presence of magazines, newspapers, or library cards in the home at age 14 provide some measure of household resources which can be expected to be related to education.[7] As column 1 of Table 42 shows, the three "home educational resource" indicators differ

[7] These measures are to be viewed solely as indicators. They are *not* meant to imply that increasingly, say, magazine sales will raise the educational attainment of black or white youngsters. The three indicators presumably represent family activities and resources that are positively related to educational achievement.

TABLE 42
Effect of home
educational
resources on
college going and
years of schooling,
17- to 27-year-old
men, by race

Group and explanatory variables	Mean values of explanatory variables (1)	Logistic curve estimates for probability of college	
		From Table 40 (2)	With educational resources in equation (3)
Black			
Index of parental occupation*	7.67	.47(.21)	.43(.21)
Years of parental education	7.9	.15(.03)	.12(.03)
Presence of magazines in the home	.45		.68(.20)
Presence of newspapers in the home	.69		−.08(.21)
Presence of library card in the home	.47		.47(.23)
White			
Index of parental occupation*	8.45	.21(.10)	.14(.10)
Years of parental education	10.5	.19(.11)	.17(.01)
Presence of magazines in the home	.80		.23(.11)
Presence of newspapers in the home	.92		.31(.17)
Presence of library card in the home	.74		.46(.10)

NOTE: All coefficients based on regressions including age, broken home, and region variables. Numbers in parentheses are standard errors. Logistic curve estimates obtained by inverse Taylor transform of linear probability estimates. Parental occupation measured as in previous tables.

greatly by race, suggesting that they may contribute to black-white differences: most strikingly, less than half of black homes were reported to have magazines compared with four-fifths of white homes.

The results of adding to the college enrollment and years of schooling equations of Tables 40 and 41 are given in columns 3 and 5 of Table 42. For comparison, the coefficients on the parental background variables are reproduced in columns 2 and 4. The major result is that home reading resources have a significant effect on both college attainment and years of schooling, which reduces the impact of parental occupation and education. The extent of the reduction varies noticeably

Linear regressions coefficients on years attained	
From Table 41 (4)	With educational resources in equation (5)
.84(.21)	.61(.20)
.20(.03)	.15(.20)
	.81(.20)
	.12(.23)
	.80(.21)
.49(.11)	.31(.11)
.31(.01)	.25(.02)
	.67(.15)
	.66(.12)
	.95(.18)

between the equations and groups, dropping by just 10 percent for the coefficient on black parental occupation in the college equation and by 38 percent for the white parental occupation coefficient in the years of schooling equation. While more detailed analysis of the resources and activities in homes is needed, the results suggest an important role for explicit household education resources in the determination of years attained and as intervening variables in the usual background-education relation. They direct attention to the absence of reading material and related environmental factors (which might be ameliorated by special school programs) in black homes as a cause of black-white educational differences.

The critical question regarding the background-education relation is the extent to which the black background disadvantage
explains black-white educational differences. As noted at the
outset of the chapter, the traditional finding has been that only
part of the education gap is due to background, leading to a
potentially large role for discrimination in access to schooling.
In Table 43 I estimate the contribution of background factors to
the gap by multiplying regression coefficient estimates of the
impact of background factors by the difference in the mean
level of the relevant factors for whites and blacks. Formally,
when $\hat{\alpha}_i$ is the estimated impact of the ith variable on educa-
tion, $\alpha_i(\overline{X}_{Bi} - \overline{X}_{Wi})$ of the black-white differential is attributed
to that variable, where $\overline{X}_{Bi}$, $\overline{X}_{Wi}$ are the mean levels for blacks
and whites, respectively. The total contribution of all variables
in explaining the education gap is $\Sigma_i \hat{\alpha}_i(\overline{X}_{Bi} - \overline{X}_{Wi})$. Since the
regression coefficients differ between blacks and whites and by
the age group covered, there are two sets of weights for each
age group and two additional possible sets using those of the
other group. In the "logistic curve" calculations, the impact of
factors on P is estimated by taking the derivative $dP/dX_i =
P(1-P)\beta_i$ at the mean level of P for blacks and whites: that is,
I multiply the estimated β_i by $P(1-P)$ for the groups.

The first column of the table gives the differences in the
proportion enrolled and years attained between blacks and
whites. Succeeding columns record the percentage point contribution of differences in family factors to the observed differential and the total percentage explained by family background.

There are two important findings in the table. First is the
greatly enhanced role of family background as a cause of black-
white differences in educational attainment among young men
when black equation weights are used—a result due to the
enhanced importance of background among blacks and convergence in background-schooling coefficients between the races.
In the older sample, the effect of family background differs
greatly depending on whether the black or white equation
weights are used: parental occupation and education account
for 110 percent of the observed differential in college going and
65 percent of that in years attained with the white equation
weights but just 50 percent and 35 percent, respectively, with the
black equation weights. A very different situation is obtained for
17- to 27-year-old men. Because the coefficient for white parental

TABLE 43　*Effect of background on black-white difference in college attainment and years of schooling*

Group and regression weights	Total difference* (1)	Contribution of family background differences				Percentage explained (6)
		Parental occupation income (2)	Parental years of education (3)	Presence of father at age 14 (4)	Home educational resources (5)	
Probability of college						
1.　48- to 62-year-olds						
White	.09	.04	.07	.00		110
Black	.09	.02	.03	.00		50
2.　17- to 27-year-olds						
White	.16	.03	.09	.00		75
Black	.15	.07	.07	.00		93
3.　17- to 27-year-olds						
White	.16	.02	.09	.00	0.5	100
Black	.15	.06	.06	.00	0.7	127
Years of schooling						
4.　48- to 62-year-olds						
White	3.6	1.4	0.8	0.1		64
Black	3.6	0.7	0.5	0.1		36
5.　17- to 27-year-olds						
White	1.7	0.4	0.8	0.2		82
Black	1.6	0.7	0.5	0.1		88†
6.　17- to 27-year-olds						
White	1.7	0.2	0.7	0.2	0.7	106
Black	1.6	0.5	0.4	0.1	0.7	106

*Adjusted for difference in age. In the younger male sample .01 of the college enrollment and 0.1 of the years of schooling differential between blacks and whites is due to their younger age, using the black equation weights with weights from the white equation the effect is too small to influence the results.

†Includes 0.1 percentage points counted in columns (2) through (4) due to rounding.

NOTE:　Estimated from regressions in Tables 40, 41, and 42 by applying differences in means to regression coefficients.

background declines somewhat between the 48- to 62- and 17- to 27-year-old samples, family background has a reduced absolute impact on the differences in attainment with the white regression weights. Because the coefficients for black family background increase for college enrollments, family background has a somewhat bigger absolute impact with the black weights. The result is that a greater percentage of the differences are attributed to background factors when the black equation weights are used, with 93 percent of differences in the proportion in college and 78 percent of differences in years of schooling attributed to differences in backgrounds.

Second, when differences in black and white home educational resources are also taken account of, the explanatory power of background increases even further to explain *all* the education differentials. As the final column shows, home educational resources and parental occupation and education differences explain 100 or more percent of the gap among 17- to 27-year-olds in 1969. In this case, while black and white regression equations attach somewhat different weights to parental education and occupation, the adjustments tell the same story: in the new market differences in family background resources were the major factor behind black-white differences in college enrollment and overall educational attainment—a far cry from the situation found in the older male cohort.

PROFESSIONAL-MANAGERIAL OCCUPATIONAL ATTAINMENT AND INCOME

How important were family background factors in the attainment of professional-managerial jobs in the new market? Did family background become more important in black labor market achievement? Are black-white economic as well as schooling differences in the young male sample attributable to background factors? Statistical calculations presented next show that family background has, in fact, a greater impact on the probability that the young black men who entered the job market in the 1960s would become professionals or managers than on the probability of older black men. Other measures of labor market achievement also show an enhanced role for family background factors. Additional data on the pattern of change in background factors over the life cycle and on the progress of black and white male cohorts suggests that the cross-sectional differences represent, at least in part, temporal rather than life-cycle developments.

Empirical Results

Least squares regression calculations were estimated linking professional-managerial job attainment to family and geographic background for the young and older male samples. In addition to the explanatory variables used in Table 40, variables relating to years of work experience were added to the regressions. Years of experience was estimated for young men from data on weeks worked per year, thereby taking account of the intermittent work experience of young men. For older men, experience was estimated as the difference between the year in which they began work and the current year.

Table 44 summarizes the results in terms of the estimated β_i parameter for the logistic model (obtained by transforming the linear probability coefficients). The odd-numbered lines record the coefficients on parental occupation and education while the even numbered lines give the coefficients with years of schooling included as an additional explanatory variable. Because so many of the 17- to 27-year-old men were still in school or did not report labor market information, lines 5–6 examine the effect of family background factors on *expected* professional-managerial job status, which enlarges the sample.

What stands out in the table is the substantial increase in the effect of parental background factors on the probability of professional-managerial job attainment among blacks. In the older male sample, parental occupation has a negative insignificant effect on "elite" job attainment while parental education has a moderate .15 effect (line 1). In the younger male actual occupation calculations, parental occupation has a positive though not significant effect while the coefficient on parental education rises to .20 (line 3); in the calculations including those still in school, where expected occupation is the dependent variable, the results are similar: a parental occupation coefficient of .34 and a parental education coefficient of .09 (line 5). Since, by contrast, lines 1, 3, and 5 show a decline in the effect of parental characteristics on white attainment of professional-managerial jobs, the table indicates that there was a convergence in background–elite-job standing, as well as in background-schooling, relations in the new market. Moreover, with both the coefficients on parental occupation and education greater for older whites than older blacks, background clearly mattered more in the elite status transmission of the former than latter; while by contrast, among the young, the coefficient on parental education was greater for blacks while that on parental occupation was smaller, suggesting a similar process linking background to professional-managerial job attainment.[8]

---

[8] Indeed, since parental education varies more in the samples than parental occupation, the figures suggest a greater impact of standard deviation change in each background characteristic on the probability of black than white professional-managerial job status.

TABLE 44
Estimated logistic coefficients for the probability of professional-managerial

		Black			
		Coefficients for:			
Age group	Parental occupation	Parental education	Own college	Sample size	F
1. 48–62 years old	−.17 (.50)	.15 (.06)		471	3.29
2. 48–62 years old	−.35 (.56)	.08 (.06)	.36 (.07)	471	4.99
3. 17–27 years old, actual	.30 (.43)	.20 (.06)		519	6.16
4. 17–27 years old, actual	.01 (.45)	.11 (.06)	.60 (.09)	519	9.86
5. 17–27 years old	.34 (.24)	.09 (.03)		769	5.91
6. 17–27 years old	.16 (.25)	.04 (.04)	.35 (.05)	769	10.30

NOTE: Logistic coefficients obtained by inverse Taylor transformation of least squares estimates. Numbers in parentheses are standard errors. All regressions include variables for age, years of experience, broken home, and region and size of residence dummies.

When own education is added to the regressions, it is clearly the dominant variable, greatly reducing the effect of parental status. This is not surprising since professional jobs, in particular, tend to require considerable education and it is unlikely that background would have much effect on professional job attainment independent of education. This does not, of course, imply that background factors do not have substantial effects on wages or on the type of professional-managerial (or other) job held.

Curvature of the Background-Achievement Locus

The analysis thus far has treated parental occupational status as a continuous variable measured in income units. Additional insight into mobility patterns can be gained by replacing this metric with dichotomous variables relating to whether or not someone is in one of the standard occupational categories. Such a procedure provides a check on preceding findings and information on possible nonlinearities in the background achievement locus. Chart 4 contains the results of such computations for the probability of professional-managerial job status, with parental occupational status decomposed into seven occupa-

White				
Coefficients for:				
Parental occupation	*Parental education*	*Own college*	*Sample size*	*F*
.81 (.18)	.17 (.02)		1486	25.9
.43 (.20)	.08 (.02)	.40 (.03)	1486	46.9
.42 (.18)	.12 (.02)	.62 (.04)	1505	22.4
.20 (.19)	.01 (.03)		1505	44.0
.29 (.13)	.12 (.02)	.34 (.02)	2145	22.3
.19 (.14)	.05 (.02)		2145	36.1

tional groups. The chart shows that the parental-occupation–managerial-professional job-attainment locus is steeper among older white than black men, but is similar for young blacks and whites. For example, among 48- to 62-year-olds, the probability of being a manager or professional was raised by just 3 percent for blacks having professionals or managers as parents relative to those with farm–farm laborer parents compared with 19 percent for whites from professional-managerial backgrounds. By contrast, in the young men sample, the probability of "elite" jobs employment was 11 percent better for blacks from professional or managerial families (relative to the farm–farm laborer group) and 13 percent for whites. A similar, though less-striking twist in the background–elite-job relation is observed among other groups of blacks.

In sum, the evidence in Table 44 and Chart 4 suggests that black youngsters from better family backgrounds advanced relative to those from disadvantaged circumstances in the new market, at least in terms of elite-job attainment. The next issue to consider is the extent to which differences in social origin and educational attainment have come to account for differences in the proportion of blacks and whites in these jobs.

CHART 4 *Loci of effect of parental occupation on professional-managerial job attainment*

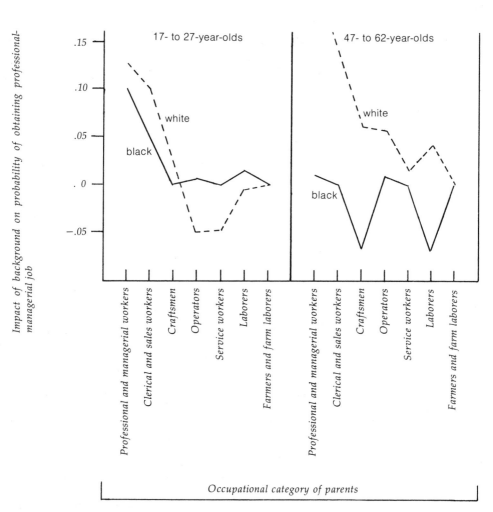

NOTE: Estimated from maximum likelihood estimate of the logistic curve parameters of $P(1 + \exp\Sigma bX)$, the logit probability curve for obtaining a professional or managerial job; unit impacts are estimated as $dP/d\beta = p(1 - p)\beta$. The farmer and farm laborer group is the base group with impact of 0.

BACKGROUND AND PROFESSIONAL-MANAGERIAL JOB STATUS Table 45 uses the estimated "logistic" coefficients from the preceding calculations to examine this issue. As before, I multiply the estimated impact of factors by the mean difference between blacks and whites (using black and white equations) to obtain their contribution to observed differences. The impact of a factor in the logistic model $[dP/dX = P(1-P)X]$ is evaluated at the average unweighted proportion of blacks and whites hold-ing professional-managerial jobs. Column 1 gives the observed differences; columns 2 and 3, the point contributions of parental occupation and education; column 4, the contribution of own education; while the final two columns present the percentage explained by the parental background variables and by those variables and own education. Lines 1 through 6 correspond to the equations for blacks in Table 44, lines 7 through 12 to those for whites in that table.

The findings can be summarized briefly. With the black equation weights, there is a striking increase in the importance of background differences in accounting for differences in professional-managerial job attainment. Among the older men, background by itself explains just 19 percent of differences. Among the young it explains 64 percent in actual attainment and 60 percent in prospective attainment. With the white equation weights, by contrast, there is a moderate drop in the explanatory power of background from lines 7 to 9 but a slight increase to line 11. Finally, the even-numbered lines show that regardless of which weights are used, when education is included as an explanatory variable, the analysis explains *all* the observed differences in the NLS data, implying that pre-labor market factors are the prime cause of differences in the proportion of young blacks and whites obtaining high-level jobs in the new market.

Other Measures of Labor Market Success

Analysis of the relation between family background and other measures of labor market achievement: wages and salary per hour, total labor market earnings, and the median income of an individual's three-digit occupation show that the results obtained above are not limited to attainment of professional and managerial jobs. By these measures of market success as well, background was more important for young blacks in the new market than among older black men and came to account for virtually all of black-white economic differences.

First, according to the calculations in Table 46, which treat the larger sample of persons who reported parental occupation but not necessarily parental education, the estimated coeffi-cients on the parental-occupation measure show a sharp increase between the younger and older black male samples. Since the coefficients in the white male sample are relatively constant, the result is a marked convergence in the impact of

TABLE 45
Contribution of
family background
and college
attainment to
black-white
differences in
professional-
managerial job

		Point contributions to difference		
	Difference	Parental occupation	Parental education	Own education
Black equation weights				
1. 48- to 62-year-old	.24	−.03	.06	
2. 48- to 62-year-old	.24	−.05	.03	.19
3. 17- to 27-year-old, actual	.14	.03	.06	
4. 17- to 27-year-old, actual	.14	.00	.03	.13
5. 17- to 27-year-old, expected	.15	.05	.04	
6. 17- to 27-year-old, expected	.15	.02	.02	.10
White equation weights				
7. 48- to 62-year-old	.24	.12	.06	
8. 48- to 62-year-old	.24	.07	.03	.21
9. 17- to 27-year-old, actual	.14	.04	.04	
10. 17- to 27-year-old, actual	.14	.02	.00	.14
11. 17- to 27-year-old, expected	.15	.04	.05	
12. 17- to 27-year-old, expected	.15	.03	.02	.10

NOTE: Contributions estimated by applying mean differences in characteristics to their estimated impact using $dP/dX = \beta P(1 - P)$ with β as estimated in Table 40 and P equal to the average of the proportion of blacks and whites in college.

background on market attainment, especially in income and wages. Although the results for occupational attainment (measured by the median income in the individual's three-digit occupation) are weaker, they move in the same direction, with an increased coefficient on parental occupation reducing the percentage (though not the absolute) difference between young blacks and whites. Somewhat greater similarity in coefficients for blacks and whites is obtained in the expected occupation regressions (which include a larger sample of young persons).

Second, as Chart 5 shows, when the discontinuous measure of parental occupational status is used to get a better handle on the curvature of the background effect on occupational attainment and income, the results for these continuous variables parallel those given in Chart 4. The effect of coming from a professional or managerial home was a bare .01 for older black men (versus the deleted group) compared with .18 for younger

| Percentage due to | |
Parental background	Parental background and own education
19	
	71
64	
	114
60	
	93
75	
	129
57	
	114
60	
	100

TABLE 46
Regression coefficient estimates of the impact of family background on wages, income, and occupational attainment

| | Coefficients on parental occupation | | | |
| | Black | | White | |
Variable*	Older	Younger	Older	Younger
1. Wages	.02(.05)	.17(.09)	.22(.03)	.16(.05)
2. Occupational position	.04(.03)	.09(.03)	.13(.02)	.18(.02)
3. Income	.03(.06)	.20(.07)	.24(.03)	.23(.04)
4. Expected occupation at age 30		.10(.03)		.15(.02)

*Lines 1 through 3 use the out-of-school sample. Line 4 relates to all persons reporting expected occupation. The samples sizes were: lines 1–3 young men, black 634, white 1607; line 4 black 769, white 2145. Older men, black 979; white 2131.

NOTE: Regressions include variables for years of work experience, family structure, and other geographic background dummies. The dependent variables are in logarithmic form; occupational standing measured by 1969 income in individual's three-digit occupation; as in previous tables parental occupation measured by 1959 income in head of household's three-digit occupation, with nonwhite incomes used for blacks.

SOURCE: NLS data tapes.

CHART 5 *Changed curvature of parental background–achievement locus, black and white men, aged 17–27 and 48–62*

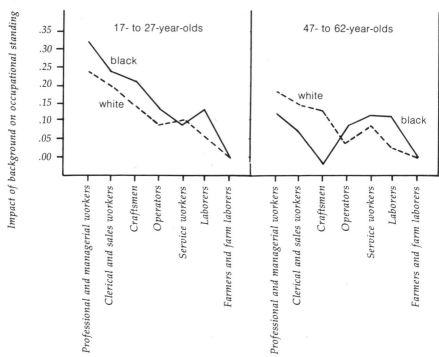

black men. As the same calculations for whites yielded nearly identical coefficients for the two age groups (.17 and .18), there is strong indication of convergence in the background-occupational attainment link between blacks and whites. When the log of income is the dependent variable, the increase in the effect of professional-managerial parental background is even more striking.

Third, in sharp contrast with the past unimportance of background factors in overall black-white labor market differences, the calculations summarized in Table 47 reveal that virtually all the differences among young persons in the new market result from background. Column (1) of the table records the percentage point differences in economic standing between blacks and whites with the same work experience.[9] Because blacks are somewhat younger in the NLS sample and have less

[9]The slight differences in the logarithmic differentials between column (1) lines 1 to 3 and lines 4 to 6 result from differences in the experience coefficients in the equations.

CHART 5   *(continued)*

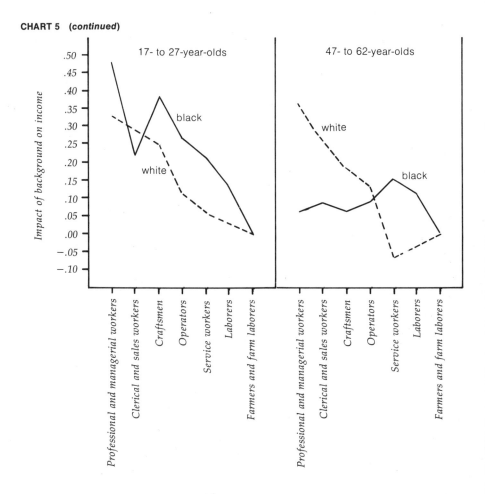

NOTE: Based on regressions including additional variables for region, place of residence, family structure at age 14, and years of work experience. Numbers in parentheses are standard errors. Dependent variables in logarithmic form, with occupational standing measured as log of 1969 income in individual's three-digit occupation.

SOURCE: NLS tapes, see Freeman (1976*b*) for precise regression coefficients.

experience, this adjustment makes a significant difference in the income, but not in other comparisons. According to column (1), there was a substantial diminution of black-white labor market differences between the younger and older male samples, a result consistent with those in other chapters. Most striking, the wage rate of whites is .62 log points above that for blacks among 48- to 62-year-olds, but only .27 points above that for blacks among 17- to 27-year-olds. In terms of the index of

TABLE 47
Contribution of family and regional background and of educational attainment to labor market differences

Measure of market position and group	Logarithmic difference, adjusted for differences in work experience* (1)	Percentage of differences due to:	
		Parental occupation (2)	Parental occupation (3)
Black equation weights			
1. Occupational standing			
17- to 27-year-olds (actual)	.20	40	25
17- to 27 (expected)	.09	78	33
48- to 62-year-olds	.30	13	7
2. Wages			
17- to 27-year-olds	.25	36	38
48- to 62-year-olds	.62	3	−3
3. Income			
17- to 27-year-olds	.44	39	27
48- to 62-year-olds	.66	5	−5
White equation weights			
4. Occupational standing			
17- to 27-year-olds (actual)	.19	.79	47
17- to 27 (expected)	.09	122	78
48- to 62-year-olds	.30	47	17
5. Wages			
17- to 27-year-olds	.27	41	26
48- to 62-year-olds	.62	37	13
6. Income			
17- to 27-year-olds	.41	49	22
48- to 62-year-olds	.68	37	12

*Years of experience differed substantially in the sample due to the fact that blacks at work in the 1969 survey were younger than whites. Sixty-two percent of blacks were below 23 years of age compared with just half of the whites. In addition, blacks tend to experience more job instability and hence accumulate less work experience in a year. Experience has a major effect on income but only a slight impact on wages and occupational standing.

†Residual discrimination obtained by subtracting estimated differences due to background from column (1).

NOTE: Contributions estimated by applying mean differences in background variables to estimated regression coefficients and dividing by figures in column 1. Regression coefficients on the parental occupation variable are given in Table 46.

SOURCE: NLS data set.

Own education (4)	Geographic distribution (5)	Residual market discrimination† (6)
40	25	.04
44	5	.01
27	17	.15
36	24	.03
31	24	.30
34	9	.10
36	18	.33
53	11	−.02
56	33	−.06
43	10	.09
33	30	.22
40	11	
39	10	.12
41	10	.25

occupational attainment, the differential drops from .30 to .20 and falls even further when the expected occupation of *all* blacks and whites, including those in college, is taken as the comparison variable. Income differences also decline, though less steeply, and remain considerable among the young. The much greater difference between young blacks and whites in income than in wages reflects strikingly different amounts of time employed, consistent with the higher unemployment rates found for young black than white men.

The next four columns of the table present estimates of the percentage contribution of parental occupation, the individual's education, and geographic locale at age 14 to the observed differentials. They are based on the regression equations similar to those summarized in Table 46 and are obtained using the same methodology—namely, multiplying estimated regression coefficients by mean differences in the background variables. In column (2) the parental occupation coefficients of Table 46 are, for example, multiplied by the black-white differences in the measure of parental occupation to obtain the estimated contribution of that variable to the differential. The estimates in columns (3) through (5) are obtained from regression equations which also include the education of the individual. The last column measures "residual labor market discrimination," black-white differences that cannot be attributed to the premarket factors.

Lines 1 through 3, which use the black equation weights, show that as a result of the increased impact of family background in black attainment equations, the percentage contribution of parental occupation to differences in income, occupation, and wages was much greater among the young than older male cohorts. Most strikingly, parental occupation accounts, by itself, for 36 to 40 percent of the differences in labor market position among the young men and 78 percent of the difference in expected occupational attainment, compared with only 13, 3, and 5 percent of the difference in occupational position, wages, and income among older men. Addition of own education to the calculations lowers the impact of parental occupation but raises the proportion of differences due to pre-labor market factors considerably. The figures in columns (3) and (4) show that 60 to 77 percent of differences among the young are attributed to education and parental occupation in the young male sample compared with about one-third of the differences in the older male samples. When differences in geographic distribution are brought into the picture, virtually all of black-white economic differences among the young are accounted for. As the last column shows, residual labor market discrimination, defined as the difference in column (1) minus the differences due to parental occupation, own education, and geographic locale, is quite small for 17- to 27-year-olds, though sizeable for 45- to 62-year-olds.

Turning to the calculations with white equation weights, there is less evidence of increases in the role of family background, because background differences already contributed substantially to differences in the older male sample. The proportion of differences in wages and income attributed to parental occupation rises moderately in column (2) while that in occupational standing rises substantially. As in the black equation estimates, residual discrimination in wages and occupational standing appears to be quite small (negative, in fact), while that in income remains nonnegligible but half as large among older men.

If the young men sample is restricted to those who entered the job market in the late 1960s, when the 1964 Civil Rights Act was operative, more striking results are obtained. For men aged 17–22 in 1969 estimates of black-white differentials yield more negative than positive residuals,[10] which corroborates the findings of Hall and Kasten (1973) using the same data file but different modeling procedures. However, because this sample leaves out so many of the young who are still in college, and relates to such an early position of the work life, it should be viewed as suggestive only. When additional years of observation on the NLS sample are available, it will be possible to compare the pre- and post-Civil Rights Act market entrants with more certainty and thus obtain better clues to the causality of the changes. For the present, the important finding is that in

[10]The logarithmic point differentials between black and white 17- to 22-year-olds are much smaller than those between 17- to 27-year-olds in total; the background-achievement regression coefficients and parental background differences are about the same. Hence, the residual differences become smaller and in several instances negative. For example, the occupational status difference is just 0.13 between 17- to 22-year-olds, the income difference is just 0.17. As a result with either black or white equation weights blacks earn a modest "premium" in the estimates.

the new market of the 1960s traditional discriminatory differences between young black and white men in the labor market declined greatly. The remaining income and occupational position differences between them are largely the result of the black background disadvantage.

INTERPRETATION OF THE CROSS-SECTIONAL DIFFERENCES The question naturally arises as to whether the differences between the young and older male background-attainment relations can be attributed to temporal, rather than life-cycle, changes. Although the changes could be due to life-cycle, temporal, or vintage effects, whose influence cannot be factored out solely with the data, a case can be made that much of the change is temporal.

First, an explanation based on "normal" life-cycle changes in the effect of background appears in conflict with data on the relation between background and attainment over life cycles and by age in cross sections. These data show no striking patterns of change as persons age. Duncan's, Featherman's, and Duncan's partial regression coefficients between occupational status of first job and family background are similar to those between current occupation and background in specific cohorts (p. 260). Hauser's and Featherman's coefficients in the 1962 OCG survey show no clear life-cycle pattern in the impact of father's occupation on the individual's occupational status by age group for nonblack men. (The coefficients rise from ages 25–34 to 45–54, then dip.) Similar rough stability (modest increase) is found for nonblack men in their analysis of the 1973 OCG survey (tabel 6).[11]

Second, for blacks, the 1962 OCG data also show no clear cross-sectional age pattern in the effect of father's occupation on son's occupation in the period preceding development of the new market of the 1960s. Of greater significance, the *differences* between black and nonblack coefficients on father's occupation also do not decline with increasing age (Hauser & Featherman, table 6). The type of cross-sectional pattern of change on the impact of background needed to explain the results—decreases for blacks relative to whites—are not found in these data, which suggest that changes over time, in fact, occurred.

---

[11] For a more detailed comparison of the NLS and OCG results, see Freeman (1976*b*).

Third and most decisively, the Hauser-Featherman analysis of the 1962 and 1973 OCG surveys yield results consistent with our interpretation of the NLS cohort differences. While their youngest age group is somewhat older than that in the NLS samples, and their regression model differs in several respects from ours, the pattern of findings tend to be similar. Between 1962 and 1973, which covers the post–1964 Civil Rights Act improved market for black workers, their data show a marked increase in the role of background in the occupational attainment of young blacks. In the 1973 OCG sample, for example, the regression coefficient for father's occupation on the occupational status of 25- to 34-year-olds as measured by the Duncan SES was .23 for nonblacks and .25 for blacks compared with .27 for nonblacks and .05 for blacks in the comparable 1962 regression.

In sum, the evidence from the NLS and other data sets provides substantial support for the hypothesis that new patterns of social mobility developed among black Americans in the improved labor market of the 1960s. The traditional finding of Duncan that black families were less able to pass on their socioeconomic status to children appears to have been overturned, at least for the cohort entering the market in the period of change. In contrast to the past, when "stratification within the Negro population [was] less severe than in the white" (Duncan, p. 88), intergenerational status transmission became quite similar for young cohorts in the "new market."

While the statistical analysis contained here cannot determine the cause of the new pattern of social mobility in black America, a reasonable case can be made that the principal determinant of change was the improved job market for blacks of the 1960s, which was likely to have contributed to the shifts in mobility shown here in several ways. First, to the extent that the historically loose background-attainment relation among blacks was due to market discrimination, the post-1964 decline in discrimination (due, presumably to the 1964 Civil Rights Act and related antibias activities) could be expected to produce a process of social mobility similar to that for whites. The tendency for the demand for more educated and skilled black workers to increase especially rapidly may also have contributed to the observed new patterns of mobility, as it could reasonably be expected to benefit those from more advantaged backgrounds, who are likely to have the skills and resources needed for white collar job success, more than those from poorer backgrounds. Finally, some of the changes in stratification may reflect supply as well as demand factors—the possibility that young persons from advantaged families adjust or respond faster to new opportunities (of whatever type) than those with less-advantaged backgrounds (say, because of better information, connections, quality of education, and the like).

IMPLICATIONS The observed changes have several implications regarding stratification, discrimination, and policy. First, they suggest that changes in the labor market and educational sector, due at least in part to national antibias policy, can alter traditional patterns of mobility. The process of mobility is, by our interpretation, a dependent function of market conditions and policies which alter the market. Second, the formation of what may be called a more "rigid" intergenerational status transmission belt, which benefits some blacks, has implications for the structure of the black community, of the type which some have alleged is producing a "schism" in black America (Moynihan). According to the data shown here, the greater division among blacks involves not only greater economic differences between the highly skilled and the less skilled, but also between those from more and less advantaged backgrounds. A major unintended consequence or by-product of the decline in discrimination may very well be the development of greater "class" differences in black America. Third, assuming that the patterns and development analyzed herein continue, it appears that the burden of background is going to be the major deterrent to future attainment of black-white socioeconomic equality. This raises issues and problems relating to equality of opportunity and policy. What responsibility should the government take for helping blacks in the short run to overcome long-run disadvantages in endowment? To what extent should it also help whites who had poor endowments in the labor market? Does the fact that part of the black background disadvantage results from past discrimination merit special compensatory or income redistributive programs or should all disadvantaged persons be aided in the same manner?

5. Antidiscriminatory Employment Policy and Demand for Black Labor

It shall be an unlawful employment practice for employers to fail or refuse to hire or to discharge or otherwise discriminate against any individual with respect to his compensation, terms, conditions, or privileges of employment, because of such individual's race, color, religion, sex or national origin.

SECTION 703A (1) OF TITLE VII, CIVIL RIGHTS ACT OF 1964

The contractor will not discriminate against any employee or applicant on employment because of race, creed, color or national origin. The contractor will take affirmative action to ensure that applicants are employed, and that employees are treated during employment, without regard to their race, creed, color or national origin.

EXECUTIVE ORDER NO. 11246, SECTION 202 (1)

An affirmative action program is a set of specific and result oriented procedures to which a contractor commits himself to apply every good faith. . . . [It] must include an analysis of areas with which the contractor is deficient in utilization of minority groups and when, and further, goals and timetables to which the contractor's good faith efforts must be directed to correct the deficiencies.

REQUIRED CONTENTS OF AFFIRMATIVE ACTION PROGRAMS, REVISED ORDER NO. 4,

OFFICE OF FEDERAL CONTRACT COMPLIANCE

The decade of the 1960s was marked by a significant effort on the part of the federal government and other groups to remove discriminatory barriers and improve the economic status of minorities. Title VII of the Civil Rights Act of 1964, Executive Order No. 11246, and 16 state fair-employment practice laws (in addition to 25 existing laws) were passed to penalize discrimination in the market place. In 1972 the powers of the Equal Employment Opportunity Commission, which administered Title VII, were substantially strengthened. Court interpretations of the law tended to favor active intervention in the employment process and, in particular, the use of affirmative action plans with numerical goals to speed attainment of a more equitable employment structure. In several important cases, employment tests and various selection procedures that were fair in form but discriminatory in practice were proscribed. Substantial penalties were placed on several discriminatory companies. If discrimination occurred after 1964, collectively negotiated seniority systems were liable to face court attacks. Voluntary private efforts to aid minorities were undertaken by big businesses, with the Plans for Progress program (1967) specifically oriented to increase corporate hiring of minorities for white-collar jobs. The NAACP shifted its focus from school and public facility integration to employment issues. While not directed toward the labor market, the Voting Rights Act of 1965 refranchised blacks in several southern states, with consequences for public employment policies.

Can the development of the new market be attributed at least in part to these and other antidiscriminatory activities by the federal government, the judiciary, state and local governments, and private groups?

This and succeeding chapters examine this important question. Because the phenomena under study are complex, involving changes in behavior throughout the society in a period of marked socioeconomic change, a clear-cut answer cannot be given. Some of the black economic advances in the new market may be attributed to an autonomous reduction in discriminatory attitudes beginning in the 1940s, resulting perhaps from knowledge of the outcome of Nazi racism or to the improved quality of black schooling in the 1940s and 1950s (Welch, 1973) or to the economic penalties placed on discriminators by the free market (Freeman, 1974a; Chiswick, 1974). While alternative explanations cannot be entirely ruled out, the evidence given in these chapters indicates that antidiscriminatory activity associated with national policy was a factor in creating the new market.

The present chapter focuses on the national effort to end labor market discrimination which commenced with the Civil Rights Act of 1964. It begins by describing federal and other equal employment policies and then analyzes the time-series link between antidiscriminatory activity and the timing of black economic advance. Evidence on the effect of antibias pressures on corporate personal policy and the findings of studies of minority employment in companies that appear to have faced especially strong equal employment pressures are evaluated next. Finally, the chapter examines the plausibility of some alternative hypotheses about the causes of the new market, using data on the progress of specific cohorts and individuals to reject the "improved schooling" hypothesis and the timing of changes to reject the autonomous decline in discriminatory attitudes and competitive market explanations.

FEDERAL ANTIDISCRIMIN- ATORY ACTIVITIES There were two major federal initiatives in the 1960s designed to reduce market discrimination against minorities and redistribute income in their favor: Title VII of the Civil Rights Act of 1964, later amended (1972), and Executive Order No. 11246, which required nondiscriminatory and affirmative action by federal contractors. Federal court decisions regarding these and other equal employment laws imposed broad penalties and stringent controls on discriminators in the marketplace, presumably stimulating demand for minority labor.

Title VII made discrimination by employers (section 703a), employment agencies (703b), and unions (703c) illegal in a wide variety of areas of employment, including hiring, firing, compensation, and the terms, conditions, and privileges of employment, and union membership. It established the Equal Employment Opportunity Commission (EEOC) to administer the law but gave the commission little *direct* power to penalize discriminators. Until 1972, the commission could investigate alleged discrimination, conciliate, and request the attorney general to prosecute, but did not have the power to go to court on its own volition or to give "cease and direct" orders, as did many state FEP agencies; in 1972, the act was amended so that the commission could bring action against alleged discriminators. While the lack of EEOC enforcement power is often cited as evidence of the weakness of Title VII, it seems as if placing the burden of enforcement on the courts has turned out to be a "strength in disguise." On the one hand, the weakness of the EEOC reduced the likelihood that enterprises or unions would attempt to control the commission, as regulatees often try to do to regulatory agencies; on the other, it produced sweeping court rulings that might not have emerged from the political and regulatory process.

The 1964 act contained one critical restriction on antidiscriminatory activity, section 703j, which states that nothing contained in this title shall be interpreted to require . . . preferential treatment . . . on account of an imbalance which may exist with respect to the total number or percentage of persons of any race, color, religion, sex or national origin . . . in comparison with the total number or percentage of persons . . . in any community . . . or in the available work force.

The weight placed upon this section by courts, as opposed to other parts of the law, has been a critical determinant of the extent to which the government can press for better treatment of minorities in the labor market.

The amount of resources and activity by the EEOC, which might be taken as indicators of the antidiscriminatory effort, is examined in Table 48. In 1974 the commission had an annual budget of $44 million or approximately $4.40 per nonwhite worker, a figure which far exceeds the total pre-1964 expenditures (approximately $2 million) of all state FEP commissions. Over 37,000 cases were handled, most dealing with the racial discrimination by employers in the South. Because of severe discrimination and the absence of state FEP laws in most southern states, nearly 60 percent of the cases in 1972 originated in that region (see line 5), with Texas, Florida, and Louisiana having the greatest number of charges investigated. Even in the early 1970s, after the commission had been active for nearly a decade, however, relatively few cases ended in successful conciliation, which highlights the reliance on court orders to obtain satisfactory solutions. Note finally that over 26 percent of EEOC charges were remanded to state and local FEP agencies, who were indirectly spurred into greater activity as a result of the federal law.

The second major federal action in the sixties was Executive Order No. 11246 (1965), which requires that federal contractors, who employ about one-third of the United States work force, "not discriminate" in employment and take "affirmative action" to recruit, employ, and promote qualified minority workers. The Executive order established a potentially powerful sanction on miscreants by giving contracting agencies and the Office of Federal Contract Compliance (OFCC) the power to "cancel, terminate, suspend, or cause to be cancelled, terminated or suspended" contracts which fail to comply with nondiscrimination provisions. Possibly the most important aspect

TABLE 48		
The antidiscriminatory activity of the Equal Employment Opportunity Commission, 1973–74	1. Budget (in millions of dollars), 1974	$44,076
	2. Number of cases (1973)	37,415
	3. Basis of discrimination: race	18,002
	4. Treatment of cases (1971), by percentage	
	Deferred for state or local FEPC action	26%
	Recommended for investigation	49%
	No jurisdiction	14%
	Additional information required	11%
	5. Breakdown of race cases by state (1973)	
	South and border	59%
	West	13%
	Northeast	8%
	North Central	24%
	6. Breakdown of cases, by type (1971)	
	Employers	82%
	Unions	6%
	Other	12%
	7. Completed conciliations	2,438
	Fully successful	1,373
	Partially successful	39
	Unsuccessful	1,026

SOURCES: Equal Employment Opportunity Commission (1970, 1971) and Executive Office of the President, (1975, p. 250).

of the order, however, was the required affirmative action programs. Under Revised Order No. 4 issued by OFCC, each federal contractor was obligated to present a program consisting of a "set of specific and result-oriented procedures," including "analysis of the areas within which the contractor is deficient in the utilization of minority groups and women," and further, "goals and timetables to which the contractor's good faith efforts must be directed to correcting deficiency." According to the order, affirmative action programs must contain analyses of utilization of minorities and women by considering such factors as the minority population of the labor area, the percentage of the minority work force, availability of minorities with requisite skills, availability of promotable and transferable minorities within the organization, existence of training institutions capable of training minority persons in the requisite skills, and the degree of training which the contractor is reasonably able to undertake. Goals and timetables must involve personnel relations staff, department adviser heads, and local and unit managers in the goal-setting process; be significant, measurable, and attainable; and be specific for planned results; and where deficiencies exist and where numbers or percentages are relevant, establish and set forth specific goals and timetables. Compliance with affirmative action programs also require many specific acts on the part of contractors. Guidelines for universities further suggest appointment of a director of equal employment programs; development of a data file on employees, including ethnic identification; and comparisons of the number of minorities with market availabilities. An additional stipulation is that "neither minority nor female employees should be required to possess higher qualifications than those of the lowest-qualified incumbent." In short, the Executive order required substantial, formal equal employment administrative procedures which, if carried out, would revolutionize traditional personnel policy.

Court Decisions The way courts have treated the Civil Rights Act and federal affirmative action programs is the *key* to their effect on the market, for the courts bear the ultimate power of interpretation and enforcement. Federal courts have generally acted to strengthen the power of the state to intervene in the employment relationship for the purpose of aiding minorities.

- *Griggs v. Duke Power* (1971) held that the Civil Rights Act "proscribes not only overt discrimination but also practices that are fair in form, but discriminatory in action," outlawing employment tests that are not demonstratably related to immediate job performance if their effect is to restrict minority hiring. According to the Supreme Court, "Congress directed the thrust of the Act to consequences of employment procedures." As a result, major changes have been required in employee selection standards and processes that adversely affect minorities.

- *U.S. v. IBEW*, local 38 (1970) explicitly held that section 703j "cannot be construed as a ban on affirmative relief against the effects of past discrimination resulting from present practices (neutral on their face) which have the practical effect of continuing past injustices."

- *Contractors' Association of Eastern Pennsylvania v. Hodgson* (1971) made it clear that "required goals with percentage of minorities" to be hired were within the purview of the law.

- *Hicks v. Crown Zellerbach* (1972) ruled that "blacks be given preference in filling vacancies at entry level jobs in previously all-white promotion ladders."

- In several cases, the use of statistics showing minority underrepresentation has been treated as prima facie evidence of unlawful discrimination and, according to one court, requires issuance of preliminary injunctions.

- Federal courts ordered substantial back pay to minorities who had been kept out of higher paying jobs by discrimination. In the American Cast Iron case (1975), after 10 years of court action, $1 million was paid to 833 former and current black employees who had not been promoted in accord with seniority.

- Seniority practice in companies that had discriminated after 1964, perpetuating past discrimination, were ordered changed by courts, to permit blacks with many years in plants to move into better departments. In the case of *Afro-American Patrolmen's League v. Duck* (1974), the seniority requirement of five years on the force before being allowed to take a sergeant's test was held illegal as having no real relation to "bona fide occupational qualifications" and freezing in past discrimination. However, in the New Jersey Center Power and Light case (1975), the existing system of seniority was ruled legal even though it made affirmative action plans unattainable.

In sum, courts have focused on results rather than intentions or overt acts of discrimination and required detailed affirmative action plans to remedy underrepresentation of minorities. Furthermore, they have not been averse to using judicial power to order changes in company policies and to penalize discriminators. While a definitive study has yet to be made, examination of cases suggests strongly that *court rather than EEOC activity has been the major factor making the 1964 Civil Rights Act effective in reducing market discrimination.* Detailed analysis of judicial decisions, their impact on affected companies, and spillovers in other companies is needed to delineate the impact of the judiciary.

Additional Antidiscriminatory Activity Partly as a result of section 706b of Title VII, which stipulated that complaints filed in states with their own antidiscriminatory laws be deferred to relevant state agencies for at least 60 days, state and local antidiscriminatory activity also intensified in the 1960s. Prior to the 1964 federal Civil Rights Act, 25 states, largely in the industrial North, had fair employment practice laws which, it is generally agreed, were relatively ineffective because they lacked strong action to curb discrimination. A 1963 Senate Labor Committee report showed, for example, that 19,000 complaints to state FEP agencies resulted in just 62 hearings, 26 cease-and-desist orders, and 18 court actions (Senate Report No. 867, 88th Congress, 2nd Session, 1964, p. 7). Reliance was placed on individual case conciliators and persuasion, with the result that court litigation and potentially powerful judicial restrictions on discrimination were limited. Commissions appear, like regulatory agencies, to have been anxious to appease business concerns rather than to use all available powers to open new job opportunities for Negroes.

In the decade following the 1964 act, by contrast, there was a significant increase in state FEP activities. Sixteen additional states passed antidiscriminatory laws so that by 1972 virtually all states outside the South had a legal commitment to nondiscriminatory employment. In addition the resources and cases handled by state FEP commissions increased significantly, with, for example, twice as many cases dealt with in 1968 as in 1965 in those states for which data are available (Kovarsky & Albrecht, 1970, p. 113–114).

Private as well as public activities designed to reduce discrimination in the labor market also increased greatly in the 1960s. The NAACP shifted its attention from education to job market issues. Federal policy encouraged participation by civil rights groups in affirmative action planning and established class actions as a legitimate mode of Title VII suits. As one indication of increased private civil rights activity, NAACP expenditures more than doubled from 1965 to 1970 after increasing relatively slowly in the early 1960s (NAACP). Private business also made a voluntary effort to improve employment of black workers. Under the Plans for Progress program over 300 companies organized to increase black employment, particularly in higher level jobs. To motivate black youngsters to seek careers in business, "some 220 Negro executives visited 72 predominantly Negro colleges at the expense of their companies to inform students of the receptivity of business and encourage them to pursue a course of studies which would lead to a business career" (*Plans for Progress*, 1967). The minority share of white-collar employment in the original Plans for Progress companies roughly tripled in the late sixties.

TIME-SERIES EVIDENCE If the antidiscriminatory activity which was initiated by the 1964 Civil Rights Act was in fact the major cause of the improved economic status of blacks, there should be a close relation between the level of such activity and improvements, holding fixed other potential causes of change such as pre-1964 trends or cyclical ups-and-downs. Regression calculations designed to see whether such a relation does in fact exist are given in Tables 49 and 50 for all black workers and for the highly qualified blacks of special concern to this book.

Table 49 presents regression coefficients linking (in logarithmic form) relative and actual incomes of black men and women and indices of occupational position to the following explanatory variables: time or the trend level of GNP (*GNPT*)—designed to pick up past trends or the effect of economic growth on the black position; differences in black and white years of education (to measure the impact of greater black attainment on income differences); cumulated real expenditures per nonwhite worker of the Equal Employment Opportunity Commission (EEOC)—an indicator of civil rights activity; and a measure of the business cycle, deviation of real GNP from its trend (*DGNP*).[1] Cumulated rather than annual spending is used to measure the intensity of antidiscriminatory activity because such activity is an investment in nonwhite opportunities, reducing future as well as current discrimination. While it would be proper to take account of depreciation (or possible appreciation) of civil rights resources, the data are not rich

---

[1] More precisely, the log of real GNP (*RGNP*) was regressed on time (*t*) for the period 1947–1972 with the following result:

$$RGNP = 7.95 + 0.037t$$
$$(0.015) \quad (0.001)$$

$R^2 = 0.99$; standard error of estimate = 0.033.

The numbers in parentheses are standard errors. Deviations from the regression line are used to measure short-run fluctuations. The deviation variable is, it should be noted, highly correlated with the deviation of GNP from potential GNP ($r = 0.98$) and is thus comparable to this cyclic measure. Alternative measures of cyclical conditions—deviation of GNP from potential GNP and from the trend level of money GNP, and unemployment—yield results similar to those in the table.

Dependent variable	Constant	Time	DGNF*	Trend level of real GNP
1. Relative median wage and salary income, male, 1947–1971	−0.58	0.0032 (0.0012)	0.91 (0.22)	
2. Relative median wage and salary income, male, 1947–1971	−1.27		0.91 (0.22)	0.087 (0.032)
3. Relative median wage and salary income, male, 1947–1971	−0.46		0.80 (0.24)	
4. Relative median wage and salary income, female, 1947–1971	−1.01	0.029 (0.002)	0.76 (0.39)	
5. Relative median wage and salary income, female, 1947–1971	−7.33		0.76 (0.39)	0.78 (0.05)
6. Relative median wage and salary income, female, 1947–1971	−0.29		0.87 (0.39)	
7. Relative year-round full-time income, male, 1955–1971	−0.59	0.007 (0.002)	−0.18 (0.25)	
8. Relative year-round full-time income, female, 1955–1971	−0.91	0.027 (0.003)	−0.36 (0.37)	
9. Relative occupational position, male, 1948–1972§	−0.28	0.004 (0.0005)	0.34 (0.085)	
10. Relative occupational position, female, 1948–1972§	−0.57	0.010 (0.0008)	0.78 (0.14)	
11. Relative mean income, male, 1947–1971	−0.68	0.005 (0.0009)	0.23 (0.17)	
12. Relative mean income, female, 1947–1971	−0.75	0.022 (0.001)	−0.15 (0.22)	
13. Relative median wage and salary income, male, 1947–1971	−0.54	0.002 (0.001)	0.99† (0.26)	
14. Relative median wage and salary income, female, 1947–1971	−1.06	0.028 (0.002)	0.85† (0.45)	
15. Mean income, black male, 1946–1971	7.47	0.030 (0.002)	1.20 (0.31)	
16. Mean income, black male, 1947–1971	−1.61	0.000 (0.008)	0.87 (0.24)	
17. Mean income, black female, 1946–1971	6.43	0.046 (0.003)	1.28 (0.49)	
18. Mean income, black female, 1946–1971	−4.28	0.022 (0.007)	0.55 (0.44)	

*Deviation of real gross national product from trend as explained in footnote 1.
†Deviation of actual from potential GNP is used in regressions (13) and (14), from George L. Perry (1971, p. 556).
‡Cumulated expenditures by the Equal Employment Opportunity Commission (see text).
§1949, 1951, and 1954 are omitted because data are lacking.
NOTE: All variables (except time) are in log form.
SOURCE: Freeman (1973).

EEOC†	Education	Income (white)	R^2	Durbin-Watson statistic
0.075 (0.02)			0.76	2.60
0.075 (0.02)			0.76	2.60
0.069 (0.19)	0.003 (0.001)		0.74	2.39
0.116 (0.03)			0.95	1.79
0.116 (0.03)			0.95	1.79
0.120 (0.027)	0.015 (0.001)		0.95	1.99
0.035 (0.015)			0.78	2.80
0.027 (0.022)			0.92	1.31
0.017 (0.005)			0.89	1.06
0.058 (0.008)			0.97	1.36
0.044 (0.012)			0.82	1.46
0.031 (0.016)			0.96	1.77
0.085 (0.020)			0.71	2.43
0.129 (0.034)			0.93	1.32
0.048 (0.021)			0.95	1.88
0.078 (0.018)		1.13 (0.28)	0.98	2.60
0.106 (0.036)			0.96	1.86
0.120 (0.028)		1.42 (0.39)	0.98	1.62

enough for such calculations. Alternative specifications, using annual EEOC spending per nonwhite worker, nondeflated spending, or a simple post-1964 trend variable, show the basic results to be impervious to the precise measure of antidiscrimination activity. Because several governmental and private equal employment pressures commenced or accelerated in the 1960s, the EEOC variable must be viewed *solely as an index of activity* and *not* as a measure of the effectiveness of the commission or of the social effect of its expenditures.

The most important finding of Table 49 is that the post-1964 period did, in fact, witness an exceptional increase in black incomes linked to antibias activity, which cannot be accounted for by previous trends, cyclical boom, or increased black educational attainment. In regressions 1 through 6, the EEOC measure has a sizeable significant coefficient, ranging from .069 to .120. Given the growth of the EEOC variable over the period, the coefficients suggest that antidiscriminatory activity was responsible for increases in the black-white income ratio of 15 percent for males and 27 percent for females, or 9 and 16 percentage points, respectively, from levels of about 60 percent in the early sixties. This is all of the male gain and 62 percent of the female gain in the 1965–1971 period covered. If the "time effect" is attributed to the growth of real GNP,[2] the regressions take the form of lines 2 and 5 of the table, which replace time with the trend level of real GNP (GNP predicted by a regression on time). The coefficients then suggest that a 1 percent change in real GNP over the long run raises the black-white income ratio by 0.1 percent for males and by 0.8 percent for females; in contrast, the cyclical coefficients imply that a change of real GNP of 1 percent in the short run, given the trend, adds 0.8 to 0.9 percent to the relative incomes of both black men and women. When the difference in black and white median education replaces real GNP as a long-term variable, the results are similar: a sizeable effect of education for females and a small one for males, with cyclical elasticities of the same order of magnitude. In each of these cases, the trend variables must be omitted to obtain reasonable statistical results. The cause of the

---

[2]Because the trend growth of GNP is just the systematic part of the regression of GNP on time, it is clearly impossible to distinguish between time and trend GNP.

trend effects, especially the large increase in the black-white income ratio for females, is not readily determined by such time-series analysis. The point is that however the trend influence is allocated to independent variables, the EEOC effect remains about the same.

Further tests of the economic effect of civil rights activity after 1964 are reported in lines 7 through 14. The dependent variable is changed to the relative income of year-round full-time workers (lines 7 and 8), indices of occupational position (9 and 10), and mean relative incomes (11 and 12). In lines 13 and 14, the deviation of GNP from its trend is replaced by the deviation of actual from potential GNP. The results confirm the hypothesized civil rights effect, though the results vary somewhat. The biggest change is the decline in the EEOC coefficient for females when either income of year-round full-time workers or mean total income replaces the wage and salary variables. In these cases, the coefficients for females no longer exceed those for men, as they did in lines 1 through 6. Comparison of lines 13 and 14 with lines 1 and 4 reveal that the use of deviation of GNP from potential GNP rather than from trend as the cyclical variable has little effect on the EEOC coefficient. It remains sizeable and statistically well determined. Other indicators of aggregate demand, such as the rate of unemployment, also show that boom conditions were not the principal source of the improvement in the black position after 1964, although they did improve the relative incomes of blacks.

Finally, the use of relative income as the income variable is checked in regressions 15 through 18, which focus on the income of black men and women. In equations 15 and 17, the calculations concerning males and females yield the familiar results that the trend and civil right variables have somewhat greater effects for women than for men, although the difference in trend coefficients for the two sexes is considerably smaller than it is in lines 1 and 4. Regressions 16 and 18 introduce incomes of white males and females, respectively, as explanatory variables. In a properly specified equation that included all the factors causing differential changes in black and white incomes, the coefficient on the white income variables would be unity. Income of white males enters regression 16 with a plausible coefficient which differs only modestly from unity; income of white females, however, shows a much larger coeffi-

TABLE 50
Regression estimates of the effect of civil rights activity on the economic position of nonwhite male college graduates, 1949–1972

Dependent variable	Constant	Time	EEOC	DGNP
		Position of nonwhites		
Percent of nonwhite college graduates who are managers				
Equation 1	−2.40	−.01 (.02)	.40 (.10)	4.84 (2.93)
Equation 2	−5.68	.03 (.02)	.31 (.09)	3.49 (2.43)
Index of nonwhite graduate occupational position				
Equation 3	9.13	.002 (.001)	.011 (.007)	.35 (.21)
Equation 4	8.91	.004 (.002)	.008 (.002)	.30 (.11)
		Position of nonwhites relative to total males		
Relative percent of nonwhite college graduates who are managers				
Equation 5	−.55	−.03 (.02)	.45 (.12)	5.56 (3.37)
Equation 6	−4.77	.02 (.02)	.34 (.10)	3.83 (2.52)
Relative index of nonwhite graduate occupational position				
Equation 7	−.09	.000 (.001)	.012 (.008)	.31 (.24)
Equation 8	−.34	.003 (.002)	.008 (.007)	.26 (.21)

*Standard error of estimate.
NOTE: Numbers in parentheses are standard errors. Regressions cover the years 1949, 1959, 1961, and 1964–1972.
SOURCES: Data for 1959, 1962, and 1964–1972 from U.S. Bureau of Labor Statistics (various editions). Data for 1949 from U.S. Bureau of the Census (1953, table 11).

cient in regression 18, indicating that the different pattern of relative incomes for females is not well explained by the model. Again, however, the size and significance of the estimated EEOC effect remain about the same as in the initial calculations.

Ratio of black to white college graduates	R^2	SEE*
	.80.	.202
−.82 (−.35)	.89	.163
	.82	.014
−.06 (.03)	.87	.013
	.70	.227
−1.00 (.37)	.86	.165
	.58	.016
−.06 (.04)	.71	.014

College Graduates   The impact of post-1964 antidiscriminatory activity on college graduate workers is examined in Table 50, which records regressions of two indicators of the status of graduates—an income-weighted index of occupational position and the proportion obtaining managerial jobs—on EEOC, time, and the cyclical deviation of GNP from its long-term trends from 1949–1972. Lines 1 through 4 focus on the position of nonwhite college men; lines 5 through 8 on their position relative to that of all college men.

The calculations show that the improved market for the black elite was closely associated with late 1960s–early 1970s antidiscriminatory activity. In each regression, the key EEOC variable obtains a positive, generally significant coefficient of a fairly sizeable magnitude. In line 1, for example, EEOC is the dominant explanatory variable, accounting for all of the long-term improvement in the representation of blacks in managerial jobs in the post-World War II period. In lines 3 and 4, the picture is more equivocal; EEOC obtains a significant coefficient on the occupational index in line 4 but only a weak positive one in line 3. The weak effect on the occupational index variable is readily explicable, however, by the fact that the vast majority of black (and other) male graduates have always worked as professionals and managers, so that there is little variation in the occupational index over time. As for time trends, the calculations reveal a modest upward trend in the occupation index, a more marked trend in incomes, but virtual constancy in the proportion of black graduates attaining managerial jobs. The cyclic coefficients, on the other hand, are positive (save for income) indicating that the status of black college graduates is especially sensitive to economic fluctuations.

In regressions 2 and 4 the ratio of black to total college graduates has been added to the calculations to examine the possibility that the market position of black graduates is adversely influenced by their relative number. While the supply variable is accorded sizeable negative coefficients, interpretation of the result is unclear: on the one hand, it could reflect movements along a negatively sloped demand curve; on the other, as the increase in supply occurs primarily among the young, the variable may also be an indicator of the relative age structure of the college work force, for which independent data are not available.

Further evidence of a governmental policy effect is given in lines 5 through 8, which accord sizeable positive regression coefficients to the EEOC variable in equations focusing in the relative rather than absolute position of blacks in the market. The most marked effect of the policy variable is, as in the preceding calculations, on the proportion of graduates obtaining managerial jobs, a coefficient of .45 in line 6 and .34 in line 7, three to four times the size of the estimated standard error. This important finding, which suggests that policy "opened" the key managerial occupation to blacks, presumably in national corporations, can be tested further with annual data on the nonwhite share of managers from 1955 to 1972. These data have the advantage of representing a continuous series with more observations and, presumably, smaller errors of measurement due to the greater population covered than the college graduate data. The resultant regression, presented below, confirms the apparent role of policy in improving opportunities for blacks in management and shows, further, a significant independent trend in the black share of managers, possibly due to increased education.[3]

Nonwhite-total male managers
$$= .93 + .07 \text{ time} + .26 \text{ EEOC} + .13 \text{ cycle}$$
$$(.01) \qquad (.07) \qquad (1.34)$$
$$R^2 = .93$$

Causes of Differential Advance

Finally, in view of the differential change of relative income and employment among various black groups shown in Tables 49 and 50 and in Chapter 1, it must be recognized that a given change in discrimination due to antidiscriminatory activity may not have the same effect on every group of workers. In particular, reductions in discrimination are likely to have larger immediate effects on occupations or groups of workers with flat age-earnings curves or short job ladders than on sectors of the labor market where investment in skill and accumulated experience count most. A decline in discrimination in athletics, for example, would show up first in new hires of black athletes and last in employment of managers, coaches, or executives. The implication is that an easing in discrimination will be most pronounced among the young and among women, in industries where entry-level jobs bulk large, and least marked for men requiring on-the-job accumulation of human capital. This is roughly consistent with the observed patterns of change.

---

[3] The data for this regression are taken from U.S. Department of Labor (1973, table A-12), with figures for 1955 and 1957 from Russell (1966).

Differences in the response of young workers or new entrants, on the one hand, and older workers on the other, to improved income opportunities are also likely to contribute to patterns of more rapid advance of younger black men and women in the 1960s. Since the young make their career decisions contemporaneously while the decisions of older workers reflect past as well as current conditions, the elasticity of supply with respect to current incentives will be higher for the young. As a result, the young will make greater gains in the job structure in periods when discrimination declines and sustain greater losses when it intensifies. Similarly, supply responses can be expected to be more rapid in labor markets where the gross turnover of the work force is normally high, as is the case among women, because older new entrants will augment the supply of occupationally mobile young people. In addition, the lower the on-the-job training or skill of an occupation, the more rapid will be the adjustment of its supply to economic change. The considerations supplement those relating to the effect of demand as possible explanations of differential rates of advance among groups of black workers.

In sum the time-series evidence on all black workers and the highly qualified is consistent with the proposition that government and other antibias activity raised demand for black labor in the late 1960s. The regressions do not, however, provide a definitive test. If some other factors specific to the period since 1964 but omitted from analysis were the cause of the observed developments, they would indeed be misleading. It is necessary to consider other evidence that policy did indeed influence the decisions of employers in the period and consider alternative hypotheses more carefully.

EFFECTS ON PERSONNEL PRACTICES Since only a relatively small number of minority workers are covered by specific discrimination cases, court, EEOC, and OFCC pressures could have a significant aggregate effect on the demand for black labor *only if they produced widespread changes in corporate personnel policies*. While a comprehensive survey of company employment practices has not been undertaken, available evidence suggests significant policy-induced changes in the 1960s. First, minority hiring has become an explicit goal of major corporations. At IBM, for example, every manager is told that his annual performance evaluation, on which promotions, raises, and bonuses critically depend, includes a report on his success in meeting affirmative action goals (Seligman, 1973). Similarly, Xerox managers were warned that "a key element in each manager's over-all performance appraisal will be his progress in the [EEO] important area. No manager should expect a satisfactory appraisal if he meets other objectives but fails here." More generally, the Conference Board has reported that as a part of an overall strategy for identifying and correcting EEO problem areas, companies "refuse promotions or substantial wage increases to those who do not produce satisfactory EEO results, no matter what other performance results they achieve" (*Nondiscrimination* . . . , 1973). Nearly all major employers in the United States have hired equal compliance executives and/or instituted EEO departments, with, according to *The New York Times* (1973), many hiring "compliance specialists who visit even the most remote installations to suggest ways to expand the number of women and minority group employees on the payroll." Second, evidence from the Bureau of National Affairs (BNA) and the Conference Board indicate that actual personnel management practices are being changed as a result of legal interpretations of Title VII of the Civil Rights Act and Executive Order No. 11246. One personnel specialist in the Conference Board survey reported, for example, that "our basic assumption is that all groups protected by Title VII ought to be moving into all our jobs at all levels on an approximately proportional basis." Another, noting the difficulty in proving that various selection factors predict actual job performance, reported the adoption of a "separate pool" strategy in using tests, selecting the top percentiles of all groups for a particular job, regardless of the cutoff share for particular groups. According to the BNA survey, the vast majority of the 113 member firms of the American Society of Personnel Administration have altered their selection procedures by revising or eliminating preemployment tests that cannot be directly related to actual performance on specific jobs. *The New York Times* cites another specialist in personnel practices who claims that, in keeping with the Duke Power decision, tests are being deemphasized. Third, as the increased recruitment visits of corporations to black colleges show, traditional modes of searching for qualified workers have also been transformed, presumably as a result of the pressures of the law.

In sum, there was a major national effort to reduce discrimination in the labor market in the 1960s, involving passage of laws, executive orders, and numerous court decisions which appear to have significantly influenced corporate personnel practices.

Company Evidence One way of potentially isolating the effect of explicit governmental antidiscriminatory policy from other forces at work in the late 1960s and early 1970s is to compare the employment experience of companies that faced particularly strong EEO pressures. Three such studies have been performed, focusing on the impact of Office of Contract Compliance and Equal Employment Opportunity Commision efforts to reduce company discrimination, with results that are generally consistent with our analysis. As none of the studies has focused on court activity, however, we lack detailed knowledge of what may be the most important mechanism for enforcing the law.

The Burman study (1973), an unpublished University of Chicago dissertation, used EEOC data on the employment and occupational position of blacks in individual companies to evaluate the activities of the Office of Federal Contract Compliance from 1967 to 1970. The policy variables considered are the existence of a government contract (which should increase the leverage of policy) and that of a compliance contact with establishments (a direct measure of antidiscriminatory pressures). Because the compliance contact is, presumably, a response to observed levels of discrimination, a two-equation model is used in the regressions, with one equation analyzing the effect of the contact and the other the contact decision. Burman's results suggest that black employment was raised by the existence of contracts and by federal compliance activity. Firms with contracts increased their black employment proportion by one-half of a percentage point in the 1967–1970 period more than those without contracts, other things being held fixed. The percentage of black male employees grew by 2.5 points. In two stage least squares calculations compliance activity appears to have increased black employment by 2 to 2.5 percentage points also. It is still likely that Burman's calculations underrate the effect of contact, for he is unable to deal with possible spillover effects: the possible impact that placing contact and pressure on one company on others who improve their minority employment practices to avoid similar troubles.

Ashenfelter and Heckman (1975) considered the link between minority employment patterns in the period 1966 to 1970 and the relative employment and occupational position of black men in firms with government contracts and without contracts on the hypothesis that affirmative action requirements and dependence on the government would increase demand for blacks more greatly in the former. They found some impact of governmental pressure on employment, with the relative employment of black male workers increasing by 3.3 percent more in firms with contracts, but only a modest impact on relative occupational position, of 0.2 percent. While they were disappointed with the size of the governmental effects, it is important to recognize that modest changes in employment which result from increased demand could be quite significant in altering relative incomes depending on the elasticity of demand. The general pervasiveness of the improvement in the black occupational structure does, however, raise some problems for the governmental pressures hypothesis, as Ashenfelter and Heckman correctly note.

Finally, Heckman and Wolpin (1976) carried out a detailed analysis of OFCC effects for establishments in the Chicago area, using more sophisticated econometric methods than other analysts. Their findings are similar to those in the other studies, with, however, statistically significant and sizeable affirmative action effects of government contracts found primarily among black men in blue-collar jobs.

INTERPRETA- TION AND EVALUATION OF THE GOVERNMEN- TAL HYPOTHESIS While most individual company studies have found some mental policy effect on demand for blacks, the empirical results are not overwhelming.

Part of the problem is that the company analyses suffer from certain problems inherent in methodology. For one thing, they generally deal with only one of a variety of governmental programs (OFCC) which by itself could not reasonably be expected to be the major cause of the observed improvement in black-white income ratios. Indeed, if enormous OFCC effects were found, this would suggest that EEOC cases, court decisions, and the like were ineffective, which is unlikely. None of the studies has investigated the impact of court decisions on demand for black labor, which—as argued earlier—is a potentially very important route of governmental impact.

Perhaps more importantly, the studies do not take account of possible *spillovers* of government effects. If certain personnel practices are found discriminatory in one company, others following the same practices can be expected to change without explicit governmental penalization. Virtually all universities with federal contracts began to reconsider their practices when severe pressures were placed on a few institutions by HEW. Because, as noted earlier, only a relatively small number of enterprises are likely to experience direct EEOC and OFCC or court cases, it is the induced change in personnel policy throughout the economy which lies at the heart of the hypothesis that governmental policies have altered demand for black workers in the private sector.

The finding that companies which have faced OFCC or other pressures have increased black *employment* only modestly does *not*, moreover, imply that the induced change in demand has had modest effects on *income*. First, most of the gains in black income have occurred among new market entrants. Since small changes in *total* black employment are likely to involve large changes in *new hiring* practices, the modest employment effects may be consistent with the observed pattern of income gain. Second, evidence on changes in employment are not readily translated into changes in income. Even small employment effects could have sizeable income effects, depending on the elasticities of demand for black labor. If demand were relatively inelastic, for example, changes in demand due to governmental pressures could cause small changes in relative employment but large changes in relative incomes. The microstudies must be put into an aggregative framework to evaluate their significance.

The direct employment effects of governmental activity represents another important route by which public policy can alter demand for black labor that deserves consideration in explorations of the new market. As Chapters 6 and 7 show, enhanced governmental demand at the state, local, and federal levels has substantially improved the market position for black workers, particularly of those with considerable education and skill of special concern to this study.

Finally, the way in which overall societal attitudes and behavior were altered by the 1964 Civil Rights Act and ensuing public pressure against discrimination remains an elusive but potentially important component of the governmental activity hypothesis. Social mores and views of what is right were likely to have been changed and new forms of behavior initiated as a result of the pressures and attention given to the discrimination question. Without governmental activity, such changes can be expected to have been much smaller.

In sum, despite these problems, the studies tend to support the argument that demand for black labor was raised in the period by governmental antidiscriminatory activity. While the precise size and routes of impact of governmental pressures for equal employment opportunities remain unclear, there does appear to be a policy impact. More detailed work, possibly combining individual case studies with econometric computations, will cast further light on the role of explicit governmental actions in the development of the new market.

ALTERNATIVE HYPOTHESIS: "IMPROVED QUALITY OF SCHOOLING" The "quality of schooling" hypothesis advanced by Welch (1973) attributes much of the new market progress of blacks to improvements in the quality of black schooling, the result of the increased public resources given black children in the 1940s and 1950s (see Chapter 2). This hypothesis is consistent with the especially rapid convergence in relative incomes or occupational structures among the young, for the increased ratio of black to white school spending would affect the young exclusively. Since educational quality is fixed for individuals over time, however, the hypothesis cannot account for the economic progress of specific individuals or cohorts. Such progress is readily explained by shifts in demand for blacks due to antidiscriminatory activity by the federal government and other social groups.[4] Did particular cohorts and individual black workers make "longitudinal" progress relative to whites in the late 1960s? The evidence presented in Table 51, which compares changes in the ratio of nonwhite to total incomes of particular cohorts by level of schooling as they aged ten years in the 1950–

---

[4] A complicated quality hypothesis in which improved quality takes time to affect individuals might account for the pattern but requires an extra unrealistic epicycle in the argument.

	Males		
	Percentage point change in the ratio of nonwhite to total incomes		Differential change column (2) − column (1)
Cohort, by education and age, in 1950–1960 or 1960–1970	1949–1959 (1)	1959–1969 (2)	(3)
All levels of education			
18–24 to 25–34*	−0.09	0.03	0.12
25–34 to 35–44	0.00	0.03	0.03
35–44 to 45–54	0.00	0.01	0.01
45–54 to 55–64	−0.02	0.02	0.04
College graduates			
18–24 to 25–34*	−0.13	−0.02	0.11
25–34 to 35–44	−0.02	0.04	0.06
35–44 to 45–54	−0.01	0.06	0.07
45–54 to 55–64	0.00	0.08	0.08
High school graduates			
18–24 to 25–34*	−0.04	0.03	0.07
25–34 to 35–44	0.00	0.02	0.02
35–44 to 45–54	0.01	−0.01	−0.02
45–54 to 55–64	0.04	0.04	0.00
Grade school graduates			
18–24 to 25–34*	−0.06	0.03	0.09
25–34 to 35–44	−0.10	0.01	0.02
35–44 to 45–54	0.04	0.01	−0.03
45–54 to 55–64	0.02	0.03	0.05

TABLE 51
Changes in nonwhite to total income ratios, over the life cycles, 1950–1970

*Due to census age grouping, the table compares 19- to 24 with 25- to 34-year-olds.

NOTE: Ratios for 1949 to 1959 are based on *median* incomes; 1959 to 1969 are based on *mean* incomes due to different modes of reporting in the census.

SOURCE: Calculated from income ratios in Freeman (1973).

1960 and 1960–1970 decades, using data on income by age and schooling from the decennial *Censuses of Population,* provides an affirmative answer with respect to cohort advances. Columns (1), (2) and (4), (5) record the changes in the ratio of incomes over the life cycle of male and female cohorts in the 1950s and in the 1960s. Columns (3) and (6) give the differences in the changes in ratios between the two decades. If black cohorts made greater progress in the 1960s as they aged than in

Females		
Percentage point change in the ratio of nonwhite to total incomes		Differential change column (5) − column (4)
1949–1959 (4)	1959–1969 (5)	(6)
0.14	0.40	0.26
0.09	0.21	0.12
−0.09	0.11	0.20
0.03	0.23	0.20
0.12	0.15	0.05
0.00	0.14	0.14
−0.07	0.09	0.16
0.04	0.16	0.12
0.26	0.46	0.20
0.17	0.24	0.07
−0.02	0.08	0.10
−0.01	0.12	0.11
0.17	0.23	0.06
0.16	0.11	−0.05
−0.03	−0.03	0.00
−0.03	0.00	0.03

the 1950s due to improved demand for their services, the figures in (3) and (6) would be positive, while if improved quality of schooling is the sole cause of black advance, the figures would be approximately zero. In fact, the table reveals a definite pattern of gains in relative income over the life cycle for blacks in the new market. Overall, each cohort of black men gained relative to whites in the later period while, at best, holding their own in the former period; also the female cohorts enjoyed accelerated gains in the sixties. Among college graduates, there are accelerations in the change in life-cycle income ratios of 11, 6, 7, and 8 points for the 18–24, 25–34, 35–44 and 45–54-year-old-male cohorts, respectively, and of 5, 14, 16, and 12 points for the comparable female cohorts. Whereas just three groups of black men in specified age and education categories advanced relative to whites in the fifties, 10 cohorts made such gains in the sixties; similarly, the rate of change in black-white income ratios accelerated among women for all but two groups over the period. While a quality-oriented explanation of these changes is not impossible (see footnote 4) the differential changes are clearly more consistent with a change in demand explanation of black progress.

Further evidence from the cohort data which runs counter to the quality argument is given in Table 52. This table compares changes in the ratio of nonwhite to total incomes of the same cohort in the sixties and in the fifties, using the previous decades' experience of the same persons rather than the life-

TABLE 52
Change in income ratios, for the same cohorts, 1950–1970

Cohort by education and age in 1950	Change in ratio of income		Column (2) − column (1) (3)
	1950–1960 (1)	1960–1970 (2)	
All			
18–24	−0.09	0.03	0.12
25–34	0.00	0.01	0.01
35–44	0.00	0.02	0.02
College graduates			
18–24	−0.13	0.04	0.17
25–34	−0.02	0.06	0.08
35–44	−0.01	0.04	0.03
High school graduates			
18–24	−0.04	0.02	0.06
25–34	0.00	−0.01	−0.01
35–44	0.01	0.04	0.03
Grade school graduates			
18–24	−0.06	0.01	0.07
25–34	−0.01	0.01	0.02
35–44	0.04	0.03	−0.01

SOURCE: Calculated from Table 51 of this volume.

cycle experiences of similarly aged workers in the fifties as the "control group," for evaluating the experience of black cohorts in the new market. The new comparisons reveal a clear-cut improvement in the relative income of specified black male cohorts in the 1960s, in sharp contrast to a general decline in the relative standing of the group in the 1950s. The change is especially marked among college graduates, with for example, the ratio of incomes in the group aged 25–34 in 1950, 35–44 in 1960, and 45–54 in 1970 dropping by 2 percentage points in the former period and rising by 6 points in the latter period. Among women, on the other hand, the evidence appears at first glance to be more equivocal, as changes in ratios decline in several groups. The deceleration in black advance is, however, misleading, for it occurs largely in groups (18- to 24- and 35- to 44-year-old college graduates and 18- to 24-year-old high school graduates) in which nonwhite total income ratios exceeded unity by 1960, making further increases unlikely. Even the "decelerated" change in percentage point increases in the income

Change in ratio		Column (5) −
1950–1960 (4)	1960–1970 (5)	column (4) (6)
0.24	0.21	−0.03
0.09	0.11	0.02
−0.09	0.23	0.34
0.17	0.11	−0.06
0.16	−0.03	−0.19
−0.03	0.00	0.03
0.26	0.24	−0.02
0.17	0.08	−0.11
−0.02	0.12	0.14
0.10	0.14	0.04
0.00	0.09	0.09
−0.07	0.16	0.23

ratio among 18- to 24-year-olds in line 1 should not be interpreted as indicating that a lessening in the rate of black progress, for the gain of the sixties was a much larger fraction of the
income gap between the groups (70 percent minus 44 percent).
In sum, the data show marked improvements in the ratio of
black to white incomes that cannot be readily interpreted in
terms of quality-induced improvements in premarket learning
power.

**Longitudinal
Progress,
1966–1969**
National Longitudinal Survey evidence, analyzed from the perspective of social mobility in Chapter 4, shows that individual
blacks progressed in the new market. To determine the extent
of individual advancement in the late sixties, the 1966–1969 rate
of change of yearly earnings was regressed on a zero-one
dummy variable for race and several control variables, region
and size of residence, years of schooling, age, estimated work
experience, parents' occupational status for older (ages 48–62
in 1969) and young (ages 17–27) men. To get a better fix on wage
rates, moreover, hours and weeks worked are entered as
explanatory variables in some regressions.

The resultant estimates of the effect of race on the rate of
change of income or wages of individuals, presented in Table
53, show a sizeable black gain in a limited span of time. In the
calculations, the dummy variables for black (1=blacks,
0=whites) obtain positive coefficients, indicating that individual blacks advanced more rapidly in the job market in this three-
year period than did comparable whites. Older black men had
increases in income of 4 to 5 percent more than whites in the
three-year span, or more than 1 percent per annum—a sizeable
differential. The evidence for younger black men is more equivocal, for there appears to be a large advantage for blacks when
time worked is fixed but only a modest insignificant advantage
when it is not. The complexities of search for a good job and
investing in human capital at the outset of life complicate the
analysis. Stronger results for the young using a sophisticated
human capital model have been presented in a doctoral dissertation by E. Lazear (1974). Holding changes in schooling, marital
status, unionization, age, and other factors fixed, Lazear's
analysis of changes in income in 1966–1969 yield a positive significant black dummy variable of .052 with a standard
error of .024. As all these coefficients relate to individual longi-

	Ages	
	58–62	*17–27*
Number of observations	2,791	1,996
Percent black in sample	30.2	29.9
Coefficient on black dummy variable income	.053	.022
	(.028)	(.085)
Income, with hours and weeks worked as explanatory variables	.041	.095
	(.027)	(.070)

NOTE: This table is based on regression calculations which include background variables, region and size of place at age 16, parental occupation, years of experience and education. Numbers in parentheses are standard errors.

SOURCE: National Longitudinal Survey Tape. See Chapter 4 for details of the survey.

tudinal changes, it requires a far-fetched argument to explain them in terms other than changes in demand for black labor. The quality-of-schooling hypothesis is rejected.

ALTERNATIVE HYPOTHESIS: ATTITUDINAL CHANGES, COMPETITIVE PRESSURES

Two other plausible hypotheses that might account for the economic progress of blacks in the new market—the attitudinal change and competitive pressure hypotheses—can, I believe, also be rejected. They fail to account for the timing of the improvement in the black position in the 1960s.

That the attitudes of white Americans toward blacks have, for whatever reason, changed greatly in the post-World War II period is shown in opinion polls and related survey data. In 1944, for example, only 45 percent of whites thought that "Negroes should have as good a chance as white people to get any kind of job" compared with 80 percent in 1963 (Schwarz, 1967, p. 24). As the answers to these and other survey questions show a significant decline in discriminatory attitudes in the 1950s and early 1960s, *before* the rapid economic improvement of the late 1960s, however, and no sudden sharp change in the latter period, it is difficult to attribute the development of the new market to attitudinal changes. Declines in racist views undoubtedly are part of the story. They might in particular underlie the gradual upward trend in black-white income and occupational position ratios obtained on trend coefficients but not the distinct timing of the upswing.

The problem with a competitive market explanation of changes in black-white economic differences is similar. To be sure, the market penalizes discriminators who pay more for labor than nondiscriminating firms that hire discriminated groups such as blacks. In the long run, as nondiscriminatory enterprises expand and additional nondiscriminators enter the market, differences due to discrimination would decline. However, the long-term history shows no significant improvement in the black economic position until the 1960s (Freeman, 1974), suggesting that competitive forces operated slowly, if at all, over the period. While it is possible that the antidiscriminatory effort of the late 1960s was a catalyst, teaching employers that blacks were in fact able employees who could increase profits, such an explanation is far-fetched and, more importantly, rests on the exogenous increase in federal and other antidiscriminatory activity of the period.

ALTERNATIVE HYPOTHESIS: MACRO-ECONOMIC EXPANSION Finally because the latter half of the 1960s, when antibias activity grew rapidly, was a period of considerable economic expansion, it has been argued that cyclic factors rather than more fundamental market changes underlie much of the improved position of black workers. The regressions in Tables 49 and 50 tend to reject such an interpretation but still leave open the possibility that there was "something different" about the late sixties expansion. The experience of blacks in the Great Recession of 1974–1975 provides reasonably clear evidence against the cyclic explanation of observed changes. Despite the economic downturn, the position of blacks did *not* deteriorate to pre-1964 levels and, in fact, showed little evidence of the normal cyclic fall in relative income and occupational position. From 1969 to 1974, for example, when aggregate demand weakened, the income of black men increased by 45 percent compared with a 37 percent gain for white men (U.S. Bureau of the Census, 1970, table 62; 1975, table 68); in the 1973–1974 period of sharp downturn, the ratio of black to white male incomes actually rose from .69 to .71 while that for women jumped from .90 to .98 (U.S. Bureau of the Census, 1974, table 69; 1975, table 68). The ratio of an index of nonwhite to white occupational standing increased for males from .84 to .87 in the 1969–1975 period and for females from .80 to .87. The proportion of nonwhite males employed as professionals relative to the proportion of white males grew *more rapidly* from 1969 to 1975 than from 1964 to 1969: in 1964 the ratio of proportions stood at .45;

in 1969, at .48; in 1975 at .59.[5] Similarly, blacks made greater advances into managerial jobs in the 1970s than in the late 1960s. While the recession did, of course, reduce employment of blacks and cause considerable economic hardship, it did not eliminate the post-1964 gains, which effectively destroys the economic expansion explanation of those changes.

CONCLUSIONS This chapter has shown that there was a major antidiscriminatory effort in the period following the 1964 Civil Rights Act, which appears to have contributed to the development of the new market. While the evidence is not conclusive, the hypothesis that the economic position of highly educated (and other) blacks improved because of antidiscriminatory activity appears to offer the best explanation of the dramatic changes of the late 1960s and early 1970s.

[5]These figures are from U.S. Bureau of Labor Statistics' *Handbook of Labor Statistics, 1974* (1974, table 19) and U.S. Bureau of Labor Statistics' *Employment and Earnings, January 1975* (1975, table A-21). The index is calculated as $\Sigma \alpha_i W_i$ where α_i is the proportion of workers in the ith occupation and W_i is the median income of male or female workers in that occupation from the 1960 *Census of Population* (U.S. Bureau of the Census 1963*b*).

6. Governmental Employment in the New Market

Public employment policies offer another tool for changing the market for discriminated workers. As the largest single employer, the federal government can significantly raise demand for blacks by its own personnel practices, particularly in specialized occupations where federal jobs are sizeable compared with the number of qualified blacks. As major white-collar employers, state and local governments can also substantially influence the market for the black elite. How have qualified black workers fared in the public sector of the new market? Did governmental employment policies play a role in improving the black economic positions? What forces determined governmental demand for black workers?

This chapter finds that public employers, particularly the federal government, offered qualified blacks better job opportunities than the private sector in the new market; that changes in governmental demand for blacks contributed substantially to the development of the new market; and that the major factor behind increased demand for blacks by governments in the period was the growth of black voting power, which resulted in the South from the 1965 Voting Rights Act and related bills and in the North from the increase in the black share of the population.

EMPLOYMENT AND INCOME IN THE PUBLIC SECTOR I examine first the economic position of high-level black workers in the public sector in the 1970s. Evidence from the 1970 *Census of Population,* the U.S. Civil Service Commission, and the National Longitudinal Survey shows clearly that blacks fared well in governmental, particularly federal, employment in the new market, obtaining a relatively large number of high-level positions and higher incomes, relative to comparable whites, than in the private sector.

The sectoral distribution of black professionals, managers, and college graduates in 1970 is considered first in Table 54, which records the percentages of black and total workers in

TABLE 54
*Federal and total
governmental
employment of
black workers,
by sex and
occupation, 1970*

| Occupation | Percentage of occupational work force in government employment | | | |
| | *All government* | | *Federal* | |
	Black	*Total*	*Black*	*Total*
Male				
Professional, technical, and kindred	47.9	29.8	11.1	7.5
Accountants	31.7	16.2	20.3	8.7
Computer specialists	33.0	17.6	23.6	10.2
Engineers	32.2	16.5	20.3	9.5
Lawyers	27.8	14.0	14.7	6.3
Life and physical scientists	37.7	30.4	26.3	18.3
Personnel and labor relations	47.5	25.3	21.7	10.7
Physicians, dentists, and related	15.5	9.8	4.9	2.9
Social scientists	50.7	33.0	18.8	12.7
Social and recreation workers	79.1	74.6	11.0	7.5
Teachers, university	66.7	65.9	3.0	1.2
Teachers, other	86.4	79.2	3.3	1.7
Technicians, engineers, and science	25.1	18.7	14.9	8.7
Technicians, health	46.2	35.8	19.0	10.0
Managers	24.4	12.5	8.6	4.3
College graduates, four or more years	51.0	27.1	12.0	6.1
TOTAL	18.6	14.0	7.4	4.6
Female				
Professional	66.6	51.0	8.0	3.9
Managers	35.4	16.7	10.4	4.8
College graduates, four or more years	72.1	56.4	6.3	3.2
TOTAL	24.4	14.4	6.9	3.8

SOURCE: U.S. Bureau of the Census (1973*e*, tables 2, 5, 6, for numbers of government workers; 1973*a*, table 223, for total numbers in occupations; 1973*c*, tables, 8, 9, for numbers of persons with four or more years of college).

various high-level occupations employed by all governments and the federal government and, as an indicator of the differential importance of governmental employment, the ratio of black to total percentages. When the latter statistic exceeds 1, proportionately more blacks than whites work in the public sector.

Percentage of blacks divided by percentage of total		
All government	*Federal*	*State and local*
1.61	1.48	1.65
1.96	2.33	1.52
1.88	2.30	1.27
1.95	2.14	1.70
1.99	2.33	1.96
1.24	1.44	0.94
1.89	2.03	1.78
1.58	1.69	1.54
1.54	1.48	1.57
1.06	1.47	1.01
1.01	2.50	0.98
1.09	1.94	1.07
1.34	1.71	1.42
1.29	1.90	1.05
1.95	2.00	2.00
1.88	1.93	1.35
1.32	1.61	1.19
1.31	2.05	1.24
2.12	2.17	2.94
1.28	1.97	1.24
1.96	1.82	1.65

The figures show clearly that high-level black workers are more likely to be governmental employees than high-level whites. In 1970 nearly half of black male and two-thirds of black female professionals worked for governments compared with less than one-third and just one-half of all male and female professionals, respectively. Among managers, black men were twice as likely as all male managers to be governmental employees. In more detailed occupations, the story is similar, with blacks concentrated in the public sector, especially in federal jobs: roughly 1 in 3 black male accountants and auditors, engineers, computer specialists held government jobs compared with proportionately half as many white men in these fields. Black lawyers and personnel and labor relations experts are also exceptionally likely to work for governments. In nearly every case, moreover, the proportion of high-level blacks employed by the federal government is relatively greater than the proportion in state and local governments.

Table 54 shows that among college graduates over one-half of black men with four or more years of college were governmental workers in 1970 compared with just 27 percent of white

TABLE 55
Employment of blacks as managers: public administration (except education) versus other industries, by state, 1970

| States | Percentage of managers who are black* | | | | |
	Total government (1)	Federal (2)	State (3)	Local (4)	Private (5)
Southern and Border					
Alabama	3.6	6.7	3.4	5.0	2.7
Louisiana	5.7	4.0	4.1	8.4	3.1
South Carolina	3.7	4.5	2.3	3.9	2.7
Virginia	3.0	2.1	3.9	4.5	2.2
West Virginia	1.8	1.8	1.6	4.0	0.9
Missouri	4.0	5.3	1.3	4.3	1.4
Northern					
California	4.0	4.9	2.8	3.8	1.5
Connecticut	3.8	3.8	3.8	3.7	0.9
Illinois	7.6	7.6	5.4	9.1	2.4
New York	7.4	7.6	4.7	8.7	3.0
Ohio	7.2	7.7	4.8	8.3	1.4

*All data for governments exclude educational services.
SOURCE: U.S. Bureau of the Census (1972a, table 171).

males while 72 percent of black female graduates were in governmental employment compared with 56 percent of white female graduates. Additional census data on the occupation of graduates by class of worker show, further, that black college men were relatively more likely to obtain managerial positions in the government than in the private sector. In 1970, 14 percent of black male graduates working for governments held managerial jobs, about the same as the proportion of white graduates (15 percent); by contrast, only 13 percent of black college men were managers in the economy as a whole compared with 20 percent of white college men. If, as seems reasonable, the upswing in black managerial employment in the early 1970s was concentrated in private companies, however, this differential may have diminished greatly.

To see whether the concentration of high-level black workers in the governmental sector is a national phenomenon or one limited to certain geographic areas, such as Washington, D.C., or northern states, I compare the black proportion of public and private managers in selected states in 1970 in Table 55. Because of the special situation of black school administrators in previ-

	Ratios	
All employers (6)	(1)/(5)	(2)/(5)
3.5	1.03	1.91
4.3	1.33	0.93
3.8	0.97	1.18
3.0	1.00	0.70
1.1	1.69	1.64
1.8	2.22	2.94
1.8	2.22	2.72
1.2	3.17	3.17
2.9	2.62	2.62
3.4	2.18	2.24
2.1	3.43	3.67

ously segregated southern schools, administrators are deleted from the computations and dealt with separately in Chapter 7. The overrepresentation of highly qualified blacks in governmental positions in the new market appears, according to the table, to be quite widespread, although of differing intensity among the states. Even in Alabama, blacks constitute a markedly larger proportion of government than of private sector managers, by 33 percent more overall and nearly 100 percent in federal employment. While the direction of the differences in employment is the same in the South as in the North, however, there is evidently a much stronger concentration of black managers in the public sector in northern states: differences in the ratio of governmental to private shares of managers on the order of 3 or 4 to 1—a pattern which, on the basis of findings later in this chapter, may result from past differences in relative black voting power among the states.

The income as well as relative number of highly qualified blacks in public employment appears to have exceeded that in private employment in the new market. First, as Table 56 shows, in 1970 black male managers, professionals, and college graduates working for the government tended to earn considerably more relative to whites than those in all industries. Black managers employed by the government, for example, had 25 percent higher earnings than all black managers while white governmental managers had about the same pay as all white managers. Similarly, black college graduates in the public sector earned more while white graduates earned less than their private sector peers. Among the young (25- to 34-year-olds),

TABLE 56
Income of federal,
total government,
and all industry
male workers,
by race, 1970

Income		Government			Federal government	
		Black	Total	Ratio	Black	Total
Total men						
1.	Managerial	$9,377	$10,925	0.86	$9,205	$11,520
2.	Professional	8,043	9,710	0.83	8,979	12,110
3.	College graduates	9,045	10,694	0.85	*	*
Young men						
4.	Managers	8,367	9,602	0.87	*	*
5.	Professional	7,603	8,732	0.87	*	*

*Not available.

SOURCE: U.S. Bureau of the Census (1973*e*, tables 10,11; 1973*c*, tables 16, 17; 1973*b*, table 7).

whose position in private employment improved greatly in the new market, some of the differences between relative black public and private standing were attenuated, with the ratios of professional and managerial incomes differing much less by sectors than among older workers: differences in ratios of 4 and 5 compared with 18 and 9 percentage points. Second, tabulations of the income of male college graduates from U.S. Civil Service Commission data for 1974 show black graduates earning $16,593 and whites $18,593 in federal jobs, which gives a black-white income ratio of 0.89, much above the economy-wide average income ratio for college graduates of 0.69 in 1973 (Eccles, 1975). Third, estimates of the impact of public employment on black and white incomes using National Longitudinal Survey data for 1966 and 1969 show that, with diverse other income determinants held fixed (including family background, years of schooling, regional location, area of birth, years of experience), black but not white public employees earn more than their privately employed peers. According to line 1 in Table 57, in 1969 all black male governmental workers earned a 14 percent premium, while whites earned 4 percent less than comparable workers in other sectors of the economy. In 1966, a similar pattern is observed, a 13 percent black advantage from governmental jobs and a 1 percent white disadvantage. Decomposed by type of governmental job in line 2, the relatively higher earnings of black government workers are found largely in federal public administration, postal services, and education, with blacks doing about the same, relative to their peers, as whites in other areas of public employment. As the regres-

| Ratio | All industry | | Ratio |
	Black	Total	
0.80	$7,502	$11,021	0.68
0.74	7,851	10,617	0.74
*	8,832	11,945	0.74
*	8,035	9,842	0.82
*	8,023	9,664	0.83

TABLE 57 *Estimates of the effect on income of governmental employment, by type, on black and white 45- to 49-year-old men in 1966 and 1969*

Equation	Variable	1966		1969	
		Black	*White*	*Black*	*White*
1	All government	.13	−.01	.14	−.04
		(.07)	(.04)	(.05)	(.03)
2	By type				
	Postal	.27	−.08	.25	−.02
		(.18)	(.14)	(.15)	(.11)
	Federal administration	.40	.20	.32	.06
		(.18)	(.09)	(.16)	(.07)
	State administration	−.12	−.10	−.01	−.06
		(.42)	(.14)	(.33)	(.12)
	Local administration	.12	−.02	−.02	−.00
		(.20)	(.11)	(.17)	(.09)
	Education	.15	−.10	.21	−.13
		(.15)	(.09)	(.12)	(.07)
	Other	.03	−.05	.08	−.06
		(.09)	(.07)	(.08)	(.05)

NOTE: All regressions include measures for parental occupation, region, and size of residence of birth, region of employment, years of experience and schooling; numbers in parentheses are standard errors.

SOURCE: Calculations from the National Longitudinal Survey. See Chapter 4 for discussion of the survey.

sion coefficients for the two years are quite similar, moreover, the income advantage to individuals of governmental employment appears to have been maintained throughout the 1966–1969 period.

The finding that blacks fared relatively better in public than in private jobs in the new market does not, of course, mean that there was no governmental discrimination against blacks. Rather, it shows that governmental discrimination was relatively less, so that public demand for black workers exceeded private demand, not that it equalized or exceeded demand for white workers. Since, on average, highly qualified black men working for governments continued to earn less than whites, there remained some discriminatory differential to be made up in the 1970s.

CHANGES IN PUBLIC EMPLOYMENT PATTERNS Did the economic position of black workers in the public sector improve in the new market, contributing to the overall black economic advance or were blacks as well off in governmental jobs in previous years?

With respect to employment, there appears to have been a sizeable increase in the proportion of blacks in governmental jobs throughout the 1950s and 1960s, giving an upward impetus to the market. In 1950, 8.3 percent of male governmental workers were black compared with 8.7 percent of all male workers; in 1960, black men constituted 9.8 percent of governmental workers and 8.4 percent of all workers; by 1970, the black share of governmental workers had risen to 11.4 percent, which suggests a large increase in relative demand.[1] Among women, the growth of black public employment is even more striking: in 1950 only 8.6 percent of women in the public sector were black compared with 12 percent of all female employees; in 1960, 10.6 percent of public and 11.6 percent of all women workers were black; in the sixties, however, the number working for governments increased to the extent that 14.3 percent of publicly employed women were black compared with 11.4 percent of all female employees (U.S. Bureau of the Census, 1955, table 13; 1967, table 25; 1973*i*, table 47). In short, at the outset of the 1950s black men and women were underrepresented in the public sector; at the outset of the 1970s, they were substantially overrepresented.

In professional and managerial occupations, however, the pattern of change in employment is somewhat different. In the 1950s, as Table 58 indicates, the proportion of black men working for the government increased sharply in most professions while the comparable white proportions were relatively stable. Between 1950 and 1960, for example, the public share of black accountants rose from 32.5 to 40.5 percent, the share of lawyers and judges from 8.3 to 20.9 percent, and so forth. By contrast, in the 1960s, the governmental share of highly qualified black workers changed differentially, rising among lawyers and health technologists and falling sharply in personnel and labor relations and accounting, with the consequence that the public share of all black professionals increased only slightly, by about as much as the public share of all professional men. However, there was an extraordinary change in the 1960–1970 decade in public employment of black managers, with the governments'

---

[1] The shift in employment is no more than suggestive of changes in demand because the changes could reflect changes in supply as well. If, however, the relative supply of blacks to the public sector was unchanged, the growth of public employment would presumably be due to increased demand.

TABLE 58 *Changes in the proportion of black (nonwhite) male professionals, managers, and college graduates employed by the government, 1950–1970*

Occupation	Proportion of black/nonwhite men in governmental sector			Proportion of all men in governmental sector		
	Nonwhite 1950	Nonwhite 1960	Black 1970*	1950	1960	1970
Professionals	33.7	47.1	49.0	24.5	27.0	29.9
Accountants	32.5	40.5	34.1	14.3	15.6	16.2
Engineers	58.3	34.7	34.2	18.7	16.9	15.2
Lawyers and judges	8.3	20.9	36.8	13.6	14.4	18.3
Chemists	25.6	28.4	31.9	12.2	12.3	15.7
Personnel and labor relation workers	60.0	76.9	45.3	31.6	28.9	25.1
Physicians	15.0	22.1	21.6	13.1	13.8	15.2
Technicians, sciences, and engineering	†	30.8	27.2	†	19.2	18.2
Technicians, health	†	38.0	44.6	†	28.8	35.2
Managers	3.9	8.9	24.6	6.2	7.5	12.0
College graduates	†	50.0	51.0	†	23.3	27.1

*1970 figures differ slightly from those in Table 54, due to differences in the census figures in different volumes, presumably the result of sampling procedures.
†Not available.
SOURCE: U.S. Bureau of the Census (1956, tables 12, 13; 1963*b*, tables 21, 22; 1973*c*, tables 43, 44; 1967, table 20).

share of these workers roughly tripling. This suggests that increased public demand was a key factor in the improved market for black managers, which was one of the most dramatic market developments in the period.

Civil service data on the number of blacks in jobs with high governmental grades, measured by the General Schedule (GS) or Postal Force System (PFS) classifications,[2] also show a significant improvement in the black position in the new market. As Table 59 shows, the proportion of persons in GS categories 12 or better and PFS categories 10 or better shot up in the early 1970s, after rising moderately in the 1965–1970 period. Between 1970 and 1973 the black share of GS 12–15 employment rose from 1.7 to 3.3 percent; the share of GS 16–18 jobs advanced from 1.3 to 2.5 percent; the share of PFS 10–16 and 17–19 employment

[2]GS and PFS classifications are governmental wage and job classification systems for the federal white-collar bureaucracy and postal workers, respectively. The higher GS or PFS jobs are the higher paying.

increased greatly, as did the black share of PFS 20 and above jobs. While the absolute number of persons in many of these categories is small, for the first time in history blacks reached the top of the civil service hierarchy, presumably as a result of changed employment policies.

Salary data from U.S. Civil Service Commission employment records files provide a measure of the impact of improved job classifications on the position of black college men. In 1965, black male graduates earned $7,848 in federal employment, in 1974, $16,593—a gain of 111 percent, which far exceeds the comparable increase in income (78 percent) of white male graduates in the civil service (Eccles, 1975).

Finally, at the state and local level, Table 60 shows clearly that black employment in two "good" jobs for which data are available in 1960 and 1970—police and management—rose sharply in the period, albeit from extremely low levels. The gains are especially large in several southern states, such as Alabama where the black share of police jumped from 0.6 to 5.3 percent, Arkansas from 0.0 to 5.6 percent, and Georgia from 1.4

TABLE 59 *Changes in black employment and income in federal jobs, by civil service classification and agency, 1965–1973*

	Percent black				Numbers of blacks
	1965	*1967*	*1970*	*1973*	*1973*
General schedule	9.5	10.5	11.1	12.2	162,203
1–4	19.3	20.5	22.2	21.9	69,051
5–8	9.6	11.6	13.9	16.2	62,585
9–11	3.4	4.3	5.3	6.5	20,339
12–15	1.3	1.8	1.7	3.3	10,087
16–18	1.0	1.3	1.3	2.5	141
Postal System	15.7	18.9	19.5	19.5	130,413
1–5	17.1	21.6	20.6	20.4	114,005
6–9	9.3	5.0	14.9	24.9	22,225
10–16	1.8	2.9	4.7	9.6	4,155
17–19	2.8	2.8	2.4	4.8	693
20–29	0.0	0.0	2.3	4.6	329
30–42				10.5	6
All pay plans	13.5	14.9	15.2	15.7	395,409

SOURCE: U.S. Department of Commerce (1970, p. 58; 1974, p. 58).

TABLE 60 *Increased employment of black men in "good public jobs," southern and border states and selected other states, 1960–1970*

	Black percentage of male workers					
	Total		Police		Managers in public administration	
States	1960 (1)	1970 (2)	1960 (3)	1970 (4)	1960 (5)	1970 (6)
Southern and border						
Alabama	22.3	19.7	0.6	5.3	0.5	2.8
Arkansas	16.5	12.4	0.0	5.6	0.3	2.1
Delaware	11.9	10.6	3.6	3.3	0.0	6.3
Florida	17.1	13.2	4.4	5.2	0.7	2.4
Georgia	23.6	20.2	1.4	8.2	0.7	4.5
Kentucky	6.1	5.6	2.0	2.8	1.2	2.0
Louisiana	24.9	22.0	1.9	7.8	0.5	3.3
Maryland	14.0	20.8	3.0	9.6	2.9	5.1
Mississippi	35.1	26.6	0.9	8.7	0.7	2.4
Missouri	7.0	7.5	1.6	6.8	1.9	3.7
North Carolina	19.9	17.2	3.0	6.1	1.2	4.3
Oklahoma	4.4	4.1	3.0	2.8	0.3	1.9
South Carolina	28.7	24.0	1.8	8.0	0.4	3.6
Tennessee	13.6	11.8	1.6	7.4	1.2	2.9
Texas	10.3	9.9	1.3	3.0	0.1	1.8
Virginia	18.2	15.7	1.6	4.2	1.2	2.2
West Virginia	3.6	2.7	0.5	2.7	0.6	1.2
Other						
California	4.5	5.3	2.1	3.7	1.4	3.7
Connecticut	3.6	4.7	2.0	2.9	1.7	3.4
Illinois	7.9	9.6	7.8	11.8	2.7	7.4
New York	7.1	9.3	5.2	7.8	3.1	5.8
Ohio	6.6	7.2	3.8	8.3	2.2	7.3

SOURCE: U.S. Bureau of the Census (1963*d*, table 122; 1972*a*, table 173).

percent to 8.2 percent. Gains in the black share of managerial jobs in the South are smaller but still sizeable—from 0.5 to 2.8 percent of managers in state and local public administration in Alabama, from 0.5 percent to 3.3 percent in Louisiana, and so forth. A similar though less marked pattern of black gain in police and public administration management is evinced in the North. The black share of police rises from .078 to .118 in Illinois and from .058 to .078 in New York in the 1960s. With the black share of all male workers falling in the South and rising only moderately in the North, black representation in "good public jobs" obviously increased in comparison to the available black population.

In sum, governments employed more black workers in better jobs in the 1960s than in the past, thereby contributing directly to the development of the new market.

PUBLIC EMPLOYMENT AND BLACK VOTING What caused the increased employment of black workers in the public sector in the 1960s? At the federal level the growth of demand for black workers is presumably due at least in part to equal opportunity policies which began with Executive Order 11246. The nondiscrimination requirements of the order, which require affirmative action programs, cover all employees and applicants for jobs in the executive branch and those in the competitive service of the legislative and judicial branches. Overall supervision and leadership in the federal nondiscrimination program is the responsibility of the Civil Service Commission, which has developed detailed regulations regarding equal opportunity. Agencies, however, conduct their own equal opportunity programs. By law, these programs involve, among other things, establishment of equal opportunity offices, collection of data on personnel, development of an affirmative action plan, and establishment of procedures to handle complaints. Each year agencies present a plan which assesses the stature of equal employment opportunity within their work force, identifies problems, and sets out "goals and timetables" for necessary improvements. All aspects of agency EEO programs must adhere to the rules of the civil service and the merit system. The Office of Federal Equal Employment Opportunity of the Civil Service Commission evaluates annual plans and agency performance.

Since employment decisions are made at the agency level, there are in effect many different government employers, who have developed different approaches to affirmative action. Some agencies have had large increases in black college graduate employment; others have had relatively small increases. Doctorate research studies at Harvard and the University of

Chicago will illuminate these and other differences in the mechanisms of improving the black position in federal agencies and determine in great detail the EEO impact on numbers hired, promotion patterns, and the overall economic standing of highly educated and other black civil servants (Eccles, 1975; Campbell, 1975).

State and Local Demand

Because national antidiscriminatory regulations were not applicable to state and local governments until 1972, very different forces appear to underlie the improvement in the position of black public employees in the 1960s. I argue in this section that much of the increase in demand at the state and local level can be attributed to increases in black political power due to the growth of the black share of the electorates and thus in part to the Voting Rights Act of 1965 and related federal efforts to guarantee blacks the suffrage in the South. The apparent role of the Voting Act in raising demand for black public employees highlights the fact that EEOC activities were only part of the governmental antidiscriminatory activities that transformed the job market in the late sixties and early seventies.

Change in Black Voting

Black political power, which can be roughly measured by the relative number of black voters,[3] increased in the post-World War II period for two basic reasons.

First, blacks migrated from the 11 southern states where they had been disfranchised to the North. In 1940, just 15 percent of blacks of voting age resided in the North; in 1970, 49 percent were citizens of northern states, which by itself more than tripled the potential number of black voters (U.S. Bureau of the Census, 1940, 1970). The movement North also, it can be argued, created pressures on Congress and the executive branch to act to reduce voting discrimination in the South (Freeman, forthcoming).

[3] The hypothesis that political power is, more or less, proportionate or at least a monotonic function of relative numbers of voters is not innocuous. If blacks and whites formed uniform groups opposed to one another, the measure of power would be which group had 50 percent or more. More broadly, according to the Riker (1962) minimum winning coalition argument, the number of voters might not matter unless it contributed to forming the winning coalition. Depending on circumstances, a small minority might be better than a large minority. I believe, however, that because groups differ in many dimensions of interest, logrolling leads to a monotonic relation. The empirical results in this and Chapter 7 support this argument.

Second, the disfranchisement of blacks in the South underwent an increasingly powerful and ultimately successful attack by the courts, Congress, and the executive branch of the national government. The first blow against traditional modes of disfranchisement was the 1944 Supreme Court decision that eliminated the "white primary" which had restricted voting privileges to whites in Democratic party primaries (*Smith v. Allwright*, 1944). Then the Twenty-fourth Amendment to the Constitution made poll taxes illegal in federal elections. In the mid-fifties and sixties, Congress attacked discriminatory voting practices with three acts. The Civil Rights Act of 1957 set up a commission to protect individuals from interference with constitutional rights, such as voting, by private persons; empowered the U.S. Attorney General to undertake civil actions in voting cases; and gave federal courts jurisdiction without the complainants' having exhausted state remedies. The Civil Rights Act of 1960 gave the Attorney General the power to examine voting records and allowed courts to appoint referees to register voters in areas deemed discriminatory. The 1964 Civil Rights Act strengthened the various provisions of the 1960 Act. Under these laws, the Department of Justice brought suits against three states (Alabama, Louisiana, Mississippi) and against voter registration officials in about 50 southern counties. Finally, in 1965 Congress passed the Voting Rights Act which was expressly designed to remove remaining barriers to the suffrage from states or districts where less than 50 percent of blacks were registered in 1964, presumably as a result of discrimination. This act suspended literacy tests and other qualification requirements in elections; provided for the assignment of federal examiners to register voters and poll watchers to observe voting and the counting of ballots in the states of Alabama, Arkansas, Georgia, Louisiana, Mississippi, South Carolina, Virginia, at least 26 counties in North Carolina, and one in Arizona. In 1970 the act, which had been given a five-year life-span, was extended to 1975.

The impact of the growth of the black population in the North and refranchisement in the South on the size of the black electorate is examined in Table 61, which displays the black proportion of persons of voting age and of registered voters in 1960 and in 1970. The number of registered blacks and whites in southern states is estimated by multiplying the number of

TABLE 61 *Black registered voters, by state, 1960–1970*

States	1960 Percentage black of voting age	1960 Percentage black of registered voters	1970 Percentage black of voting age	1970 Percentage black of registered voters
Southern				
Mississippi	35.5	4.3	30.3	27.3
Louisiana	28.2	13.7	26.0	20.7
South Carolina	29.2	9.0	25.4	23.3
Georgia	24.5	14.4	22.7	19.0
Alabama	26.0	7.0	22.1	18.1
North Carolina	20.8	10.1	8.7	12.4
Virginia	18.5	10.2	16.2	14.7
Arkansas	18.2	12.2	14.7	16.1
Tennessee	14.8	12.4	13.4	12.4
Florida	14.7	8.9	11.9	10.2
Texas	11.5	9.8	11.0	12.7
Selected northern				
Illinois	9.3	8.6	11.0	10.2
New York	8.1	7.5	10.7	9.9
Michigan	8.7	8.1	10.2	9.5
New Jersey	7.7	7.1	9.1	8.5
Missouri	8.1	7.5	8.7	8.1
Ohio	7.6	7.0	8.2	7.6
California	4.2	4.0	6.1	5.7
Indiana	5.3	4.9	6.0	5.5
Connecticut	3.8	3.7	5.0	4.6
Massachusetts	2.0	1.9	2.6	2.4
Wisconsin	1.6	1.5	2.3	2.2
Oregon	0.9	0.9	1.0	1.0
Iowa	0.8	0.8	0.9	0.9
Maine	0.3	0.3	0.2	0.2

NOTE: Percentage of registered obtained by multiplying numbers of voting age by proportion registered in state for southern states and dividing black by the total. Individual state data used for southern states; northern and western average for other states.

SOURCE: U.S. Bureau of Census (1973*h*, tables 614, 610; 1972*b*, table 92).

voting age (U.S. Bureau of the Census, 1973*h*, table 614) by the proportion registered in each state (ibid., table 610) for the southern states and, in the absence of registration percentages by state for other states by the national nonsouthern average percent registered in 1966 (ibid., 1972*b*, table 92).[4]

The table reveals a sizeable gain in the black share of voters, notably in the South. Between 1960 and 1970 the black share of the electorate jumped from 9 percent to 23 percent in South Carolina, and from 4 percent to 17 percent in Alabama, despite declines in the relative number of blacks of voting age. In the North, there was a much smaller but still noticeable increase in the black share of the electorate. By 1970 blacks made up an especially large share, though by no means a majority, of the electorate in the traditionally discriminatory southern states and a large share of voters in the major industrial states of the North.

One consequence of the growth in black voters was a sharp increase in the number of blacks elected to public office. In 1962, there were just 4 blacks in Congress and 52 in state legislatures (U.S. Bureau of the Census, 1971, table 117). In 1968, the first year for which data are available for all elected officials, there were 1,125 blacks elected to office (ibid.). By 1974, 2,991 blacks were in public office, over half (1,609) in the south. There were 17 blacks in the Congress and 239 in state legislatures (ibid., Census, 1974, table 88). In addition to changing the racial composition of elected officials, the growth of the black share of voting also "altered" the attitude of southern white politicians. Previously extreme segregationists began campaigning for black voters, employing blacks as campaign aides, as legislative assistants, and so forth.

VOTING AND PUBLIC EMPLOYMENT To see whether or not the growth of the black electorate raised demand for black public employees (as well as politicians), I have calculated regression equations linking employment to the

---

[4]More precisely for the southern states in which the proportion of blacks and whites registered is available (table 610), I multiplied the estimated population of voting age (table 614), by race, to obtain black and white voters. For other states, I multiplied the number of white voters by 0.75, the proportion of whites outside the South who reported voting in 1966 and the number of blacks by 0.69, the comparable figure for blacks, with data from U.S. Bureau of the Census (1972*b*, table 92).

ratio of black to white voters and other variables using data on states for 1960 and 1970 pooled into a single sample. Because data for both years are available only for public administration, the regressions refer to that portion of governmental employment rather than the total. The equations are "reduced form" estimates of the impact of voting power, linking the voting variable and other demand and supply factors to the standing of blacks in the public sector. The major dependent variable is the relative number of blacks employed in total, state and local, and federal nonpostal public administration. Relative demand for black public employees is expected to depend on the black share of the eligible voters, estimated as described earlier;[5] the percentage of voters who supported Governor Wallace in the 1968 Presidential election, which is supposed to reflect discriminatory attitudes that will reduce demand for black workers; and a regional dummy variable for southern and border states, which have traditionally discriminated most against blacks. Lagged dependent variables are entered into several calculations because of the adjustment time needed to alter relative employment patterns. The relative supply of black workers is taken to depend on the black share of all employees in each state and black and white median years of school completed, which will affect supply because public administration tends to employ relatively educated workers. Median years is entered separately for blacks and whites in the regression because I expect the educational attainment of blacks to be a more critical determinant of relative supply than that of whites, large numbers of whom have enough schooling to qualify for white-collar jobs in public administration. In all the pooled regressions, a dummy variable for 1960 is also entered to pick up any unmeasured changes in demand or supply which alter the level of employment between the periods. Finally, unless otherwise stated, all variables are in logarithmic form, making parameter estimates elasticities.

The basic regression results, given in Table 62, provide strong support for the hypothesized impact of black voting power on demand for black workers in public administration.

[5]The share of eligible voters is not necessarily the best measure of black voting power, which could depend on other factors as well, ranging from divisions in the white community to cohesiveness of blacks to political leadership. The share is, however, the best quantitative measure currently available.

In line 1, the black share of voters is estimated to increase total employment in public administration with an elasticity of 0.61; the Wallace vote and Southern and border state dummies are given their expected negative coefficients; relative supply has a positive impact. In line 2, which includes the education of the groups, the coefficient on voting falls to a lower but still significant number. Black years of schooling has a sizeable positive impact on employment while white years has a modest negative impact. When the lagged dependent variable is entered into line 3, the share of all workers is considerably weakened, while the size of the voting coefficient is reduced to 0.35—still over four times its standard error. In this case, the short-run elasticity of employment to voting power is 0.35; the "long run" elasticity is 0.83 by the standard partial adjustment model.[6]

Lines 4 through 7 of the table decompose the number of workers in public administration into those in state and local employment and those in federal nonpostal public administration. Because voters in a state are likely to have a greater impact on state and local than on national decisions, I expect larger impacts for the voting variable in these regressions. The results support this expectation and provide additional evidence in favor of the hypothesized relation between voting power and employment. In line 4, the coefficient on the share of voters suggests that a 10 percent increase raises black public employment by 5 percent; in line 5 the estimated impact is 0.45 in the short run and 0.90 in the long run. The corresponding coefficients on federal nonpostal public administration are smaller, with a short-run impact of 0.23 and a longer-run effect of 0.51 (line 7).

Turning to the other variables in the equation, they yield reasonable coefficients, though the estimated impact of discriminatory feeling embodied in the Wallace vote is rather weak. The dummy for 1960 also is generally insignificant, suggesting no autonomous change in the black share of public workers, while the southern-border region dummy has a substantial negative effect, presumably the result of the discriminatory past and greater discrimination in the present. All told, while the calculations suffer from too many weaknesses in

[6] In this model the long-run elasticity is obtained by dwindling the parameter on the variable of concern (0.35) by one minus the parameter on the lagged dependent variable $(1 - 0.58 = 0.42)$.

TABLE 62
Regression
estimates of the
effect of the black
share of voters on
relative employment
of blacks in public
administration
1960 and 1970

Group	Constant	Share of all workers	Share of voters	Southern and border region	Time 1960
Total public administration					
Equation 1	.04	.35 (.13)	.61 (.13)	−.49 (.12)	−.10 (.08)
Equation 2	−.56	.55 (.12)	.51 (.11)	−.34 (.11)	.05 (.10)
Equation 3	−.16	.11 (.10)	.35 (.08)	−.22 (.08)	.06 (.07)
State and local public administration					
Equation 4	−1.06	.54 (.12)	.50 (.12)	−.25 (.12)	−.01 (.10)
Equation 5	−.91	.12 (.12)	.45 (.09)	−.12 (.01)	.05 (.08)
Federal nonpostal					
Equation 6	−.20	.62 (.15)	.43 (.14)	−.44 (.14)	.03 (.12)
Equation 7	.29	.23 (.13)	.24 (.12)	−.31 (.13)	.01 (.10)

*Standard error of estimate.

NOTE: The dependent variable is the log of the ratio of black to total workers in public administration. Numbers in parentheses are standard errors of estimates. All variables except dummies are in log form. Shares of workers relate to men and women. 1968 Wallace vote is the same in 1960 and 1970 in the states as it is a "structural" factor supposed to reflect discriminatory attributes.

Based on data for 37 states (omitting Hawaii, Alaska, Delaware, Idaho, Maine, Missouri, Montana, Nevada, New Hampshire, North Dakota, South Dakota, Rhode Island, Vermont, Utah, and Wyoming because they have too few blacks).

SOURCES: Data on public administration workers, U.S. Bureau of the Census (1963*d*, table 129; 1972*a*, table 186). Data on share of voters, U.S. Bureau of the Census (1973*h*, tables 610, 614; 1972*b*, table 92). Data on percent Wallace vote, U.S. Bureau of the Census (1971*a*, table 550). Data on median years of education, U.S. Bureau of the Census (1972*e*, table 156; 1964*c*, table 115).

specification and measurement to be viewed as "conclusive," they tend to support the argument of this book.

Changes 1960–
1970

Further tests of the impact of black voting on relative employment are given in Table 63, which treats changes in variables from 1960 to 1970 rather than levels of variables in a pooled cross section. This has the desirable feature of "holding fixed" omitted factors specific to each state which may be correlated

Percent Wallace vote	Median years of education		Lagged share of public workers	R^2	SEE*
	Black	White			
−.09 (.05)				.87	.337
−.01 (.05)	.021 (.004)	−.009 (.005)		.91	.287
−.06 (.03)	.007 (.003)	−.002 (.004)	.58 (.07)	.96	.200
−.06 (.05)	.013 (.004)	−.003 (.005)		.91	.294
−.07 (.04)	.007 (.003)	.003 (.004)	.49 (.08)	.94	.235
.01 (.06)	.021 (.005)	−.012 (.006)		.85	.363
−.07 (.05)	.005 (.005)	−.004 (.005)	.55 (.09)	.91	.287

with the dependent and explanatory variables and may produce spurious correlation at the expense of treating all cross-state differences in the level of black public employment as reflecting factors beyond the purview of analysis. By estimating both pooled cross-section and changed cross-section models, we are able to check the "robustness" of findings to the precise econometric specification.

The calculations in the table link 1960–1970 changes in the

TABLE 63
Regression
estimates of the
effect of black
voting on 1960s
changes in the
black share of
public
administration
workers

Equation number	Group	Constant	Changed share of:		Lagged share of:
			Workers	Voters	Voters
1	Total public administration	0.41	0.28 (0.10)	0.19 (0.07)	0.34 (0.07)
2	State and local	0.33	0.33 (0.20)	0.17 (0.13)	0.43 (0.11)
3	Federal	0.26	0.12 (0.13)	0.23 (0.09)	0.41 (0.09)

*Standard error of estimate.

NOTE: Dependent variable is the change in the logarithm of the ratio of black to all public administration workers. Numbers in parentheses are standard errors of estimate.

SOURCE: See Table 62.

logarithm of the black share of total employment (line 1), state and local employment (line 2), and federal employment (line 3) in public administration to: changes in the relative supply of blacks; the South and border state dummy; changes in the black share of the electorate and two lagged variables; the black share of public employment in 1960; and the black share of the electorate in 1960. Relative public employment in 1960 is expected to obtain a negative coefficient reflecting "abnormally" high or low 1960 figures which results in regression to the means, or alternatively the legacy of the past in the context of a partial adjustment model. With the dependent variable in change form, the coefficient on lagged public employment provides an estimate of the adjustment parameter. The black share of voters in 1960 is entered in the computations on the hypothesis that public employment had not yet adjusted to black political power in 1960, so that 1960 voting strength would enhance the growth of employment. Since the regressions contain the 1960 share of voters in two places, with a negative coefficient in the change in voting variable and a positive coefficient in the 1960 level variable, if the sum of the two is positive, one can interpret the results as showing that changes in public employment depend on a weighted average of the 1960 and 1970 vote shares, presumably indicative of overall black political power in the decade in which employment decisions were being made.[7]

[7] That is, I have X_0 and $X_1 - X_0$ as right-hand variables, where X_0 refers to 1960 voting power and X_1 to 1970 voting power. Then, regression equation $Y = aX_0 + b(X_1 - X_0)$ can be rearranged to $Y = (a - b)X_0 + bX_1$.

blic administration *rkers*	*Southern and border states*	R^2	*SEE**
−0.30 (0.06)	−0.10 (0.07)	0.51	0.122
− 0.44 (0.10)	−0.14 (0.13)	0.42	0.057
−0.38 (0.08)	−0.03 (0.09)	0.48	0.162

Whatever the precise model used to interpret the regressions, the results in Table 63 provide strong confirmation of the impact of black voting power on public employment. In line 1, both changes in the black share of registered voters and the 1960 share have significant positive coefficients: treated as two separate variables, the 1970 share has a coefficient of .19; the 1960 share has a coefficient of .15 (.34 − .19), indicating that the 1970 and 1960 fractions of voters had roughly similar impacts on the changes in the black share of state and local public administration employment. In lines 2 and 3, on the other hand, the 1960 voting variable is more important, suggesting a more sluggish response to the growth of black voting over the period. In all cases, the lagged share of public employment has a coefficient of about 0.30–0.40, which also suggests a relatively slow movement toward equilibrium in the context of the lagged adjustment model. From the perspective of this chapter, however, the important result relates not to the specific features of the computation but to the fact that the cross-sectional change specification supports the finding that black voting power was a major element in the demand for black workers by state and local governments and even by the federal government in states.

CONCLUSION Public employers, particularly the federal government, were especially good employers of highly qualified blacks in the new market, employing an exceptionally large share of black professionals, managers, and college graduates in general, and offering relatively better pay and occupational positions than private employers. In the 1960s and early 1970s, the position of blacks in public employment improved, contributing directly to the development of the new market. At the federal level, federal equal opportunity activities are the likely factor behind the improvement; at the state and local level, the principal forces appear to have been the growth of black voting power, which resulted from the 1965 Voting Rights Act, selected antidiscriminatory voting laws and activities, and the growing concentration of blacks in the North.

7. Desegregation, Political Power, and Employment of Black Schoolteachers

Largely because of segregated schooling in the South, teaching has traditionally been the major occupation of highly qualified black Americans, accounting in 1950 for nearly half of black professional workers, compared with less than one quarter of white professionals (U.S. Bureau of the Census, 1956, table 3). In the 1960s and to a lesser extent in the fifties as well the institutional and market forces that made teaching so important underwent substantial change: de jure segregation in schooling, outlawed by the Supreme Court in 1954, came to an end in the late 1960s (Southern Educational Reporting Service, 1967); southern blacks were effectively refranchised by various voting rights bills, culminating in the 1965 Voting Rights Act; the proportion of blacks in northern cities rose, and industrial and nonacademic governmental demand for black college graduates increased markedly after the 1964 Civil Rights Act. What effect did these diverse developments have on the market for black school teachers? Did desegregation substantially reduce demand, as the standard theory of discrimination would suggest?[1] Did refranchisement and increased black political power in the North increase demand, as might be expected if black political resources were spent on obtaining additional black teachers?

In this chapter cross-state data for 1950, 1960, and 1970 are used to analyze the impact of post-World War II civil rights developments on the market for black schoolteachers. The principal finding is that demand for black schoolteachers was main-

[1] According to the standard theory, because whites have discriminatory tastes from associating with blacks, they will seek to segregate blacks. Segregation of professional services and jobs like teaching will raise demand for blacks in segregated activities. Desegregation will reduce demand. See Becker (1971, pp. 56–58) and Colberg (1965, pp. 55–73).

tained in the 1960s. The demand-reducing effects of desegregation were offset in part by the demand-increasing effects of increased black voting power. In the South, where segregation had created an especially favorable market for black teachers, some teachers and many principals were displaced, but the potentially disastrous effects of desegregation on teacher employment—predicted, for example, by Colberg (1965, p. 72)—did not occur. In the North, demand increased greatly. Since blacks were a minority in all states save the District of Columbia, the apparent effect of their share of the electorate on demand suggests that a group need not form a "minimum winning coalition" to exercise political influence. Presumably because of logrolling and the absence of majority groups with uniform interest, changes in a minority's share of the voting population lead to changes in its share of public "goods," such as teachers' employment.[2]

The chapter begins with a brief examination of cross-state and time-series patterns of black teacher employment and income in postwar years, the empirical phenomenon under study. Then I develop a supply-demand model of the teachers' labor market focusing on desegregation, political power, and other factors likely to shift demand for black schoolteachers. The model is estimated with pooled cross-state data from the 1960 and 1970 censuses.

ECONOMIC STATUS OF BLACK TEACHERS, 1950–1970

A broad overview of the changing market for black schoolteachers after World War II is given in Table 64, which records the number and salary of black and all teachers and relative numbers and salaries, by sex, from 1950 to 1970. The table shows that, despite desegregation of education, the economic position of black teachers did not deteriorate in the fifties or sixties. The black share of male teachers rose somewhat in the 1950–1960 decade and fell somewhat in the following decade, while the black share of female teachers moved in the opposite direction (line 1). As a result the proportion of all teachers who were

[2]By the "minimum winning coalition" argument of Riker (1962), a group must form 50 percent or more of the voting population to influence policy. If the group has less than 50 percent, it has no direct input into decisions. With groups divided by color, the black minority would have no say in decisions (as, for example, has been true of the Catholic minority in Northern Ireland in the 1970s). If, however, the white and black groups have divergent interests and if there is logrolling over issues, there will be no "grand winning coalition" and a minority can have an effect on specific issues.

TABLE 64   *Black teachers in the United States, 1950–1970*

	Male			Female		
	1950	*1960*	*1970*	*1950*	*1960*	*1970*
1. *Numbers of school teachers*						
Black	18,420	32,243	50,548	67,500	101,609	177,240
Total	287,910	441,925	819,243	774,180	1,205,514	1,966,040
Ratio of black to total	0.064	0.073	0.062	0.087	0.084	0.091
2. *Income of school teachers*						
*Black**	$2,477	$4,731	$7,777	$1,923	$3,599	$6,620*
Total	$3,465	$5,709	$8,711	$2,265	$4,122	$6,369
Ratio of black to total	0.71	0.83	0.89	0.85	0.87	1.04

*Incomes refer to previous year; 1950 and 1960 are for nonwhites.
SOURCE: U.S. Bureau of the Census (1956, tables 3, 20, 11; 1963*b*, tables 3, 25, 26; 1973*c*, tables 2, 16, 17).

black was virtually unchanged over the entire interval, standing at 8.1 percent in 1950 and 1960 and 8.2 percent in 1970. The income figures (line 2) tell a more positive story, revealing a significant improvement in the ratio of black to total teacher incomes among both men and women. Between 1949 and 1969, black male teachers improved their relative income position by 17 percentage points; black female teachers gained 19 percentage points until they had a 4 percent advantage over white female teachers in 1969.

The surprising stability in the ratio of black to total teachers and improvement in relative incomes are examined further in Table 65, which records the black share of teachers and pupils, ratios of teachers to pupil shares, and the ratio of black to white teacher incomes in selected states. These data indicate that the national employment pattern resulted from divergent and offsetting trends among states, with relative black teacher employment falling unevenly in the South, where it had traditionally been high, and rising in the North.[3] Columns (1) through (3)

[3] Despite the general maintenance of black teacher employment in southern and border states, there was a great decline in the employment of blacks as principals during the period of desegregation. When black and white schools were consolidated, the usual pattern was to retain white principals and administrators and to demote or dismiss their black counterparts. The result was the virtual elimination of black high school principals from many state school systems—a drop from 350 to 36 in Kentucky, from 134 to 14 in Arkansas, and so forth (U.S. Senate, 1971). By the time court and federal actions were initiated in the late 1960s–early 1970s to prevent further displacement of black school officials and endangered teachers as well, desegregation and consolidation of school districts had eliminated most black principals in the South.

Selected states	Shares of teachers and pupils					
	1950			1960		
	Teachers (1)	Pupils (2)	Ratio (1)/(2) (3)	Teachers (4)	Pupils (5)	Ratio (4)/(5) (6)
Southern and border						
Alabama	31.1	37.0	0.84	33.2	34.4	0.97
Louisiana	26.9	36.4	0.74	31.7	36.0	0.88
South Carolina	37.2	44.2	0.84	35.0	41.1	0.85
Virginia	21.7	24.9	0.87	20.7	22.6	0.91
Kentucky	7.4	6.4	1.16	5.1	6.7	0.75
Northern						
Connecticut	0.4	3.0	0.13	1.5	4.5	0.33
Illinois	3.4	7.7	0.44	5.6	11.5	0.49
New York	1.6	6.4	0.26	2.8	8.6	0.32
Ohio	2.0	6.7	0.30	3.7	8.7	0.43

*Based on salaries calculated as means of elementary and secondary school teachers using the proportion teaching at these levels as weights.

†1960 data relate to nonwhite-total salaries.

‡Not available.

SOURCE: U.S. Bureau of the Census (1953*b*, tables 65, 77; 1963*d*, tables 46, 122, 124; 1972*a*, tables 146, 172, 175, 176).

document the apparent impact of segregation on relative employment in 1950, when the ratio of the black share of teachers to the share of pupils was much higher in the segregated southern and border states than in the North, ranging from 1.16 in Kentucky and 0.80 and 0.90 in other segregated states to 0.26 in New York and 0.13 in Connecticut. From 1950 to 1960, when Kentucky and Missouri desegregated, black teacher employment fell sharply in those border states but held steady or increased in the still segregated South, and increased in the North. From 1960 to 1970, when the South was finally desegregated, the relative number of black teachers to pupils fell, though only modestly, in the Southern states while increasing in the North and continuing to drop in Kentucky and Missouri. As a result of these divergent patterns, there was a substantial redistribution of black teachers across all states: a sharp decline in the cross-state coefficient of variation in the ratio of the black share of teachers to pupils, from 0.56 (1950) to 0.35 (1960) to 0.28 (1970) for those states with data for each year.

In contrast to the differential change in shares of teachers, the

| | | | Black-white salaries | | | |
| | 1970 | | 1960† | | 1970 | |
Teachers (7)	Pupils (8)	Ratio (7)/(8) (9)	Male (10)	Female (11)	Male (12)	Female (13)
28.1	32.6	0.86	0.81	1.01	0.97	1.08
30.7	34.7	0.88	0.85	0.99	0.99	1.16
31.3	38.3	0.82	0.84	0.91	0.92	0.98
16.4	22.3	0.74	0.92	1.05	0.95	1.14
4.5	8.3	0.54	1.03	1.03	1.15	1.15
2.9	7.0	0.42	‡	0.84	1.05	1.06
8.2	15.7	0.52	0.91	1.16	1.10	1.22
4.5	13.8	0.32	0.84	0.97	0.98	1.07
5.9	10.7	0.55	0.94	1.12	1.09	1.18

relative income of black teachers increased almost uniformly between 1960 and 1970 (columns 10 through 13). The ratio of black to white male teacher incomes rose in the North, in the border areas, and even in such southern states as Louisiana and Alabama, where the incomes of black male teachers virtually equaled those of white male teachers by 1970. As for women teachers, even though the ratio of black to white incomes was approximately unity in 1960, black women made further advances in the sixties, with their incomes surpassing those of whites in most of the states examined.

Regional Patterns: Effect of Segregation To obtain a more detailed picture of the changing regional pattern of black teacher employment and of the effect of segregation on employment, the log of the number of teachers was regressed[4] on the log of the number of pupils, by race, and measures of segregated education and regional dummy varia-

[4] The precise regression equation was

$$\log T = a \log P + bSEG + cRGN + d\,TIME$$

bles (RGN) for the southern and border states that were segregated by law prior to 1954.[5] The index of segregation is the proportion of black students in school districts *not* in compliance with the 1954 Court Order as given in Southern Educational Reporting Service (1967) and U.S. Department of Health, Education, and Welfare (1971). The segregation and regional variables are closely related: in 1950 all the states in the southern and border group were de jure segregated, in 1960 most were still largely *not* in compliance, while in 1970 none were. Hence there is perfect collinearity between the regional dummy and segregation in 1950, strong collinearity in 1960, but no relation in 1970. In the calculations, I treat the three cross sections as a single pooled sample, with separate intercepts for the years and, in some cases, separate region intercepts as well.

Table 66 presents the segregation index and regional dummy coefficients of interest: lines 1 through 3 deal with blacks, 4 through 6 with whites, and 7 through 9 with the ratio of blacks to whites. In each, results are given first for regressions with only the segregated school index, then for those with the index and the regional dummy, and finally for regressions that include separate regional intercepts by year as well. The table confirms the hypothesized effect of segregated education on black teacher employment. In line 1, the coefficient on segregated schooling suggests that 100 percent segregation raised black teacher employment by nearly threefold [exp (1.05) = 2.86] while reducing white teacher employment (line 4), thereby raising the ratio of black to white teachers (line 7). When the southern and border dummy variable is introduced, it takes up some of the effect of segregation, but most remains attributed to segregated schooling. In 1960 when the variables differ, black teacher employment is relatively greatest in states not in compliance with the law; while in 1970 there remains a

---

where T = number of teachers (black, white, or ratio)

P = number of pupils (black, white, or ratio)

SEG = index of segregation as defined in the text

RGN = dummies for region

$TIME$ = dummies for time period

[5] Eighteen states had de jure segregation in 1954. They were Alabama, Arkansas, Florida, Georgia, Louisiana, Mississippi, North Carolina, South Carolina, Tennessee, Texas, Virginia, Delaware, District of Columbia, Kentucky, Maryland, Missouri, Oklahoma, and West Virginia.

TABLE 66 *Regression coefficients on southern and border regional dummy variables and estimates of school segregation*

Group and equation number	Index of segregation	Southern and border region			
		Total	1950	1960	1970
Black teachers					
Equation 1	1.05 (.13)				
Equation 2	.71 (.15)	.43 (.12)			
Equation 3	.33 (.24)		.66 (.31)	.34 (.24)	.28 (.11)
White teachers					
Equation 4	−.14 (.04)				
Equation 5	−.10 (.06)	−.04 (.04)			
Equation 6	−.00 (.09)		−.17 (.11)	−.07 (.09)	−.01 (.05)
Ratio of black to white teachers					
Equation 7	1.16 (.14)				
Equation 8	.82 (.16)	.57 (.14)			
Equation 9	.42 (.24)		.72 (.33)	.34 (.25)	.41 (.16)

NOTE: All regressions include constants, number of pupils (black, white, or ratio of blacks to whites) and time dummies for 1950 and 1960. Teachers and pupils are in logarithmic form. Numbers in parentheses are standard errors of estimate. Number of pupils who were black in 1960 estimated by multiplying number who were nonwhite by the black share of 5- to 18-year-olds in U.S. Bureau of the Census (1963 *d,* table 96). Number of nonwhites in 1950 used to measure black pupils.

SOURCE: U.S. Bureau of the Census (1963*d*, tables 46, 96, 122; 1972*a*, tables 146, 172; 1953*b*, tables 65, 77).

southern and border "effect" despite de jure desegregation. When separate state and border dummies are introduced, moreover, though most of the desegregation effect is reflected in the separate dummy variables, there continues to be a "pure" segregated schooling impact on black teacher employment, though with only marginal statistical significance (line 3). In these calculations changing segregation is reflected in the time dummies, which are greatest in 1950 and smallest in 1970. The impact of desegregation can thus be measured in one of two ways: with the segregation index or with separate regional dummies for each time period. The latter measure also "picks up" other changing regional factors; because I am concerned with the effect of black voting power, which also changed largely in the southern and border states, in ensuing regressions, I use the regional dummy as the indicator of segregated education and related regional factors. This minimizes the possibility of misconstruing the voting effect for some other regional change without losing much information about segregated schooling.[6]

FORCES FOR CHANGE

There were several important institutional and market developments in the 1960s that could be expected to alter the demand and supply of black schoolteachers.

First, the traditional pattern of de jure segregation came to an end in the South. While some states with de jure segregation complied with the 1954 Court decision in the late 1950s, most did not act until the sixties. Desegregation was likely to reduce demand in the sixties.

Second, however, blacks attained greater political power in the sixties as well, especially in the South following the Voting Rights Act of 1965. In a "median voter" model of public decision making, where the state acts as if it were the median voter, the greater the black share of the electorate, the smaller will be the level of public discrimination and the greater the demand for black workers. Under more complex models of the translation of political power into public jobs, a similar result is likely, though not certain due to "logrolling." In addition, black political power will shape the effect of segregation or desegregation on demand: when blacks count politically, black teachers can expect better treatment under segregation and are less likely to be displaced when schools are desegregated.

Third, although teachers were not protected by the Equal Employment Opportunity Act until 1972, courts placed legal constraints on the employment policies of desegregating districts in the sixties, outlawing several practices designed to reduce black teacher employment. The U.S. District Court in Mississippi ruled in 1971, for example, that the Columbus Municipal School District could not suddenly require teachers to score above 1000 on the National Teachers Examination (on

---

[6] If both the regional dummies and the segregation index are included in calculations with other variables, the index drops to negligible significance.

which blacks do markedly worse than whites) as a condition of employment in the newly desegregated schools. Other courts have required "clear and convincing" evidence that dismissals of teachers are not discriminatory (U.S. Senate . . . , 1971). In the 1969 Singleton case, the court held that:

> If there is to be a reduction in the number of principals, teachers, teacher-aids, or other professional staff employed by the school district which will result in a dismissal or demotion of any such staff members, the staff member to be dismissed or demoted must be selected on the basis of objective and reasonable non-discriminatory standards from among all the staff of the school district. In addition if there is any such dismissal or demotion, no staff vacancy may be filled through recruitment of a person of a race, color, or national origin different from that of the individual dismissed or demoted, until each displaced staff member who is qualified has had an opportunity to fill the vacancy and has failed to accept an offer to do so.
>
> Prior to such a reduction, the school board will develop or require the development of nonracial objective criteria to be used in selecting the staff member who is to be dismissed or demoted. These criteria shall be available for public inspection and shall be retained by the school district. The school district also shall record and preserve the evaluation of staff members under the criteria. Such evaluation shall be made available upon request to the dismissed or demoted employee (*Singleton v. Jackson Municipal Separate School District*, App. A, 1969).

Fourth, on the supply side of the market, the increased number of black workers with college training or professional job skills substantially raised the supply of potential teachers in postwar years. At the same time, however, demand for highly qualified blacks in nonteaching occupations also increased markedly, especially after the passage of the 1964 Civil Rights Act and subsequent antidiscriminatory activity. Whether the net effect of those two developments was to increase or decrease supply to elementary and secondary schools remains to be seen.

Supply-Demand Model for Analyzing Change To analyze the effect of the factors described above on employment of black teachers in the 1960s, I develop a two-equation supply-demand model of the market for black schoolteachers focused on the impact of desegregation and black voting power on demand. The first equation is a structural demand equation, in which demand for blacks depends on the total number of teachers in the school system, the black share of pupils and voters, the effect of segregation (and other regional factors) as reflected in the dummy variable for states which practiced de jure segregation in education, and the salary of black and white teachers:

$$BT = f(SHR, TT, VOTE, RGN, BSAL, WSAL) \tag{1}$$

where BT = number of black teachers

TT = total number of teachers

SHR = black share of pupils

$VOTE$ = black share of voters

RGN = dummy variable for the segregated southern and border states

$BSAL$ = income of black school teachers

$WSAL$ = income of white school teachers

and all variables are in logarithmic form so that the coefficients are elasticities. The teacher variable (TT) is expected to obtain a roughly unit coefficient, reflecting scale homogeneity. SHR is expected to increase demand for black teachers, on the hypothesis that parents and school administrators have some preference for more black (white) teachers when the student body contains more blacks or white. $VOTE$ will also increase demand, with blacks assumed to spend some of their voting power to obtain more favorable treatment in public employment, including the school system. Pressures to displace black teachers are presumably less effective and affirmative action more vigorous, the greater the black share of voters. The salary variables are expected, given logarithmic functional form, to have opposite signed coefficients of approximately similar magnitude.

In addition to Eq. (1), some calculations are made with a slightly modified demand equation in which the total number of teachers was taken as dependent on the total number of pupils (TP) and the latter used as the educational scale variable. Empirically, the two yield similar results.

The second equation relates the supply of black teachers to teaching salaries and two additional variables:

$BALT$ = alternative salaries available to blacks

$BQUAL$ = the number of blacks "qualified" to teach, as measured by the number in professional, technical, and kindred jobs

$$BT = f(BSAL, BALT, BQUAL) \qquad (2)$$

With all variables in logarithmic form, the coefficient on *BQUAL* is expected to be unity and that on *BSAL* and *BALT* opposite in sign and of comparable magnitude, given reasonably valid specification of the equation.

The two equations yield a system with two endogenous variables: *BT, BSAL,* and seven exogenous variables. By substitution, the reduced form equation for employment is

$$BT = f(SHR, TT, VOTE, RGN, BALT, BQUAL, WSAL) \quad (3)$$

Because there are several demand-and-supply shift variables, the model is overidentified. Accordingly, I estimate the structural equation by simultaneous equation techniques, using the reduced form equation to summarize the "final" effects of the exogenous variables on black teacher employment.

ANALYSIS AND DATA The model is estimated from pooled cross-sectional data for states for 1960 and 1970. Pooling has the advantage of providing two types of variation in the segregated education and political power variables of interest: difference among states in a particular year (i.e., North versus South, 1960) and within a state over time (South 1960 versus South 1970). The equations are estimated first for the pooled sample as a whole, with time and regional dummy variables; and then in "cross-sectional change" form with changes within states from 1960 to 1970 as the key variables. The latter form amounts to having individual state constant terms in the regressions and thus to the econometric models which ignore cross-state variation to focus on within-state changes.[7]

[7]To see the equivalence of the cross-sectional change and individual state constant models in the case of two cross sections, consider the observations for a given variable X_{it} where i relates the state i and $t = 0,1$ to the time periods. The variable that enters the least squares formulas in the cross-sectional change model is $X_{i2} - X_{i1}$. In the individual state constant model, all variables are compared to their mean so that we have $X_{i2} - X_i = X_{i2} - \frac{1}{2}(X_{i1} - X_{i2})$ for period 1. Since in regressions with all variables multiplied by $\frac{1}{2}$, the scale factor $\frac{1}{2}$ drops out, the models are the same save for the fact that there are "twice" as many observations in 2. Since a degree of freedom is used up to estimate the individual state dummy, however, degrees of freedom are the same.

Data on teachers, pupils, and qualified workers (professional, technical, and kindred workers) are taken from the state volumes of the 1960 and 1970 *Census of Population* reports as described in the table notes.[8] Because of the predominance of women in teaching and the absence of data on incomes for nonwhite men in several states, female teacher salaries are used to measure *BSAL* and *WSAL*. The number of qualified black personnel is estimated as a weighted average of all male and female professionals in a state, using the share of teachers who are men or women as weights. Alternative incomes are measured as a weighted average of the median incomes of black men and women in the state, also using the share of teachers by sex as weights. Nonwhite incomes are used for 1960 due to the absence of black income figures. Regional dummy variables (*RGN60* for 1960 and *RGN* for 1960 and 1970) are used to measure the effect of desegregation and related regional changes on demand for black teachers. A time variable (*T60*) is entered to reflect national changes in demand over time.

The most difficult factor to measure is the political strength of the black population. In the absence of a theory of group political activity and the translation of such activity into public jobs, there is no obvious theoretically best measure. Empirically, data on what is probably the most reasonable proxy— registered voters—are not available by race and state, except for the 11 southern states which had disfranchised blacks prior to 1965. With the data that are available, however, an estimate of black registered voters in each state is obtained, as described in Table 61, by multiplying the number of persons eligible to vote (U.S. Bureau of the Census, 1973*h*, table 614) by percentages registered, using the actual percentages from the southern states (ibid., table 610) and the national non-Southern average percentage for other states (ibid., 1972*b*, table 92). These estimates yield *VOTE*, the black share of voters, which is the political variable used here, as in Chapter 6. Other aspects of political power and its effect on demand for black schoolteachers, such

[8]These data have some problems. The census reports nonwhite pupils in 1960 rather than black pupils. To correct for this, I multiplied the number of nonwhite pupils by the proportion of 5- to 19-year-old nonwhites who were black in each state (U.S. Bureau of the Census, 1965*a* individual state volumes, table 96). In 1960 teacher incomes are medians for nonwhites and total workers or other than for blacks and whites.

as the cohesiveness of black voters, their desire for black teachers, and the effectiveness of the voting bloc, though presumably important, are not treated.

Regression Results: Pooled Cross Sections

Tables 67 through 71 present the basic regression findings, as obtained by the pooled cross-sectional calculations.

The reduced form employment computations in Table 68 provide substantial support for the model, in particular for the hypothesized impact of the black share of voters on teacher employment. In line 1, which holds fixed total number of teachers, and line 2, which uses total pupils as the scale variable, all the explanatory variables are accorded sensible effects, though the standard errors on white teachers' salaries are relatively large. The critical *VOTE* variable has a sizeable coefficient of 0.16–0.17 with a standard error of 0.09–0.10, suggesting that a 10 percent increase in the black share of voters increases black teacher employment by 1.6–1.7 percent. The dummy variables for *RGN* show a substantial drop from 1960 to 1970 of 24 and 28 percent in lines 1 and 2, respectively, which can be viewed as reflecting the demise of segregated education (among other factors). The overall time coefficient reveals an increase in the employment of black teachers, all else the same, over the period and when compared to the South dummy, the convergence in regional patterns noted earlier. The number of professionals raises and alternative salaries reduce employment, as would be expected given their effect on black teacher wages.

The reduced form income equations in lines 3 and 4 tell a similar story about the relation between the hypothesized determinants of demand and supply and black teachers' income. The black share of voters is estimated to raise the income of black teachers by 0.08–0.09, with a standard error of just 0.04. All the demand variables obtain positive coefficients in the income equation while on the supply side *BQAL* reduces while *BALT* increases black incomes. The overall result is that the exogenous variables of the model do a good job in accounting for income as well as employment, with the political factor under study having its posited positive effect on both variables. This suggests the value of estimating the structural equations of the model directly, using simultaneous equations techniques.

Table 68 presents estimates of the demand for black teachers by the two-stage least squares technique with the instrumental

TABLE 67
Regression estimates of reduced form employment equations, 1960–1970

Dependent variable	Constant	TT (TP)	SHR	VOTE	BALT	BQUAL
1. Employment	1.85	.64	.58	.16	−.57	.35
		(.17)	(.19)	(.10)	(.21)	(.16)
2. Employment	.00	.62*	.54	.17	−.54	.36
		(.15)	(.16)	(.09)	(.20)	(.15)
3. Income	2.01	.23	.15	.08	.42	−.19
		(.07)	(.07)	(.04)	(.08)	(.06)
4. Income	1.51	.20*	.12	.09	.42	−.17
		(.06)	(.06)	(.04)	(.08)	(.06)

*Number of pupils *(TP)* used as scale variable.

†Standard error of estimate.

NOTE: Numbers in parentheses are standard errors of estimate. All variables are in logarithmic form except for dummies. BQAL, BALT, estimated as weighted average of male and female wages or numbers of professionals, using the fraction of teachers in the year by sex as weights, as described in the text. WSAL is the median income of all teachers in state, obtained as weighted average of male and female teacher salaries.

SOURCE: U.S. Bureau of the Census (1963*a*, tables 46, 96, 122, 124; 1964*c*, table 139; 1972*a*, tables 146, 172, 176; 1973*f*, table 344; 1973*h*, tables 610 and 614).

TABLE 68
Two-stage least squares estimates of structural demand equation, 1960 and 1970, pooled sample

Equation number	Constant	TT(TP)	SHR	VOTE	BSAL	WSAL
1	3.95	1.03	.87	.28	− 1.33	.82
		(.05)	(.11)	(.13)	(.58)	(.62)
2	.48	1.01*	.81	.31	− 1.35	.92
		(.05)	(.13)	(.57)	(.57)	(.61)

*Used TP as scale variable.

†Standard error of estimate.

NOTE: Instrumental variables are: supply of qualified blacks, salary of white teachers; alternative salary of blacks; the proportion of teachers who were female for whites and blacks; and the exogenous variables in the table. All variables are in log form.

variables listed in the note. The calculations support the demand model: the number of teachers (line 1), or pupils (line 2), is accorded a roughly unit coefficient, as required of "scale" variables and the black share of pupils and voters given sizeable significant effects on employment. Roughly, demand for black teachers is raised by 0.28 to 0.31 percent by each 1 percent gain in black voting power. The coefficient on black teaching salaries is, moreover, negative and the coefficient on white teacher salaries opposite in sign, though of smaller magnitude

WSAL	T60	RGN	RGN60	R^2	SEE†
.28	−.37	.06	.30	.974	.193
(.42)	(.14)	(.12)	(.11)		
.27	−.61	.04	.32	.976	.188
(.41)	(.13)	(.11)	(.11)		
.37	−.04	.11	.05	.952	.074
(.16)	(.05)	(.04)	(.04)		
.37	−.13	.10	.05	.952	.074
(.16)	(.05)	(.04)	(.04)		

T60	RGN	RGN60	R^2	SEE†
−				
.40	.22	.38	.964	.228
(.16)	(.12)	(.13)		
−				
.80	.16	.42	.964	.225
(.16)	(.12)	(.13)		

than that on black teacher salaries. As for the regional and time dummies, the coefficient on the southern and border states is large and positive in 1960, presumably as a result of segregation in schooling, and drops from 1960 to 1970 by 16 and 26 percent, presumably as a result of desegregation. The negative coefficient on *T60* shows that overall there was a significant *upward* shift in the demand for black teachers, the other factors in the model held fixed.

Turning to the supply side of the market, Table 69 presents

TABLE 69						
Two-stage least squares estimates		Constant	BSAL	BALT	BQUAL	T60	RGN

		Constant	BSAL	BALT	BQUAL	T60	RGN
of structural supply equation, 1960 and 1970, pooled samples	1	−4.08	1.87 (.44)	−1.60 (.18)	.96 (.03)	−.13 (.13)	
	2	−5.76	2.27 (.65)	−1.81 (.34)	.95 (.04)	−.21 (.14)	−.17 (.14)

*Standard error of estimate.

NOTE: Used same instrumental variables as Table 69.

TABLE 70 Reduced form employment and income equations using cross-sectional change observations	Equation number	Constant	TT (TP)	VOTE	RGN	SHR
Employment						
	1	.34	.34 (.18)	.11 (.05)	−.39 (.06)	.01 (.22)
	2	.50	.52* (.25)	.17 (.06)	−.35 (.06)	.23 (.25)
Income						
	3	.00	.27 (.10)	.01 (.03)	−.03 (.03)	−.07 (.12)
	4	.09	.15* (.15)	.04 (.03)	−.00 (.04)	.01 (.05)

*Used TP as scale variable.

†Standard error of estimate.

NOTE: All variables are in logarithmic form. There are 29 states in this sample.

ments) of the structural supply equation. Line 1 excludes the two-stage least squares estimates (with the same set of instru-region and region-time interaction terms on the hypothesis that segregation of schooling and other regional factors operated solely on the demand side of the market. Line 2 includes those variables in the computations. In both cases, the results yield a significant positive coefficient on black teachers' salaries and a roughly similar significant negative coefficient on black alternative salaries, which suggests that the supply of black school-teachers is responsive to economic incentives. The near unit coefficient on the supply of qualified personnel indicates, further, that the increased number of high-level black workers in the sixties shifted the schedule to the right in the expected manner. Finally, the relatively small coefficient on *RGN* suggests that the major source of high black teacher employment in southern and border states in years past was due to segregated schooling rather than supply factors. Even the greater supply of black teachers in the South, however, may be attributed to the

RRGN60	R^2	SEE*
	.963	.049
.21	.960	.055
(.13)		

BALT	BQUAL	WSAL	R^2	SEE†
−.18	.58	−.07	.962	.091
(.20)	(.14)	(.31)		
−.19	.56	−.18	.959	.095
(.21)	(.16)	(.32)		
.15	−.04	.69	.753	.050
(.11)	(.08)	(.17)		
.18	−.01	.57	.678	.057
(.13)	(.10)	(.19)		

segregated system, which led public Negro colleges to concentrate on preparing teachers for segregated schools.

Regression Results: Cross-Sectional Changes The effect of *changes* in black voting power and in the other variables of the model on employment and income of black teachers is examined in Table 70, which focuses on changes within states from 1960 to 1970. In these calculations, the logarithmic change in the number or income of black teachers is regressed on log changes of the various explanatory variables. The regressions are equivalent to an econometric specification which includes individual state constant terms: each state is compared to its own position rather than to the average position of all states in the sample. By deleting cross-state variation, which is reflected in individual state constants, I am putting the model to a strict test.

The resultant employment (lines 1 and 2) and income (lines 3 and 4) equations indicate that the model does a tolerably good job of explaining the intrastate changes. In lines 1 and 2 where the complete reduced form employment equation is fit, the key *VOTE* variable obtains a sizeable significant coefficient of magnitude somewhat below that in the pooled cross-sectional regressions; all the other variables are accorded reasonable coefficients, except that on white teachers' salaries, which should increase rather than decrease black teacher employment. The weakest part of the cross-sectional change model appears to relate to the cross-elasticity between white teachers' salaries and black teachers' employment, a peripheral issue in this chapter.

Turning to the reduced form income equation, while all of the variables obtain coefficients of the right sign, including teacher salaries, the vote coefficients are relatively small, indicating that most of the increase in demand for black teachers due to the vote effect occurred in employment, not incomes, presumably because of a relatively elastic supply schedule.

Two-stage least squares estimates of the structural demand equation for black teachers, given next in Table 71, show that, consistent with the voting power hypothesis, demand was significantly enhanced by the growth of the black share of voters. When the total number of teachers (*TT*) is the scale variable (line 1), *VOTE* is accorded a significant coefficient of 0.13 while the other variables obtain reasonable coefficients, though in some instances of only marginal significance: *WSAL*, in particular, has a positive but small coefficient relative to its standard error. In line 2, when the number of pupils is the scale

TABLE 71
Estimates of structural demand equations using cross-sectional change observations

		Constant	*TT (TP)*	*VOTE*	*SHR*	*RGN*	*BSAL*
1		.71	.97	.13	.39	−.47	−.89
			(.30)	(.07)	(.26)	(.08)	(.83)
2		.84	.88*	.20	.82	−.40	.24
			(.28)	(.07)	(.23)	(.07)	(.61)
3		.76	1.16*	.25	.89	−.39	−.53
			(.22)	(.06)	(.23)	(.07)	(.38)

*Used TP as scale variable.

†Standard error of estimate.

NOTE: All variables are in logarithmic change form. There are 29 states in the sample.
   In the two-stage least squares regressions, the instrumental variables were changes in: alternative salaries of blacks; female share of black and white teachers; the number of qualified blacks; along with the exogenous variable in the equations.

variable, the effect of *VOTE* increases but the teachers' salary coefficients obtain incorrect signs, which confirms the implication of Table 70 that the weakest part of the model relates to the response of demand to salaries. If *WSAL* is deleted, the coefficient on *BSAL* becomes negative while that on *VOTE* rises further to 0.25. Problems with the salary variables notwithstanding, the results in Table 71 tend to support the key hypothesis of this chapter: that the increased share of voters who were black in the 1960s raised demand for black teachers.

Turning to the supply side of the model, two-stage least squares regressions using the cross-sectional change data set, given below, provide confirmatory evidence of the supply responses revealed in Table 69, though the estimated elasticities or supply are smaller and the standard errors are relatively large:

$$BT = -.09 + .68\ TSAL - .68\ BALT + 1.16\ BQUAL$$
$$\quad\quad\quad (.66) \quad\quad (.36) \quad\quad\ (.13)$$
$$R^2 = .849 \quad SEE = .167 \quad (4)$$

Extensions The model of (1) and (2) estimated in Tables 67 through 71 takes white teachers' salaries and total employment of teachers as exogenous and focuses on just one indicator of black political power, the black share of registered voters. Alternative models of the market can also be developed, in which the supply and demand for white teachers are also made endogenous and in

WSAL	R^2	*SEE†*
.13	.933	.119
(.75)		
−.83	.933	.118
(.53)		
	.926	.121

which other measures of political power are entered in demand equations. Such extensions, given in Freeman (1977*a*), yield results that are quite similar to those in this chapter, with the critical voting variable accorded a roughly similar effect to that uncovered herein. This strengthens the reliability of the results, for they are robust with respect to alternative model structures.

CONCLUSIONS AND PROVISOS

While the calculations in this chapter and in Freeman (1977*a*) provide support for the argument that black political power is an important determinant of demand for black schoolteachers and played a role in offsetting the predicted deleterious effect of desegregation on demand, they fall short of a "complete" explanation of the political element in demand in several ways. First, as pointed out in the data section, the available census information has numerous shortcomings with regard to incomes and alternative opportunities, especially in 1960, with the consequence that at least some of the variables contain considerable measurement error. Second, the interrelation between the market for white and black teachers was not as well estimated as might be desired. The weakest results pertain to the effect of white teachers' salaries, alternative incomes, and supply on demand for blacks. Third, many of the institutional and market features of the teaching profession, such as unionization or the availability of experienced women out of the work force to teach, have been ignored in order to focus on the relation between voting and demand. Fourth, the mechanism by which voting power is translated into employment and the effect of other political forces, such as court rulings, was also not treated in the regressions. These provisos and problems notwithstanding, however, the evidence does indicate a significant relation between black political power and desegregation and demand for teachers. The findings with respect to the impact of the black share of voting lend support to the general thesis of the book that some of the development of the new market of the late 1960s can be attributed to changed political power and governmental activities.

8. Black Faculty in the New Market

The economic situation of black faculty has been historically bleak. Until the 1960s, employment was largely restricted to the predominantly black colleges of the South. In 1946 less than 2 percent of black doctorates were employed in national (white) colleges and universities (Greene, 1946). C. Johnson's 1936 survey of black college graduates found that male college teachers earned about $2,000 annually or just 64 percent of the earnings of faculty nationwide (Johnson, 1936, p. 137; Stigler, 1950, p. 44). Despite the obvious talent of such black scholars as W. E. B. DuBois, Horace Mann Bond, Charles Johnson—among others—there was no demand for their services by the major research universities. As late as the 1950s and early 1960s, black academicians were rarely found in northern much less southern nonblack institutions of higher education.

In this chapter I examine the changed economic standing of black academicians in the new market. I briefly review the state of the market for black faculty in the early 1950s and 1960s, consider the forces that could be expected to alter the market, and then analyze the income and academic employment of black faculty in the early 1970s. The evidence reveals a sizeable improvement in the job market for black faculty in the period under study: employment of black faculty in primarily white institutions increased substantially; black faculty incomes came to equal or exceed those of comparable white faculty; the most productive black scholars, in terms of articles published, obtained a sizeable salary premium over equally productive whites; and somewhat lower hiring standards appear to have been applied to black faculty appointments. Some of those improvements are found in the 1968–69 academic year prior to initiation of significant affirmative action pressures, which suggests that despite the substantial publicity given affirmative action, other factors and pressures were also at work to improve the position of black faculty. On the other hand, some improvement occurred after 1969, so that the federal program does appear to have had an impact.

BLACK FACULTY, AFFIRMATIVE ACTION, AND THE ACADEMIC JOB MARKET

What was the economic status of black faculty in the years preceding the pressures for affirmative action of the late 1960s and early 1970s? How did affirmative action programs operate to alter university personnel policy? What features of the academic marketplace shaped the response to these programs?

Census of Population evidence regarding black faculty is summarized in Table 72, which records the number and income of black (nonwhite) and total faculty, by sex, from 1950 to 1970. The table shows that the relative number of black male or

TABLE 72
Economic status of nonwhite (black) faculty, 1950–1970

	1950	1960	1970
Male			
1. *Numbers of faculty**			
Black	2,490	3,518	8,851
Total	96,030	138,889	354,671
Ratio	0.026	0.025	0.025
2. *Incomes of faculty†*			
Nonwhite (black)	$3,300	$5,738	$8,867
Total	$4,366	$7,510	$11,657
Ratio	0.76	0.76	0.79
Female			
3. *Numbers of faculty**	1,410	1,897	7,535
Black	1,410	1,897	7,535
Total	27,780	38,859	139,278
Ratio	0.051	0.049	0.054
4. *Incomes of faculty†*			
Nonwhite (black)	‡	$4,154	$5,637
Total	‡	$5,013	$6,220
Ratio		0.83	

*Numbers in 1950 and 1960 include college presidents and deans.

†Incomes for preceding years.

‡Not available.

NOTE: Incomes refer to nonwhites in 1950 and 1960 and to blacks in 1970.

SOURCE: U.S. Bureau of Census (1956, tables 3, 19, 21; 1963*b*, tables 25, 26; 1973*c*, tables 2, 16, 17; 1973*f*, table 205).

female faculty changed little in the 1950–1970 period preceding affirmative action pressures: in 1950, 2.6 percent of male and 5.1 percent of female faculty were black; in 1970, 2.5 percent (male) and 5.4 percent (female). With regard to income, while the census data suffer from several problems, such as failure to control adequately for levels of education (notably, whether or not the individual has the Ph.D.) and refer to nonwhites in 1950 and 1960 but to blacks in 1970, they suggest some improvement, particularly for black female faculty, whose income relative to total female faculty rose from 0.83 to 0.91 in the 1960s. The gain for black male faculty is smaller but nevertheless probably indicative of real changes, as the shift in the average from nonwhite to blacks is likely to bias changes downward. With some increases in relative incomes but little or none in relative employment of black faculty, the general picture is of only slight advances in the market in the decades preceding initiation of significant equal employment pressures.

The Shift in Demand

Two basic sets of forces operated to raise demand for black faculty in the late 1960s–early 1970s and thus to bring to an end traditional patterns of employment discrimination. First, there were substantial student and related pressures from various social groups for black faculty appointments in predominantly white institutions. Student pressures often focused on the demand for "black studies" programs and led a wide variety of colleges and universities such as Cornell and Harvard to institute such areas of study. The faculty tended to support demands, with over two-thirds agreeing in 1969 that "any institution with a substantial number of black students should offer a program of black studies if they wish it" (American Council of Education, 1970, p. 17). A reasonably large number of faculty also felt that, black studies aside, preferential treatment should be given to prospective minority faculty to break down all-white staffs: in 1969, 33 percent favored "preferential hiring" (American Council on Education, 1973, p. 30). With these pressures of students and sentiments of faculty, colleges and universities began to alter traditional employment practices. Many initiated a serious effort to find and hire black faculty, with the consequence that demand rose rapidly from historically low levels.

The second and possibly more important force changing the

market was federal pressure for affirmative action, which began in 1968 when Revised Order No. 4 of Executive Order 11246 (1965) required institutions with federal contracts to "develop and maintain a written affirmative action program." This program is submitted to the Higher Education Division of the Office of Civil Rights of the Department of Health, Education, and Welfare for approval. Failure to produce an acceptable plan carries the potential penalty that federal contracts will be blocked by HEW. Under the Higher Education Guidelines of the Office of Civil Rights (October 1, 1972) such a plan requires:

- Establishment of a basic data file with data on the ethnic identification, salary, job position, education, and various personnel action.

- Organization of the data for ready analysis by department, rank, and job classification across department lines so that comparisons of duties, educational requirements, and pay can be made easily.

- Construction of an availability index using data on the percentages of blacks (others) holding doctorates by field to show the potential supply of minority faculty.

- Comparison of current work force with available supplies and setting of goals to overcome deficiencies. The goals are to be set in numbers or percentages and "should reflect not only the number of new hires but also the projected overall composition of the work force in a given community."

- Compilation of data to determine the success or failure of minorities in attaining promotion or tenure.

The detailed written plans and numerical goals of the guidelines involved substantial changes in university personnel policy, which can be expected to raise demand for black faculty. In conjunction with other pressures from black (and other) students demanding black faculty directly or indirectly by the establishment of black studies curricula, from the faculty, and from related social groups, the affirmative action programs appear to have produced a major reorientation in the academic job market. According to some observers, in fact, the institution of minority employment as a goal of academic institutions led to "reverse discrimination," favoring less-qualified minority applicants over more-qualified majority applicants in employment. Lester (1974), in particular, argued that federal antibias regulations were having adverse consequences on the quality of appointments, with "the likelihood of an increasing number of mistakes in the selection of tenured faculty." Whether or not hiring standards were in fact lowered in the new market, it is clear that federal affirmative action and related pressures did significantly raise demand for black faculty.

Effect of Increased Demand The way increases in demand affect the market for minorities that are relatively underrepresented in academia depends on supply conditions and the institutional features of the marketplace. Because of the lengthy training period for Ph.D.'s and the limited stock of black doctorates in the 1960s–1970s, the supply of black faculty was relatively fixed or inelastic in the period under study, suggesting that increased demand would improve the income status of black faculty, possibly substantially, but raise employment only moderately. Because of the importance of quality dimensions in academia, there are several distinct ways in which an improvement might be effectuated. Institutions could reduce hiring standards for the group in heavy demand, producing the type of quality deterioration which some have feared. If only standards were changed, one would find average incomes roughly the same but incomes adjusted for quality rising, the relative number of persons in the group attaining "good academic" jobs increasing, and sizeable quality differences (say, in terms of publications) within specified institutions. On the other hand increases in demand could show up largely in the willingness to pay a premium for persons with strong qualifications for a job and thus in an increase in income for the more qualified and in the slope of the curve linking income to "qualifications." Under this adjustment mode, persons with many publications or related accomplishments in the group having great demand would receive a premium, their number would increase modestly in top jobs, (given inelastic supply), and there would be no substantial quality differences within those institutions desiring members of the group. Third, there could develop a "pure" premium for members of the group, much like the traditional discrimination coefficient. Quality standards and the reward for quality would be unchanged but every member of the group would receive a given amount of extra income. Which, if any, of these various adjustment modes operated in the late sixties–early seventies is

an empirical question which the remainder of this chapter seeks
to answer.

**FACULTY
CHARACTERIS-
TICS: AMERI-
CAN COUNCIL
ON EDUCA-
TION SURVEY**

Evidence on the status of faculty in the new market is taken
from the 1968–69 and 1972–73 surveys of the American Council
of Education (ACE), which covered over 60,000 and 42,000
faculty, respectively, at more than 300 institutions.[1] A major
advantage of the data is that they contain relatively detailed
information on individual "productivity" or skill, including
numbers of publications and quality of graduate school of
highest degree, as well as on standard human capital indicators, years of schooling, and years of experience. While articles
or books published are by no means optimal measures of
academic productivity (they ignore teaching skills, quality of
publications, and committee work), they do provide a finer
comparison of individual output than is common in earnings
equations analysis.

Table 73 compares characteristics of black and white male
and female faculty in the survey. The figures for blacks are
obtained from a complete count of black respondents to the
ACE questionnaire; the figures for whites, from a random
sample of about 3,500 respondents. Both are weighted by the
ACE stratification sample weights (see ACE, 1970, 1973). Comparisons of the characteristics of whites in the random sample
with those of the entire population reported in the ACE publications indicate that the 3,500 is a representative sample.

Line 1 of the table shows that blacks were substantially
underrepresented in academia, though at a decreasing rate, in
the period. In 1969 just 1.8 percent of male and 3.9 percent of
female faculty were black; when the market improved in the
early 1970s, the proportions rose to 2.4 percent and 4.8 percent,
respectively, large percentage gains for a four-year span but
ones which still left a sizeable gap between academic employment of the two groups. Underlying the increase in black
employment were substantially greater numbers of job offers
tendered black as compared with white faculty, with 65 percent
of the former but just 34 percent of the latter reporting in 1973
offers "within the past two years."

[1] The surveys are described in detail in American Council of Education (1970, 1973).

The salaries in line 2 show that, without adjusting for differences in academic qualifications, white male faculty earned a moderate premium over blacks in 1969 and 1973, of $877 (7 percent) in the former and $1,140 (also 7 percent) in the latter year, while black women faculty did about the same as white faculty in both periods.

Turning to academic and personal qualifications, there appear to be sizeable differences between the blacks and whites in training and productivity, measured by publications of black and white faculty (lines 3 and 5) but not in age and experience, measured by years since the highest degree (line 4). White academicians are more likely than blacks to hold doctorates and correspondingly less likely to have master's degrees as their highest qualification. They also have a greater number of publications, with 61 percent of white men and 42 percent of women faculty reporting one or more articles compared with 46 percent of black male and 24 percent of black female faculty.

With respect to fields of specialization, line 6 reveals different distributions of blacks and whites among academic specialties. White men, but not white women, are more likely than blacks to be scientists, while both white men and women are found proportionately less frequently in the conglomerate "other fields" than blacks. But these and other differences in the field distribution of teachers appear to be diminishing over time: in 1969 the summation of the absolute value of the difference in the distributions was 40 for men and 32 for women; in 1973, 28 (men) and 16 (women). Finally, line 7 shows a moderate white advantage in academic rank with no indication of diminution over time.

QUALITY-ADJUSTED INCOMES To examine the income of black and white faculty with similar qualifications, it is necessary to estimate the effect of various faculty characteristics, such as number of publications, on income and to use these estimates to calculate quality-adjusted incomes. If $\hat{a}_i$ is the effect of the ith income determining variable X_i and if blacks and whites differ in their level of X_i by say $X_i^w - X_i^b$, then $\Sigma_{i}a_i[X_i^w - X_i^b]$ of the black-white difference represents the quality-adjusted or hedonic market differential.

Step one in this adjustment procedure is taken in Table 74, which records the coefficients of income determination equations for black and white faculty. Since whites constitute 95 or

		Male			
		1969		1973	
		Black	*White*	*Black*	*White*
1.	*Percentage of total faculty*	1.8	96.6	2.4	95.1
2.	*Salary*	$12,526	$13,403	$16,169	$17,309
3.	*Age*	44	42	44	44
	Years since completed highest degree	10	12	12	13
4.	*Academic training (percentage with degrees)*				
	Ph.D.	23	40	20	37
	Education and other professional degrees	25	16	9	10
	Master's	39	35	62	44
	Less than master's	12	9	9	8
5.	*Publications (percentage who published)*				
	1 or more articles	47	58	46	61
	5 or more articles	15	27	16	38
	1 or more books	20	29	30	42
6.	*Field (percentage)*				
	Social science	21	25	28	25
	Science	18	28	23	31
	Humanities	13	19	18	24
	Other	48	28	31	20
7.	*Rank (percentage)*				
	Professor	21	24	23	31
	Associate professor	20	20	23	24
	Assistant professor	28	29	30	26
	Other	31	27	24	19

SOURCE: Calculated from ACE tapes for 1968–1969 and 1972–1973 using sampling weights.

more percent of the faculty, the white equations show the overall process of faculty income determination while the black equations pinpoint distinctive factors at work among black faculty. The dependent variable in the regressions is the log of academic salary; regressions with the dollar value of salary

	Female		
1969		1973	
Black	*White*	*Black*	*White*
3.9	94.7	4.8	93.6
$10,461	$10,202	$14,425	$14,589
44	42	43	45
10	9	10	11
12	17	7	17
24	16	5	5
57	57	69	62
7	10	19	11
28	36	24	42
6	8	3	11
20	16	119	27
25	22	23	19
12	9	12	9
14	30	28	27
49	39	37	45
4	8	5	10
17	16	15	24
35	30	35	29
39	46	45	37

yielded similar patterns of results. The independent variables relate to degree held and quality of graduate institution awarding the Ph.D.; age and experience, measured as years since receipt of higher degree, with squared terms entered to pick up the downward curvature of income profile near retirement;

TABLE 74 *Coefficients for faculty income determination equations, by sex and race, 1973*

	Men		Women	
Explanatory variables	White (1)	Black (2)	White (3)	Black (4)
Training				
Ph.D.	.04(.02)	.09(.08)	.04(.06)	.26(.08)
Ed.D.	.10(.04)	−.03(.12)	.14(.09)	.31(.11)
Other	.05(.03)	−.44(.10)	−.05(.10)	−.11(.26)
Master's	−.08(.02)	−.07(.07)	−.17(.04)	−.00(.06)
High-quality Ph.D.*	.02(.02)	.05(.06)	.04(.05)	−.01(.08)
Age and experience				
Age	.039(.007)	.049(.017)	−.030(.013)	.042(.015)
$(Age)^2$	−.0004(.00008)	−.0005(.0002)	.0004(.0001)	−.0004(.0002)
Years since highest degree	.016(.003)	.006(.008)	.022(.006)	.006(.008)
$(Years)^2$	−.0002(.003)	−.0001(.0003)	−.006(.002)	−.0001(.002)
Scholarly productivity				
Articles				
1–2	−.05(.020)	.01(.06)	−.04(.04)	.02(.05)
3–4	.01(.02)	.08(.06)	−.04(.05)	.05(.09)
5–10	.01(.02)	.22(.08)	−.07(.06)	.22(.15)
11–20	.11(.03)	.15(.12)	.08(.08)	.24(.16)
21 or more	.16(.03)	.33(.10)	.20(.11)	.23(.20)
Books				
1–2	.06(.02)	−.04(.05)	.09(.04)	.01(.06)
3–4	.07(.02)	.10(.09)	.15(.08)	.10(.10)
5 or more	.07(.03)	−.07(.14)	.11(.08)	−.08(.13)
Hours of activity				
Administrative	.008(.0007)	.008(.002)	.013(.002)	.005(.002)
Teaching	.002(.0001)	.002(.002)	.007(.002)	−.001(.003)
Preparing class	.002(.0009)	.003(.002)	.004(.002)	−.000(.002)
Advising students	.002(.002)	.002(.003)	−.008(.003)	−.001(.004)
Research	.005(.001)	.006(.003)	.006(.003)	.003(.004)
Institution of employment†				
University				
High-quality	−.00(.085)	.04(.090)	−.17(.06)	−.01(.23)
Medium-quality	.05(.024)	.26(.105)	−.13(.06)	.06(.25)
Other	−.05(.028)	.07(.114)	−.24(.06)	.16(.25)
High-quality college	.13(.03)	.29(.088)	−.11(.05)	.08(.22)

TABLE 74 *(continued)*

	Men		Women	
Explanatory variables	White (1)	Black (2)	White (3)	Black (4)
Other college	−.08(.03)	.09(.11)	−.28(.05)	.03(.23)
Two-year college	.12(.02)	.22(.10)	−.14(.05)	.31(.22)
Black college	−.08(.08)	−.01(.01)	−.07(.15)	−.01(.22)
R^2	.446	.413	.281	.601
SEE ‡	.291	.339	.409	.202

*Quality Ph.D. is defined as having obtained a degree from an institution in the ranking by K. Roose and C. Anderson (*A Rating of Graduate Programs,* 1973). The Roose-Anderson ratings are based on a detailed survey of over 6,000 scholars. They represent the best available indicator of the quality of institutions. Over 100 major schools are rated—those that are not rated can be treated as being of relatively low quality.

†High-quality universities are defined as having student SAT scores of 600 or more; medium quality, 500–599; other, less than 500; good colleges (public and private), 500 or higher scores; other colleges (Protestant, Roman Catholic, and private), four-year schools. The scores are from ACE surveys and relate to the approximate year of the survey. The deleted group is public colleges with SAT scores below 500.

‡Standard error of estimate.

NOTES: The dependent variable is the log of income; numbers in parentheses are standard errors; all regressions include variables for the basis of pay (9 or 12 months) and dummies for field (social science, humanities, other).

Regressions for women include additional variables for number of dependents and whether or not the woman is married.

scholarly productivity in terms of articles and books published and hours spent at various academic tasks; and institution of employment, which can be viewed as an indicator of perceived quality or simply as a control that focuses on the incomes of persons in similar types of institutions. In the cases where the variables are dummy classifications, the coefficients compare the effect of having a specified characteristic with that of the omitted group: persons with a B.A. or less (a very odd group for faculty) in the first set; those with 0 articles and books in the third set; and those employed in lower quality public colleges, defined as public institutions whose students score below 500 in the Scholastic Achievement Tests, in the last set. In addition to the variables in the table, each calculation also includes the "basis of pay" (on a nine- or twelve-month basis), field dummies (social sciences, science, humanities versus "other"), and a constant whose coefficients are not recorded as being of little concern.

The table reveals both differences and similarities in the income determination process for black and white male faculty. The estimated coefficients for age and experience, for hours of work, and, to a lesser extent, for training, are roughly similar.

The age coefficient is higher for blacks than whites but the experience coefficient is lower, which nets out to approximately similar life-cycle earnings profiles. The coefficients on Ph.D. and master's degrees differ by .12 for whites and .16 for blacks, a modest black advantage, while the other educational attainment coefficients, which reflect small often disparate groups, differ unevenly. The coefficients on the hours of work by activity, which measure the impact of an hour of work time spent per week in administration, teaching, and research, are virtually identical. By contrast, there are marked differences in the coefficients on articles published, with blacks apparently receiving greater marginal rewards for articles than whites (the coefficients in books are mixed): a black with three or four articles, for example, earned 8 percent more than a black with no publications compared with a 1 percent advantage for white faculty with three or four publications over one with no publications. Blacks with 21 or more articles earned 33 percent more than their peers with no articles and 18 percent more than those with 11 to 20 articles—differences much above those for white male faculty (16 percent and 5 percent, respectively).

A second and very different finding relates to the marked difference in the income determination equations for white and black women. While, save for the B.A. or less group, the training coefficients are quite similar, there are. substantial differences in the age-experience, scholarly productivity, and hours coefficients. As black female faculty age, they obtain similar gains in income to those of black or white men while, by contrast, white women lose: the age coefficient is negative in column (3), suggesting a distinct age-income profile for white women. With respect to articles, the figures show that among women as among men, blacks earn a sizeable marginal premium, compared with whites, from publishing. In this case, however, white women with articles in the range from 1 to 10 do relatively poorly while black women earn more than those with 0 articles. On the other hand, white women appear to have a greater return to hours of research than black women. Finally, the institution coefficients also show a strikingly different pattern, with white women earning relatively more in low-quality public colleges (the omitted group) than blacks, who do particularly well in junior colleges and lower quality universities. In short, the evidence suggests distinct and quite different income determination processes for black and white women faculty, an issue which merits detailed consideration but lies outside the scope of this chapter.

The regressions in Table 74 provide several sets of weights for evaluating the impact of academic qualifications on income (white male, female and black male, female coefficients). Because the white male coefficients reflect the predominant pattern of income determination in the market, they are used as the chief weights for adjusting incomes for qualifications; the other weights were employed, however, to check the results. Table 75 summarizes the adjustments. It lists the major contributing factors, their contribution to black-white income differences $[a_1(X_i^w - X_i^b)]$, and then gives the sum of the contributions. The difference between the sum and the actual differential is the quality-adjusted differential.

The resultant adjustments are clear-cut. With the white male weights, the academic and related qualifications of white men yield an approximate 13.7 percent advantage, while white women have a 9.9 percent advantage. That is, if all were paid by the white male income equation, white men and women would earn somewhat more than their black peers. In fact, they do not earn that large a premium, with the result that the quality-adjusted incomes show black faculty earning 6.6 and 8.9 percent more than white faculty, somewhat more than $1,000 with 1973 faculty salaries. While the quantitative results are moderately different when other income equation weights are used, the overall result is that in each case black faculty earn somewhat more than white faculty in quality-adjusted terms

TABLE 75 Logarithmic differences between white and black faculty incomes in 1973 due to "characteristics of persons and institutions of employment"*		
Contributions to differences	*Men*	*Women*
Differentials expected		
Training, articles, books published, hours worked	.068	.019
Experience and age	.018	.022
Type of institution	.069	.053
All other†	−.019	.005
All characteristics	.137	.099
Actual differential	.071	.010
Difference between actual and income differences	−.066	−.089

*Calculated from equations 1 through 4 of Table 73 as described in text.

†Field of teaching, basis of pay, and marital status and dependents for women.

TABLE 76
Black-white male
faculty incomes
and income
differences, by
numbers of articles
and field,
1969 and 1973

Numbers of articles	Total			Science		
	Black	White	Difference	Black	White	Difference
	Income, 1973					
5 or more	22,071	20,398	1,673	21,497	19,623	1,874
1–4	16,398	16,094	304	14,301	15,653	−1,352
0	14,320	15,015	−695	12,229	14,371	−2,142
	Income, 1969					
5 or more	15,777	16,908	−1,131	13,881	16,444	−2,563
1–4	12,692	12,676	16	11,839	12,549	−710
0	10,503	10,554	−51	10,562	10,605	−43

SOURCE: Calculated from ACE tapes.

(see Freeman, 1977b, table 3). However, it is important to note that much of the adjustment is due to differences in institutions of employment. If national institutions with higher salaries are rewarding qualifications that are not measured by the variables in the calculations, black faculty earn a premium in the market. If, on the other hand, the high-salary institutions discriminate against blacks, so that this part of the quality correction should be deleted, the results can be interpreted to indicate that, while within given types of institutions blacks do better than comparable whites, in the market as a whole, the two groups have approximately the same income.

Comparable estimates for 1969 reveal a similar picture, as quality characteristics have the same magnitude effect on incomes and initial differentials are similar (see Table 72). We conclude that in the new market of the 1960s and early 1970s, black faculty earned as much as, or more than, comparable whites depending on the computations and interpretations. In any case, income differentials of the type shown in Table 71 have obviously been eliminated.

REWARDS TO THE HIGHLY QUALIFIED The apparently greater premium[2] to black than white faculty with the highest scholarly qualifications can be pursued further by comparing the income of blacks and whites with different numbers of publications. Table 76 presents such comparisons for 1973 and 1969 for all male faculty and for faculty in science and social science fields where publications of articles are espe-

---

[2] More detailed analyses of the reward structure to blacks with greater or lesser academic qualifications are given in R. Freeman (1977b).

| | Social science | |
Black	White	Difference
23,081	20,291	2,790
16,301	16,216	85
17,002	15,663	1,339
14,174	16,343	−2,169
12,675	12,800	−125
10,559	10,787	−228

cially important. The table shows a drastically different impact of scholarly productivity on black as compared with white incomes in 1973 and a markedly different pattern in 1969. In 1973, highly "productive" black scholars appear to have been much more heavily rewarded than their white compatriots while less productive scholars did not do much better. More specifically, blacks with five or more articles earned $1,673 more than whites in 1973 compared with a $205 advantage for those with one to four articles and a $695 deficit for persons with no articles. By contrast, exactly the opposite pattern is found in 1969, with the most able blacks earning less than comparable whites by greater amounts than the least productive.

More refined estimates of the greater rewards to black than to white academicians with high qualifications given in Freeman (1977*b*, table 5) using the regression results of Table 72 to estimate the income differential between black and white faculty with specified characteristics, other income determining variables held fixed, show similar results. While there are difficulties in before and after attribution of causality, the fact that federal affirmative action pressures were exceptionally severe in the 1969–1973 period covered suggests that they had a major effect on the return to quality. This is not unreasonable since affirmative action was concentrated in the top universities, where scholarly production is the major criterion for employment.

EMPLOYMENT BY INSTITUTION The pattern of black and white faculty employment by type of institution is examined in Table 77, which records the proportion employed in universities, four-year colleges, two-year colleges, and predominantly black colleges in the 1969–1973

TABLE 77
Percentage of
black and white
faculty in
universities,
predominantly
black, and other
colleges and
universities,
1969 and 1973

	1969		1973	
	Black	*White*	*Black*	*White*
Male				
Universities	10	51	18	44
Colleges	15	36	24	936
Predominantly black colleges	71	1	51	1
Two-year colleges	4	12	7	19
Female				
Universities	10	41	10	37
Colleges	15	40	21	37
Predominantly black colleges	70	1	51	1
Two-year colleges	5	18	18	25

SOURCE: Calculated from ACE tapes for 1968–1969 and 1972–1973.

period under study. Two important aspects of the differential pattern of black and white faculty employment stand out in the table. First is the extraordinary difference in the proportion of blacks and whites employed in the various institutions. In 1969 and 1973 black faculty tended to be concentrated in the predominantly black colleges of the South and were much less likely to be employed in universities, colleges, and junior colleges (save for women in 1973) than whites, a pattern which reflects the historic virtual exclusion of black scholars from primarily white institutions. Second, however, is the marked change in the black distribution in the 1969–1973 period of severe affirmative action pressures. In four years, the proportion of black faculty in the predominantly Negro schools fell from nearly three-fourths to about one-half; the fraction of black men in universities increased by 8 percentage points while, as a result of the slow-down in the academic marketplace, the fraction of white men dropped by 7 percentage points. While the direction of change was clearly toward greater similarity in the distributions, however, sizeable differences still remained in 1973.

Hiring Standards

Evidence pertaining to the complex and controversial issue of differential hiring standards is presented in Table 78, which compares the number of articles published by black and white men in various types of academic institutions in 1973. If the number of articles is taken as a measure of academic qualifications, black faculty would have fewer publications in particular types of schools than whites if lower academic standards were applied to black appointments and conversely if white faculty had fewer publications. The data reveal sizeable differences in articles between black and white male faculty in the institutional categories considered, with blacks reporting fewer published articles than whites. Correcting for the broad field of employment, moreover, does not, it turns out, greatly affect these differences as the relatively small supply of black men in sciences (where many publications are common) is balanced by relative underrepresentation in humanities (where publications are less frequent) and ages are quite similar (see Table 73). While more detailed analysis of faculty employed in particular types of institutions based on a larger data set is needed to

TABLE 78
Scholarly productivity of black and white male faculty in academic institutions, 1973

Institution of employment	Mean number of articles
High-quality university	
Black	8.2
White	15.9
Medium-quality university	
Black	6.4
White	12.4
Other university	
Black	4.1
White	10.0
Private four-year (non-sectarian)	
Black	1.7
White	4.3
Public four-year	
Black	1.8
White	5.9
Predominantly black	
Black	4.2
White	6.6

SOURCE: Calculated from ACE survey, 1972–1973.

determine whether other factors account for the observed patterns, the articles data suggest that reduction of hiring standards as well as increased demand for the highly productive characterize the new market.[3]

The fact that black faculty report fewer published articles does not, it should be stressed, mean that affirmative action pressures diluted the overall "academic quality" of institutions. For one thing, colleges and universities could be selecting black faculty with about the same number of publications or overall qualifications as would be held by marginal white appointments. That is, differences in mean numbers of publications between the groups cannot be used to infer the effect of demand on the average number of publications of all faculty in the relevant institutional group. Given the choice of similarly productive or qualified black and white faculty, colleges and universities may "tilt" in favor of the black candidate, with the result that the average black faculty would have fewer articles than the average white, while the institution average is unchanged. Whether this process or some other reason explains the observed difference in articles published remains to be seen. In addition, numbers of publications are, of course, indicators of only one aspect of academic quality and an imperfect indicator, at that.

CONCLUSION This chapter has shown that, presumably because of the broad social changes of the late 1960s, ranging from student and related pressures to federal affirmative action, demand for black faculty increased in the new market. As a result, the employment and income position of black academicians, especially those with many publications, improved substantially relative to that of whites. By 1973, black faculty appear to have had, by

[3]Estimates of the impact of various characteristics on articles published show that the differences observed in the table cannot be attributed to differences in age, years since degree, or field. In particular a regression of number of articles on age, field, and related characteristics yielded coefficients (and standard errors, in parentheses) for the variables of concern: age, .025 (.023); years since highest degree, .24 (.02); science (versus humanities), 1.2 (.37); social science, .9 (.4); other fields, 2.5 (.4). The differences in black and white male distributions among fields would, by these estimates, account for less than one article in the black-white differences. Even a difference in years since receipt of highest degree of 10 years would produce a difference in articles of just 2.4 below the observed differentials. In fact, according to Table 71, black and white men have nearly the same years since highest degree, on average.

some measures at least, a modest advantage over their white peers—a far cry from past discriminatory disadvantages.

The extent to which the divergence of the market in the late sixties and early seventies from the historic past can be attributed to federal or other specific antidiscriminatory activity, however, is unclear. While certain aspects of the market, notably growth of employment of black faculty outside the traditional black colleges of the South and the sizeable reward to publications, appear to have changed in the 1969–1973 period of intense affirmative action pressure, rough equality of salaries was found in the 1969 as well as in the 1973 ACE survey.

9. Interpreting the New Market

The evidence analyzed in this book tells a remarkable story of social and economic change in the market for the black elite. Discriminatory differences that had persisted for decades began collapsing with surprising speed in the 1960s and early 1970s. Black students and highly qualified personnel responded to newly created opportunities by moving rapidly into remunerative but once "closed" occupations. The development of the new market for highly educated black Americans raises several questions about the operation of discrimination in the economy, the value of standard economic analysis of discrimination, and the likely future economic status of the black elite. In this chapter I summarize the major empirical findings of the study, examine their implications for the analysis of discriminatory differences in the job market, and speculate, albeit cautiously, about the future.

SUMMARY AND FINDINGS
The principal results of this investigation can be conveniently grouped into those relating to the development of the new market; the response of black students and highly qualified personnel to new opportunities; and the role of national antidiscriminatory policy in establishing the new market.

The New Market
The socioeconomic position of the black elite and other black Americans improved along many dimensions in the new market of the sixties and early seventies:

1 The income of blacks improved substantially relative to that of whites—in some instances continuing trends that had begun earlier. Specific groups of black workers—women, young and older male college graduates, young men in general—experi-

215

enced especially large economic gains. By the 1970s black women earned as much as or more than whites with similar educational attainment; black female college graduates obtained a moderate premium over their white peers; young black male college graduates attained rough income parity with young white graduates; and all black male graduates had more rapid increases in income than whites, ending the historic pattern of declining black-white income ratios with ascending education. Despite the advances, however, a sizeable overall black to white male income gap remained in the early seventies, the legacy of years of discrimination.

2 The occupational position of black workers was substantially improved, with women moving from domestic service to factory and office jobs, and men moving into white-collar and craftsmen's jobs. Among college-trained men there was a sharp increase in representation of blacks in managerial jobs and a general convergence in the distribution of blacks and whites by detailed field, especially among the young. Most of the improvement in the black position is attributed to differences in the occupations of entering and leaving cohorts.

3 Young black college-trained men enjoyed the most significant gains in income and job opportunities of any group, with large national corporations actively recruiting them for the first time. As a result of the increased income of college men and attainment of equality in starting salaries, the rate of return to black male investments in college came to exceed that of whites, and was so perceived by students. The return to investments in graduate training also came to surpass that of whites.

4 The relation between family background and educational and labor market achievement, traditionally quite weak among black Americans, was greatly strengthened for young persons in the new market to approach that found among whites. Because of the enhanced curvature of the background-achievement locus for blacks and declines in discriminatory differentials, differences in family background resources became the chief deterrent to attainment of educational and economic equality among the young. While even young black men from the poorest backgrounds, those born in the rural South, pro-

gressed in the new market, persons from higher socioeconomic backgrounds made the most rapid improvements, creating greater "class" cleavages in black America.

5   The number of blacks enrolling in college rose rapidly in the new market, with nearly all the increase occurring in primarily white institutions, as northern white institutions began to recruit blacks, often on a preferential basis, while southern white colleges were legally desegregated. By 1970, for the first time in history, the majority of black students, especially the most academically able, were enrolled outside the primarily black institutions of the South.

6   Highly qualified blacks made substantial gains in employment and income in specific markets. The number of blacks employed by state and local governments as managers rose, the number teaching outside southern schools increased, the number attaining high General Service and Postal Service federal job classifications increased, the number teaching in primarily white colleges went up sharply. Except in elementary and secondary school teaching, however, blacks continued to be substantially underrepresented in high-level occupations.

7   While the new market advances of the black elite meant that young highly educated black men and all black women were beginning their careers on rough parity with comparable whites for the first time in history, the relatively slow progress of older black men meant that overall parity was not attained and is unlikely to be attained for many decades. Even among the young, moreover, background and related factors create a disparity in starting positions that will persist—all else the same—for a long time. While the new market is a sharp break from the past, it is not the millenium.

8   The educational and career decisions of black students and qualified personnel were significantly altered by the new opportunities of the 1960s. Large numbers of students selected business-oriented fields and occupations rather than traditional teaching and professional service or nonvocational black studies curriculum. In the freshman class of 1973, for example, proportionately more black than white male students planned

to enter management—a sharp change from past patterns of occupational choice.

9 Economically rational supply behavior appears to underlie the changed educational and career patterns of black youngsters and high-level workers. Black students expressed especially great interest in pecuniary factors. The elasticity of supply of blacks to colleges and universities and to various professions appears to be quite high and probably exceeds the comparable elasticity for whites. Traditional differences between blacks and whites in the occupational structure and the new market convergence in structure are attributable, in large part, to supply responses to different wage structures.

10 Antidiscriminatory activities contributed to improving the economic status of highly educated (and other) black Americans in the sixties and early seventies, with the Civil Rights Act of 1964, Executive Order 11246, and various other governmental actions helping to create the new market. Federal antidiscriminatory activities were enhanced by court decisions favoring affirmative action programs and penalization of discriminators. Corporate personnel policies were substantially altered by legal and administrative decisions. The bulk of new market gains occurred in the period following institution of governmental antidiscriminatory programs and cannot be attributed to past cyclical or trend patterns. While the evidence supporting a governmental policy explanation of the new market is not unequivocal, it offers little support for competing hypotheses. The sizeable gains of given cohorts and longitudinal advance of individuals rule out the "improvement in school quality" hypothesis. The timing of the upswing in the black relative economic position is inconsistent with a change-in-attitude or competitive-pressures-on-discriminators explanation of developments.

11 The direct employment practices of federal, state, and local governments also contributed to the new market increase in demand for black labor. At the federal level, there was a sizeable increase in employment of black managers, in the number of blacks in high GS and PFS jobs, and in the relative income of black male college graduates. At the state and local level, the relative income of black school teachers rose and the number employed as managers in public administration increased. The improved position of educated and skilled blacks in state and local governments is associated with the increase in the black share of the electorate in the period, which is attributable in the South to the Voting Rights Act of 1965 and related legislation.

12 Although de jure segregation in education raised demand for black teachers in southern and border states prior to the 1954 Supreme Court decision, the desegregation of the 1950s and 1960s was not accompanied by a substantial decline in demand. The effect of desegregation in the South was roughly offset by that of increased black voting power, which raised demand in the North and stabilized it in the desegregating South. In 1970, the black share of teachers was about the same as in 1950, the ratio of black to total teaching incomes was considerably greater than in 1950, and a much larger proportion of teachers were employed in the North.

13 Demand for black academicians increased greatly in colleges and universities in the late 1960s, apparently as a result of pressure from students, faculty, and other social groups and of affirmative action programs. The shift in demand, coupled with the limited supply of highly qualified (Ph.D. or its equivalent) scholars, greatly improved the economic status of black faculty: the proportion employed in primarily white national institutions rose sharply; lower hiring standards may have been applied to black faculty in some institutions; blacks with many publications obtained a sizeable salary premium over comparable whites. On average, blacks did somewhat better than whites with the same nominal qualifications in similar academic institutions.

In sum, there was a pronounced improvement in the market for the black elite, which appears to have been influenced by federal and related antidiscriminatory policies. Black students and qualified personnel responded to new opportunities quickly, increasing black representation in many "traditionally closed" high-level occupations. If the developments of the 1960s and early 1970s continue into the future, the decade will mark a major turning point in black economic history.

THE NEW MARKET AND ECONOMIC ANALYSIS The extent and rapidity of black economic advance in the new market contrasts sharply with the pattern of roughly unchanged black-white economic differentials that characterized the preceding half-century. Can this distinctive time path of change be explained by the market behavior of individual prejudiced whites in the context of the standard utility analysis of discrimination? Does an alternative view of discrimination offer a better account of observed phenomena?

I argue here that the historic pattern of persistence and change in black-white economic differences is not readily explicable by the standard theory of discrimination in a competitive market. It is necessary to supplement this theory with an analysis which makes collective, especially governmental, rather than individual market behavior, the critical factor in the system.

Problems of Standard Theory The competitive market theory, which relates discriminatory differences to the actions of whites who dislike associating with blacks at the work place, faces problems with both the historic persistence of economic differentials and recent sharp changes. In the first place, one must account for the failure of capitalist competition to eliminate differentials during the decades since emancipation. Why didn't nondiscriminatory white businessmen, workers, or consumers take advantage of the profit possibilities of associating with black workers? Possibly there were too few such whites in the market and conditions did not permit those few to expand sufficiently as to eliminate discriminating differentials. In that case, what prevented the black elite of businessmen and skilled workers from undercutting their discriminatory white competitors and eventually eliminating market discrimination? Capitalism was relatively successful among Oriental Americans, why not among black Americans? Attempts to explain the failure of competition in terms of turnover costs of replacing white employees with black employees fail to come to grips with the long period over which such adjustments could have been made and the fact that many white companies did, in fact, search for black employees. The more recent signaling theory, in which self-fulfilling, initial incorrect signals preserve discriminatory differences by reducing black productivity, while ingenious, does not adequately allow for innovative acts during the period in which productivity and signals move to equilibrium—acts which would alter views of black productivity (McCall, 1975).

The other side of the coin is the need to explain sharp changes in the context of a theory designed to generate stable long-term differentials. The chief moving force in labor market discrimination, individual discriminatory attitudes, presumably changes gradually and cannot account for sudden shifts except as a deus ex machina. Similarly, it is difficult to argue that competitive pressures, favoring nondiscriminators, have suddenly improved or become effective in the market. Though the theory can usefully explain the response of firms to changes in the "price" of discrimination due, say to passage of fair employment practice laws or boycotts, analysis of these collective activities lies outside its usual scope.

Governmental Discrimination: A New View

By contrast, an analysis that focuses on governmental or other collective acts of discrimination or antidiscriminatory policy appears to be readily consonant with observed patterns of change. During the decades preceding the new market, southern governments engaged in truly extraordinary discrimination designed, at least in part, to benefit whites economically at the expense of blacks. Among the major types of discrimination were inequitable provision of public education, which appears empirically to be the most important factor preventing blacks from advancing in the occupational hierarchy from 1890 to 1940; discriminatory employment of public workers; passage of laws designed to enhance the market position of whites; unequal protection of life and property; and discriminatory treatment under law. Beyond the government, moreover, collective discrimination by organized or other groups of whites, such as trade unions, restricted access to apprenticeship and job training, and thus prevented blacks from progressing rapidly in skilled crafts. Violence, often sanctioned by the government; ostracization; and related "social pressures" provided whites with additional means of penalizing black (or white) nondiscriminatory competitors to preserve community "norms." Just as collective discrimination appears to be a major factor in the lack of black advance, the empirical findings of this book point to an important role for governmental policy in the improvements of the new market. Traditional discriminatory patterns in education and the labor market were significantly reduced by antidiscriminatory activity, which commenced with the 1964 Civil Rights Act, 1965 Voting Rights Act, Executive Order 11246, and so forth.

In short, the evidence suggests that, as a working hypothesis, the major force in discriminatory and antidiscriminatory activity is the government and collective actions, rather than the behavior of individuals in the competitive market. Since governmental policies redistribute income among groups, moreover, there appears to be a substantial role for discrimination for economic gain in past public activities against blacks and of redistributive motives in the antidiscriminatory policy in the new market. The "new view" further directs attention to the link between political and economic discrimination and suggests a key role to the political position of blacks in their economic progress or lack thereof. From this perspective, the disfranchisement of the 1890s was the underlying cause of ensuing decades of persistent differentials while increased black political power contributed significantly to the antidiscriminatory policies of the federal government in the 1960s and to the changed employment practices of southern and northern states and local governments. All of which raises a host of issues regarding the interactions between political power and discrimination whose resolution lies beyond the scope of this study.[1]

WHAT THE FUTURE MAY BRING The critical question that remains is whether or not the improvements of the new market are likely to continue into the future, until labor market differences between comparable black and white workers are entirely eliminated. What factors can be expected to improve or maintain the new market of highly qualified (and other) black workers? What might prevent further advances or possibly restore previous discriminatory differences?

The new market movement of blacks into professional and managerial jobs in national corporations is, by itself, likely to have a positive effect on the demand for black labor by increasing the number of decision makers potentially favorable to blacks. As blacks obtain positions of authority, especially as

[1] In my forthcoming book *The U.S. Discriminatory System,* I analyze these diverse issues.

supervisors or as labor and personnel relations experts, and economic importance within company hierarchies, their preferences will be weighed, along with those of discriminatory and nonprejudiced whites, in forming policy, reducing the average "taste" of firms for discrimination. Firms which hired high-level blacks in the new market will find it difficult to reverse hiring policies without arousing internal opposition from black staff, making a return to the past costly. By influencing firm policies, the black elite may reduce discrimination in markets for less-skilled workers, providing an important but different type of "spill-over" to that expected by DuBois of "the talented tenth."

As black students obtain business, accounting, and technical skills in college and on-the-job training in large corporations, moreover, the qualifications of the black business community should be significantly upgraded and the possibilities of "black capitalism" enhanced. Beyond the job market, the leadership of the black community will also be altered, as business-oriented persons become more important and college-trained ministers and teachers less important.

The observed response of young black students and other qualified personnel to the new opportunities of the sixties has an important implication for the persistence of economic differences among the young. Declines in discrimination are, assuming similar responsiveness of less-educated young black men, likely to yield surprisingly large "payoffs" in the form of changes in career patterns and income ratios. Put another way, sluggish supply responsiveness will not hamper the attainment of economic parity among the young.

Finally, as the black educational and occupational structure approaches that of whites, discrimination due to the necessity of blacks working for or with "complementary" discriminatory whites—one of the chief causes of economic differences, according to the standard theory—will disappear.

There are, however, other forces at work which will act to limit and possibly halt the further improvement in the black economic positions. First, the sizeable, rapid supply response of young blacks on the new market may overshoot long-run equilibrium in the classic cobweb fashion (Freeman, 1971) with a consequent worsening in the relative black position in the future. This scenario will occur if companies continue to distinguish between blacks and whites in employment and have limited (token) demands for blacks which were relatively unfulfilled in the 1960s due to the paucity of qualified personnel but which will be quickly met in the 1970s. While the number of qualified black workers would seem to be still far below "desired" levels as of 1976, such a cobweb overadjustment is not implausible toward the end of the decade.

Second is the danger that nonnegligible numbers of newly recruited black college students or high-level workers will fail to perform up to expectations, leading firms and colleges to reverse currently favorable recruitment policies. The relatively poor family backgrounds of black youngsters, lack of educational resources at home, generally low academic achievement scores, and psychological stresses of minority life in a discriminatory world, together with well-intentioned but possibly ill-advised attempts to obtain proportionate minority representation even when the supply of those qualified was limited, could create such productivity problems. A "weeding out" process is likely to result, with the graduation, passage of occupational licensure exams, promotions, or salary increases of the less-able new recruits delayed or denied. The failure of some, moreover, could also generate faulty expectations, beliefs, and information about the likely productivity of future cohorts, creating a barrier to further progress when, paradoxically, there will be a larger pool of able candidates.

Third, some of the mechanisms used to alter demands for black workers and create new opportunities in the 1960s— near quotas, preferential treatment, and the like—may produce significant opposition from whites. While useful as a transition strategy for breaking down traditional discriminatory barriers and justifiable as a way of redressing past patterns of discrimination, these practices also redistribute opportunities and income in ways that run counter to widely held views of fairness and could, as a consequence, generate a legal and political counterreaction. Given the apparent importance of governmental policies in creating the new market, such a turnabout would pose a serious threat to continued rapid relative economic gains by blacks. Nonetheless, barring extraordinary social change or political upheaval, it is difficult to see how the advances of the sixties and early seventies could be reversed and the relative position of blacks deteriorate. While some redistributive tools may be discarded, reducing the speed of catching up, the strong opposition of black and many white Americans to restoring traditional patterns of discrimination would appear to make such a possibility infeasible.

Even if the relative economic status of blacks continued to improve, however, and market discrimination disappears as an economic problem, black Americans will still face obstacles in the "pursuit of life, liberty, and happiness." Some employers and individuals will continue to discriminate; the problems of broken family life, urban housing and crime, and low socioeconomic backgrounds will remain as significant impediments for some time to come. All of which is not to gainsay the fact that a major step toward eliminating economic differences between blacks and whites was made in the new market of the 1960s and early 1970s.

References

American Council on Education: *College and University Faculty: A Statistical Description,* ACE report, vol. 15, no. 5, Washington, 1970.

American Council on Education: *The American Freshman National Norms for 1971,* vol. 6, no. 6, 1971.

American Council on Education: *The Black College Freshman: Characteristics and Recent Trends,* vol. 7, no. 3, 1972.

American Council on Education: *Teaching Faculty in Academia, 1972–3,* ACE report, vol. 8, no. 2, Washington, 1973.

American Council on Education: *The American Freshmen National Norms for 1974,* with the U.C.L.A. Cooperative Institute Research Program, 1974*a.*

American Council on Education: *Enrollment of Minority Graduate Students at Ph.D. Granting Institutions,* Higher Education Panel reports, no. 19, 1974*b.*

Ashenfelter, O., and J. Heckman: "Measuring the Effect of the Federal Government on the Change in the Labor Market Position of Black Male Workers Relative to White Male Workers: 1966 to 1970," 1973. (Mimeographed.)

Badger, H.: "Statistics of Negro Colleges and Universities: Students, Staff, and Finance, 1900–1950," Federal Security Agency, Office of Education, circular no. 293, Washington, 1951.

Becker, Gary: *The Economics of Discrimination,* The University of Chicago Press, Chicago, 1971.

Bowles, Frank, and Frank DeCosta: *Between Two Worlds,* McGraw-Hill Book Company, New York, 1971.

Burman, G.: *Economics of Discrimination: Impact of Public Policy,* unpublished Ph.D. dissertation, Graduate School of Business, University of Chicago, 1973.

Campbell, T.: Thesis Research, University of Chicago, 1975.

Chiswick, B.: "Comments" in M. Intriligator and D. Kendrick (eds.), *Frontiers of Quantitative Economics*, vol. II, North-Holland, Amsterdam, pp. 559–562, 1974.

Colberg, M.: *Human Capital in Southern Economic Development 1939–1963*, University of North Carolina Press, Chapel Hill, 1965.

Coleman, J. S., et al.: *Equality of Educational Opportunity*, U.S. Office of Education, Washington, 1966.

College Placement Council: *Salary Survey: A Study of Beginning Offers*, Bethlehem, Pa., 1969–70.

Dubois, W. E. B.: "The Talented Tenth," in Booker T. Washington (ed.), *The Negro Problem*, James Pott & Co., New York, pp. 33–75, 1903.

Duncan, O: "Inheritance of Poverty or Inheritance of Race?" in D. P. Moynihan (ed.), *On Understanding Poverty*, New York Basic Books, pp. 85–110, 1968.

Duncan, O., D. Featherman, and B. Duncan: *Socioeconomic Background and Achievement*, Seminar Press, New York, 1972.

Eccles, Mary: Thesis Research, Harvard University, 1975.

Educational Testing Service: *Graduate and Professional School Opportunities for Minorities*, Princeton, N.J., 1971.

Edgarton, J.: *State Universities and Black Americans*, Southern Education Reporting Service, Atlanta, Georgia, 1969.

Equal Employment Opportunity Commission: *Annual Reports*, 1970 and 1971.

Executive Office of the President: *Budget of the U.S. Government, 1975*, Washington, 1975.

Festinger, L.: *A Theory of Cognitive Dissonance*, Stanford, Calif., 1957.

Fichter, J.: *Young Negro Talent*, National Opinion Research Center, Chicago, 1964.

Fichter, J.: *Negro Women Bachelors*, National Opinion Research Center, Chicago, 1965.

Freeman, R.: *The Labor Market for College Trained Manpower*, Harvard University Press, Cambridge, Mass., 1971.

Freeman, R.: *Labor Economics*, Prentice Hall, New York, 1972.

Freeman, R.: "The Changing Labor Market for Black Americans," *Brookings Papers on Economic Activity*, Summer 1973.

Freeman, R.: "Labor Market Discrimination: Analysis, Findings and Problems," in M. Intriligator and D. Kendrick (eds.), *Frontiers of*

Quantitative Economics, North-Holland Publishing Company, Amsterdam, 1974*a.*

Freeman, R.: "Alternative Theories of Labor Market Discrimination: Individual and Collective Behavior," in G. Furstenberg (ed.), *Patterns of Labor Market Discrimination,* Heath-Lexington, Lexington, Mass., 1974*b.*

Freeman, R.: "Overinvestment in College Training?" *Journal of Human Resources,* vol. X, no. 3, pp. 287–311, Summer 1975.

Freeman, R.: *The Overeducated American,* Academic Press, New York, 1976*a.*

Freeman, R.: "Socioeconomic Mobility and Black-White Economic Differences in the New Market for Black Labor," 1976*b.* (Mimeographed.)

Freeman, R.: "Political Power, Desegregation and Employment of Black Schoolteachers," *Journal of Political Economy,* 1977*a.*

Freeman, R.: "A Premium for Black Academicians," *Industrial Labor Relations Review,* 1977*b.*

Freeman, R.: "Family Background and Black Socioeconomic Progress," 1977*c.*

Freeman, R.: *The U.S. Discriminatory System,* forthcoming.

Greene, H. W.: *Holders of Doctorates among American Negroes,* Mead Publishing Company, Boston, 1946.

Griliches, Z.: "Wages and Earnings of Very Young Men," *Journal of Political Economy,* Summer 1976.

Haggstrom, G.: "Logistic Regression, Discriminant Analysis," *Rand Memorandum.*

Hall, R. and R. Kasten: "The Relative Occupational Success of Blacks and Whites," *Brookings Papers on Economic Activity 3,* pp. 781–798, 1973.

Hanoch, Giora: "An Economic Analysis of Earnings and Schooling," *Journal of Human Resources,* 2, pp. 310–329, 1967.

Hauser, R. and D. Featherman: "Changes in the Socioeconomic Stratification of the Races, 1962–1973," Center for Demography and Ecology, University of Wisconsin Working Paper, 75-26, 1975.

Heckman, J., and K. Wolpin: "Does the Contract Compliance Program Work? An Analysis of Chicago Data," *Industrial Labor Relations Review,* July 1976.

Johnson, G.: "Public Higher Education in the South," *Journal of Negro Education,* p. 320, Summer 1954.

Kovarsky, I., and W. Albrecht: *Black Employment,* Iowa State University Press, Ames, 1970.

Lazear, E.: *The Timing of Technical Change: An Analysis of Cyclical Variations in Technology Production,* unpublished dissertation, Harvard University, August 1974.

Lester, R.: *Antibias Legislation of Universities,* McGraw-Hill, 1974.

Lewis, Sir W. A.: "The Road to the Top Is through Higher Education, Not Black Studies," *The New York Times Magazine,* pp. 34–35*ff,* May 11, 1969.

Mincer, J.: *Schooling, Experience, and Earnings* NBER, Columbia University Press, New York, 1974.

McCall, J.: "Racial Discrimination in the Job Market: The Role of Information and Search," RM-6162-OEO, Rand Corporation, Santa Monica, Calif., 1975.

McCord, J. H.: *With All Deliberate Speed,* University of Illinois Press, Urbana, 1969.

Mommsen, K.: "Black Ph.D.'s in the Academic Market Place," *Journal of Higher Education,* April 1974.

Mommsen, K.: "Black Doctorates in American Higher Education: The Case for Institutional Racism," Southwestern Sociological Association, San Antonio, Tex., 1973.

Moynihan, D. P.: "A Schism in Black America," *Public Interest,* pp. 3–24, Spring 1972.

NAACP: *Annual Reports,* various editions.

National Academy of Sciences: *Minority Groups among United States Doctorate Level Scientists, Engineers, and Scholars, 1973,* Washington, 1974.

National Academy of Sciences: *Summary Report 1974: Doctorate Recipients from United States Universities,* Washington, 1975.

National Science Foundation: *American Science Manpower, 1970,* Washington, 1971.

National Science Foundation: *Characteristics of Doctoral Scientists and Engineers in the United States,* detailed tables, Appendix B, 1975.

Nerlove, M. and Press, J.: "Multivariate Log-Linear Probability Models for the Analysis of Qualitative Data," Northwestern University, 1976. (Mimeographed.)

Nondiscrimination in Employment, The Conference Board, New York, 1973.

Office for Advancement of Public Negro Colleges: *Public Negro Colleges: A Fact Book,* Atlanta, 1969.

Perry, G.: "Labor Force Structure, Potential Output and Productivity," *Brookings Papers on Economic Activity,* 3, 1971.

Planning Commission for Expanding Minority Opportunities in Engineering: *Minorities in Engineering,* Alfred Sloan Foundation, New York, 1974.

Plans for Progress, a report, National Voluntary Equal Employment Program for American Business, Washington, D.C., 1967.

Riker, William: *The Theory of Political Coalitions,* Yale University Press, New Haven, Conn., 1962.

Roose, K., and C. Anderson: *A Rating of Graduate Programs,* American Council on Education, Washington, 1973.

Russell, J. L.: "Changing Patterns in Employment of Nonwhite Workers," *Monthly Labor Review,* vol. 89, May 1966.

Schwartz, Mildred: *Trends in White Attitudes toward Negroes,* report no. 119, National Opinion Research Center, University of Chicago, Chicago, 1967.

Scientific Manpower Commission: *Manpower Comments,* vol. 12, no. 4, Washington, 1975.

Seligman, D.: "How Equal Opportunity Turned into Employment Quotas," *Future,* vol. 87, p. 167, March 1973.

Sharp, Laure: *Education and Employment: The Early Careers of College Graduates,* The Johns Hopkins Press, Baltimore, Md., 1970.

Shoemaker, D. (ed.): *With All Deliberate Speed,* Harper & Brothers, New York, 1957.

Southern Regional Education Board: *New Careers and Curricula,* Atlanta, 1968.

Southern Educational Reporting Service: *A Statistical Survey, State by State, of School Desegregation—Desegregation in the Southern and Border Area from 1954 to the Present,* Nashville, 1957–1964.

Stigler, G.: *Employment and Compensation in Education,* National Bureau of Economic Research, paper 33, New York, 1950.

Thurow, L.: *Poverty and Discrimination,* Brookings Institution, Washington, 1969.

U.S. Bureau of the Census: *Census of Population, 1950: Education,* ser. P-E, no. 5B, Washington, 1953*a*.

U.S. Bureau of the Census: *Census of Population, 1950,* detailed state volumes, Washington, 1953*b*.

U.S. Bureau of the Census: *Census of Population: Industrial Characteristics,* ser. P-E, no. 1B, Washington, 1955.

U.S. Bureau of the Census: *Census of Population, 1950: Occupational Characteristics,* ser. P-E, no. 1B, Washington, 1956.

U.S. Bureau of the Census: *Census of Population, 1960: Earnings by Occupation and Education,* ser. PC(2)-7B, Washington, 1962.

U.S. Bureau of the Census: *Census of Population, 1960: Detailed Characteristics,* ser. PC(1)-D, individual state volumes, Washington, 1963*a.*

U.S. Bureau of the Census: *Census of Population, 1960: Occupational Characteristics,* ser. PC(2)-7A, Washington, 1963*b.*

U.S. Bureau of the Census: *Census of Population, 1960: Educational Attainment,* ser. PC(2)-5B, Washington, 1963*c.*

U.S. Bureau of the Census: *Census of Population, 1960: Characteristics of Professional Workers,* ser. PC(2)-7E, Washington, 1964*a.*

U.S. Bureau of the Census: *Current Population Reports: Educational Attainment,* ser. P-20, no. 194, Washington, 1964*b.*

U.S. Bureau of the Census: *Census of Population, 1960: U.S. Summary,* Washington, 1964*c.*

U.S. Bureau of the Census: *Census of Population, 1960: Industrial Characteristics,* ser. PC(2)-7F, Washington, 1967.

U.S. Bureau of the Census: *Census of Governments, 1969: Topical Studies No. 1, Popularly Elected Officials of State and Local Governments,* Washington, 1968.

U.S. Bureau of the Census: *Current Population Reports: Consumer Income,* ser. P-60, no. 75, Washington, 1970.

U.S. Bureau of the Census: *Statistical Abstract of the United States, 1971,* 92nd edition, Washington, 1971*a.*

U.S. Bureau of the Census: *Current Population Reports: The Social and Economic Status of Negroes in the U.S., 1970,* ser. P-23, no. 38, Washington, 1971*b.*

U.S. Bureau of the Census: *Census of Population, 1970: Detailed Characteristics,* ser. PC(1)-D, individual state volumes, Washington, 1972*a.*

U.S. Bureau of the Census: *Current Population Reports: The Social and Economic Status of the Black Population in the U.S., 1971,* ser. P-23, no. 42, Washington, 1972*b.*

U.S. Bureau of the Census: *Current Population Reports: Population Characteristics,* ser. P-20, no. 243, Washington, 1972*c.*

U.S. Bureau of the Census: *Census of Population, 1970: General Social and Economic Characteristics,* ser. PC(1)-C1, Washington, 1972*d.*

U.S. Bureau of the Census: *Detailed Occupation of Employed Persons by Race and Sex . . . ,* supplementary report, ser. PC(S1)-32, Washington, 1973*a*.

U.S. Bureau of the Census: *Census of Population, 1970: Educational Attainment,* ser. PC(2)-5B, Washington, 1973*b*.

U.S. Bureau of the Census: *Census of Population, 1970: Occupational Characteristics,* ser. PC(2)-7B, Washington, 1973*c*.

U.S. Bureau of the Census: *Census of Population, 1970: Earnings by Occupation and Education,* ser. PC(2)-8B, Washington, 1973*d*.

U.S. Bureau of the Census: *Census of Population, 1970: Government Workers,* ser. P7(2)-7D, Washington, 1973*e*.

U.S. Bureau of the Census: *Census of Population, 1970: Detailed Characteristics, U.S. Summary,* Washington, 1973*f*.

U.S. Bureau of the Census: *Current Population Reports: The Social and Economic Status of the Black Population in the U.S., 1972,* ser. P-23, no. 46, Washington, 1973*g*.

U.S. Bureau of the Census: *Statistical Abstract of the United States, 1973,* 94th edition, Washington, 1973*h*.

U.S. Bureau of the Census: *Census of Population, 1970: Industrial Characteristics,* ser. PC(2)-7B, Washington, 1973*i*.

U.S. Bureau of the Census: *Current Population Reports: Consumer Income,* ser. P-60, no. 90, Washington, 1973*j*.

U.S. Bureau of the Census: *Current Population Reports: The Social and Economic Status of the Black Population in the U.S., 1973,* ser. P-23, no. 48, Washington, 1974.

U.S. Bureau of the Census: *Current Population Reports: Consumer Income,* ser. P-60, no. 97, Washington, 1975*a*.

U.S. Bureau of the Census: "Income and Expenses of Students Enrolled in Post-Secondary Schools: October 1973," *Current Population Reports: Population Characteristics,* ser. P-20, no. 281, 1975*b*.

U.S. Bureau of the Census: *Current Population Reports: Consumer Income Series,* ser. P-60, Washington, 1947–1975.

U.S. Bureau of the Census: *Current Population Reports: Population Characteristics,* "School Enrollment in the U.S.," ser. P-20, nos. 110, 148, 162, 190, 222, 272, 278, Washington, various years.

U.S. Bureau of the Census: "Educational Attainment," *Current Population Reports: Population Characteristics,* ser. P-20, nos. 169 and 172, various editions.

U.S. Bureau of Labor Statistics: *Educational Attainment of Workers,* special labor force reports, Washington, 1960–1974.

U.S. Bureau of Labor Statistics: *Handbook of Labor Statistics, 1971,* and *1974,* Washington, 1971, 1974.

U.S. Bureau of Labor Statistics: *Employment and Earnings, Jan. 1975, Feb. 1975* and *June 1975,* Washington, 1975.

U.S. Department of Health, Education and Welfare: *Graduates of Predominantly Negro Colleges: Class of 1964,* Public Health Service, no. 1571, Washington, 1967.

U.S. Department of Health, Education and Welfare: *News Release,* Washington, June 18, 1971.

U.S. Department of Labor, Manpower Administration: *Career Thresholds,* Manpower Research, Monograph, No. 16, Washington, D.C. 1970.

U.S. Department of Labor: *Manpower Report of the President, 1968, 1973* and *1974,* Washington, 1968, 1973, and 1974.

U.S. Equal Employment Opportunity Commission: *Annual Reports,* Washington, 1970, 1971.

U.S. Executive Office of the President: *Budget of the U.S. Government,* Washington, 1975.

U.S. Office of Education: *Earned Degrees Conferred, 1967–68,* Washington, 1969.

U.S. Office of Education: *Digest of Educational Statistics, 1972,* Washington, 1973.

U.S. Office of Education: *Projections of Educational Statistics to 1978–79,* Washington, 1970.

U.S. Senate Select Committee on Equal Education Opportunity Hearings: *Part 1: Displacement and Present Status of Black School Principals in Desegregated Districts,* 92d. Cong., Washington, June 14, 1971.

U.S. Labor Committee: *Report,* U.S. Senate, 88th Cong., no. 867, Washington, 1964.

Vroman, W: "Changes in Black Workers' Relative Earnings: Evidence for the 1960s," in G. Von Furstenberg (ed.), *Patterns of Racial Discrimination,* vol. II, Heath-Lexington, Lexington, Mass., 1974.

Weiss, R: "The Effect of Education on the Earnings of Blacks and Whites," *Review of Economics and Statistics,* no. 2, pp. 150–159, May 1970.

Welch, F.: "Black-White Returns to Schooling," *American Economic Review,* vol. 63, No. 5, pp. 893–907, December 1973.

Welch, F. and J. Smith: *Black/White Male Earnings and Employment: 1960–1970,* Department of Labor, R-1666-DOL, June 1975.

Willingham, W. W.: *Admission of Minority Students in Midwestern Colleges,* report M-1, Higher Education Surveys, College Entrance Examination Board, New York, 1970.

Index

NOTE: Page numbers in italics indicate tables or charts.